HISTORICAL SCHOLARSHIP IN THE UNITED STATES, 1876-1901:

As Revealed in the Correspondence of Herbert B. Adams

HISTORICAL SCHOLARSHIP IN THE UNITED STATES, 1876-1901:

As Revealed in the Correspondence of Herbert B. Adams

EDITED BY

W. STULL HOLT

Department of History
The Johns Hopkins University

GREENWOOD PRESS, PUBLISHERS
WESTPORT, CONNECTICUT

TO THE MEMBERS OF THE

JOHNS HOPKINS HISTORY SEMINAR,

PAST AND PRESENT

HISTORICAL SCHOLARSHIP IN THE UNITED STATES, 1876-1901:

As Revealed in the Correspondence of Herbert B. Adams

INTRODUCTION

The purpose dictating the selection of these letters from the many hundreds in the files of Herbert Baxter Adams was to make available data that will contribute to a better understanding of historical scholarship in America during the most significant period of its development. More exactly, those letters were chosen which show what the historical scholars of that generation were doing, what problems interested them, what courses they gave, what books they used, what contacts they had with each other and with foreign scholars, and what kind of an intellectual atmosphere they worked in. Most of the writers were members of a pioneering group who for the first time in America were making the study and teaching of history a profession. Consequently their letters, even those concerned with the routine of academic life, are invested with an added significance to anyone interested in the establishment of that profession and in the conditions which determined its early progress.

To the student of American historiography there is no period comparable in interest to the years between 1876 when Herbert B. Adams was appointed a fellow in the Johns Hopkins University and 1901 when he died. In part this is because of the presence of certain ideas which either as avowed philosophy or as unconscious prepossessions affected the history written. Prominent among these were that complex of ideas labelled Darwinism and the related belief that history is or should be a science. In part the period is so rich a one to study because of the achievements of the historians during it. Both in quantity and in quality the historical output was remarkable. Moreover, two distinct forms of historical writing, the broad canvas and the miniature, flourished side by side. It was the golden age of the Titans who scaled the historical heaven by piling volume on volume. It was also the period during which the monograph, born of the new specialization, became the characteristic form of scholarly history.

But what gives the last quarter of the nineteenth century a unique interest is the fact that historical scholarship then became a profession. Only a bare handful of men had previously made a career of historical study and writing. In no sense of the word had the study of history been a profession. Historical scholarship and the writing of history had been the avocation of lawyers, clergy or businessmen.

When Herbert Adams began his career at the Johns Hopkins in 1876 almost no history had been written by American university professors. Indeed there had been almost no professors of history to write any. Andrew D. White noted that before he accepted the professorship in history at Michigan in 1857, " there was not at that time a professor of history pure and simple in any American University." [1] The teaching of history in most universities had been left to men primarily interested in other subjects so that history received, as Charles Kendall Adams complained, " only such charitable attention as could be given it by some benevolent professor after his energies had already been too much exhausted by the absolute necessities of what was thought to be more important instruction." [2] By 1880 there were only eleven professors of history in the United States. [3]

---

[1] Andrew D. White, *Autobiography of Andrew Dickson White* (New York, 1905), I, 255.

[2] Charles Kendall Adams, *A Manual of Historical Literature* (New York, 1888), p. 1. Some of the combinations seemed ludicrous after a generation of specialization. Thus Brander Matthews, as a student at Columbia in the seventies, found one professor teaching mental and moral philosophy, political economy, logic, English literature and history. " It was," Matthews observed, " not only a chair that he filled, or even a settee; it was a series of settees rising row on row." Brander Matthews, " College in the Seventies," *Columbia University Quarterly*, XIX, 134.

[3] *Historical Scholarship in America* (New York, 1932), p. 4. The statement is in the Introduction written by J. Franklin Jameson.

Within one generation a revolution had been effected. Its results can be seen in the personnel of the two notable co-operative histories of the period. In the earlier one, Justin Winsor's *Narrative and Critical History of America,* two of the thirty-four authors were professors of history and only eight others were university professors of other subjects. Of the entire number only one had received graduate training in history. In the American Nation Series, which appeared between 1904 and 1907, twenty-one of the twenty-four authors were university professors and all but two of them had done graduate work in history. That shift marked the trend of the times. When Herbert Adams died in 1901, no one could doubt that historical scholarship in America and the writing of history with any pretense to scholarly qualities were, for better or for worse, in the custody of university professors.[4]

Herbert B. Adams not only witnessed the process but played a larger part than any other one man in America in the establishment of the historical profession. Consequently his correspondence is a proper source for the study of various significant aspects of the movement.[5] Although it is expected that the letters here presented will speak for themselves, a little judicious prompting may help.

In the first place it is necessary to remember that these letters are distinctly written by one member of a profession to another. They are about courses being given, the number of students, textbooks, subjects being investigated, jobs and other similar professional matters. To people who consider such things trivial the letters will have no significance. To

---

[4] Curiously, although the fact is a commonplace, no one has yet studied the results to ascertain in what ways the history written under the new regime is better or worse or different. The most thoughtful discussion I have found is in the inaugural address of J. Franklin Jameson as professor of history in the University of Chicago. *University Record* (Jan., 1902), VI, 294-300.

[5] Adams kept no copies of the letters he wrote except in a few instances and then usually when discussing business rather than scholarly matters. The letters of his printed below constitute a fairly large proportion of those that have been found. Several are from the Andrew D. White Papers in the Cornell University library; and Dr. Frederic Bancroft generously permitted copies to be made of the letters Adams had written to him.

persons seeking the observations of intelligent men on contemporary events they will be intensely disappointing. The several hundred letters written during the period of the Spanish American War and of the contest over the ratification of the peace treaty contain only several passing references to those exciting events.[6] Although the writers were students of history they were, if one judged by these letters alone, so absorbed in their professional problems as to be oblivious to life surrounding them. Such a judgment would probably be incorrect. Herbert Adams certainly insisted that " Politics is present history." It is more accurate to conclude that in this correspondence they were writing not in the spirit of Horace Walpole but as one chemist might describe test tubes, laboratory technique and experiments to another.

For that very reason the letters will be of value to persons interested in the historical profession—a value artificially enhanced because there are practically no similar letters available in print. They cast some light, for instance, on the spread of historical scholarship through the country. This subject greatly interested Adams. He liked to refer to other universities where his students had gone to introduce the new scholarly methods as colonies.[7] He had a map on the wall in which he stuck pins wherever a former student was teaching, and in numerous articles he dwelt with emphasis on the various university positions held by Hopkins graduates.[8] Some letters are included to illustrate how university positions were filled, the salaries paid, the stipulations made, the services expected—all of these factors being obviously important to students of the profession.

Another subject on which the letters cast light is the con-

---

[6] For one such reference see the letter of Edward Eggleston. No. 153. One of the interesting instances of non-professional comment is John S. Bassett's account of race riots in Wilmington, N. C. No. 156.

[7] See the letter of Charles H. Levermore from the University of California. No. 44.

[8] See letter No. 44, n. 1. It is not difficult to understand how unfriendly critics might have attributed this to professional advertising rather than to enthusiasm.

tact between Adams and European scholars. The situation
revealed is one that surprised me greatly. I had assumed that
Adams, the graduate of a German university, the historian
of the Germanic origins of New England towns and the man
who is supposed to have introduced German seminar methods
at the Johns Hopkins, would have held German scholarship
in the greatest esteem and would have kept in the closest
possible touch with many German scholars. Apparently the
reverse is nearer the truth. Among the thousands of letters
preserved there are only a scant dozen from Germany and
most of them are of no consequence. It is also obvious from
other letters that Adams neither wrote to his former German
professors nor sent them his historical publications, and that
his admiration for German scholarship was by no means
unqualified.[9] On the other hand the letters testify to a much
more intimate contact with English scholars. The number
and eminence of the Englishmen who visited the Johns
Hopkins and with whom Adams corresponded suggests the
possibility that the orthodox account of the dominant influence of German scholarship in America during this period
may need revision.

Interesting as is the question of the European influences
on the new scholarly profession, its American environment
was of more concern, certainly to the men who wrote to
Adams. Accordingly many of the letters contain references
indicating the general intellectual atmosphere and the condition of education. Many were written by young men fired
with professional zeal and in a hurry to succeed in their chosen
career so that allowance must be made for complaints of
discouraging conditions. Nevertheless, there is an explanation
of much in the intellectual scene in Trent's description of
his surroundings or in Bassett's wish that someone would
present a picture of Lincoln so that he could make an address
on that subject at Trinity College in North Carolina.[10]

---

[9] See letters Nos. 25, 49, 172. Frederic Bancroft and David Kinley
wrote some interesting comments on German scholarship. Nos.
36, 181.
[10] Letters No. 150 and No. 161.

One of the first things that the members of a scholarly profession are apt to do is to form an organization for mutual encouragement, for the promotion of the interests of the group and for increasing the aids to research. So it was with the professional historians. Herbert Adams was the moving spirit both in the formation of the American Historical Association in 1884 and in the conduct of its affairs for many years afterwards. A number of the letters refer to its activities and career. It is possible to appreciate fully the fact that great history cannot be organized into being and yet recognize the many important ways in which the organization of scholarly work prevents wasted effort and raises the standards of the profession. The independent suggestions that a scholarly journal for the profession be started is evidence of how keenly the need for that particular piece of machinery was felt.

Enough has, perhaps, been said to indicate some of the reasons for which these letters were selected and some of the uses to which they may be put. They can, however, be more wisely interpreted if certain of the facts concerning the career of Herbert Adams and the work in history at the Johns Hopkins are borne in mind.[11]

The fellowship to which Adams was appointed in 1876 was something new in America, for post-doctoral grants to enable young scholars to engage in research had been unknown. Although no teaching duties were required of him, he had two classes in his first year. Both were entirely voluntary for students as well as teacher. One class of two students met once a week with European history as the subject. The other class with one student consisted of a walk and a talk on American constitutional history twice a week.

---

[11] The fullest sketch of Herbert B. Adams is that by John Martin Vincent in *American Masters of Social Science* (New York, 1927), edited by Howard W. Odum. A number of appreciation accounts of his career were published in 1902 as an extra volume of the Hopkins *Studies*. In this memorial volume is a bibliography of the published scholarly work of the faculty and students who had been in the department.

In 1878 Adams was promoted to the rank of Associate and to a salary of $1,000. In the academic year 1878-1879 he taught his first regular classes. They included a class in European History during the Middle Ages meeting four times a week during the first half year, a class in German History meeting twice a week for two months and a class in Political Economy meeting twice a week for two months. In addition to these courses he gave ten public lectures on the Beginnings of Church and State. During the second half of the year and similarly during the next several years Adams taught at Smith College. One other course claimed his presence. This was the seminar in history directed by Dr. Austin Scott, who once each week left his regular work in Washington as assistant to George Bancroft and took charge of the new seminar in Baltimore. Scott, with an appointment as Associate, had begun this work when the University opened in 1876 and continued in it until 1882.

Obviously the slight contact of Scott, the courses of the young Herbert Adams and the occasional series of lectures by visiting scholars did not constitute a program of graduate work in history that satisfied President Gilman. Between 1876 and 1881 a number of men then enjoying established reputations as historical scholars were invited to take charge of the work in history at the Hopkins. Professor J. L. Diman of Brown University had been offered a permanent position on the Hopkins faculty by Gilman in May, 1876, but replied that domestic circumstances prevented him from considering it. In December, 1877, Henry Adams was approached and at one time apparently consented to accept a temporary appointment. Nothing came of these conversations. In July, 1879 and again in the summer of 1880, Professor Hermann E. von Holst of Freiburg was offered a professorship in history. After protracted negotiations he refused. In November, 1880, T. M. Cooley, a judge and a professor of law at the University of Michigan, was offered a professorship in jurisprudence and with it was to go the responsibility of leadership in related subjects including history. He, too, declined the appointment.[12]

Gilman had warned Adams that the appointment of a senior professor might jeopardize his position, but whatever danger there might have been became remote after 1881. In the autumn of that year Adams for the first time was placed in charge of the Historical Seminary which he devoted to original investigations of what he called American Institutional History. The publication of the results of the research done by his students and by himself began in 1882 when the first numbers of *The Johns Hopkins University Studies in Historical and Political Science* appeared. This was the first such series in history in the United States and its appearance created something of a sensation. The new University had previously made possible the publication of several scholarly journals in other fields, and nothing Gilman and his associates did contributed more to the reputation of the Hopkins as a center of advanced scholarly work. The period had begun in the United States when the publication of research was the great desideratum among members of university faculties.

Adams had by this time won an assured place on the Hopkins faculty. In 1883, the year in which he was offered the professorship at the University of Pennsylvania to which McMaster was subsequently appointed, he was promoted to the rank of Associate Professor with a salary of $2,750. The program of studies he then considered best for a graduate student was described at length in the draft of a statement dated February 6, 1884. It reads:

Requirements and Discipline in the Course for Ph. D.
History and Political Science

1. The candidate must pass all required examinations, some of which occur the first year of his graduate course, in (1) his principle [*sic*] subject which may be either History or Political Science and

---

[12] The correspondence relating to these offers is in the files of President Gilman in the archives of the Johns Hopkins University. A brief account of the negotiations with Henry Adams is in *The New England Quarterly* (Sept., 1938), XI, 632-638.

(2) in two subordinate subjects, both akin to his major course. For example, History may [be] associated as major with International Law and Political Economy as minors.

2. The Ph.D. course presupposes an acquaintance with general hist. & with polit. econ. equivalent in amount to that obtained in the undergraduate courses of this University & this matter will be tested.

3. The course absolutely requires a reading acquaintance with French and German authors representing the most advanced stage of Hist. & Polit. Sci. as seen in special lit. & the regular journals.

4. A thorough knowledge of some special field is requisite for a major course in Hist. or Political Science, which though limited shall nevertheless be sufficiently broad to illustrate general truth, the theory being that the way to the general is through that which is special or *universalia in rebus*. For example, when History is taken as the major subject, the student may specialize upon Institutional History (embracing Ancient Society, Classic & Modern European States); or, he may pursue the subject of Church History (including Church and State); or, again, the Const. Hist. of Eng. and of the U. S. When Political Science is taken as a major course, a very special knowledge of some one large subject is demanded, as Political Economy, including all its subdivisions (Theory, Hist. of Economics, Finance, Social Questions) or a Science of Gov. including Polit. Philos. Con. Politics & Administration. For minor course any two branches of a major subject akin to the major course actually taken may be offered, e. g. Polit. Philos. & Finance with Hist or Classical Hist. & Engl. Hist. with Polit. Sci.

5. In all subjects, major or minor, an acquaintance with original sources of information for some limited period & upon some special topic will [be] exacted.

6. In all subjects an extension of private reading will be demanded, e. g. in Eng. & Amer. Hist. Elton, Allen, Guest, Stubbs, Hallam, May, Madison, Elliotts Debates, Bancroft, Von Holst, in Polit. Econ. as major.

7. Attendance upon all lectures class-exercises & sem. work required of grad. students in Hist. & Polit. Sci. This attendance averages from 10-12 hours per week.

8. The lectures in Hist. & Pol. Sci. aim at the presentation of (a) the best sources of information, primary & secondary, (b) representative & suggestive topics, which shall not only convey pos. knowledge but open up lines of special reading & original research.

9. Class-exercises for graduates comprise (a) oral reports & joint discussions upon appointed themes; (b) the exposition of original texts such as Stubbs Select Charters & medieval Latin chronicles, French & German economists, Bluntschli, Voelkerrecht, the Madison Papers, Elliotts Debates, Stat Laws, Records &c.

10. Sem. work consists of the individ. preparation & joint discussion of original papers upon histor. & polit. subjects of the char. frequently reported in the Univ. Circular. The best of these papers find their way into the Univ. Studies or other special avenues for publica.

11. The natural outgrowth & highest requirement of the above system is a graduating thesis, wh must be a positive contribution to special knowledge in the candidates chosen field.

The enviable reputation which Adams enjoyed increased rapidly after 1884 because of his services in the organized effort to gain recognition for the new profession of historical scholars. In that year the American Historical Association was founded and Adams became its secretary. As such he more than anyone else arranged the programs of its annual meetings, edited its publications, and generally directed its affairs. Occupying this position he inevitably became one of the leaders of the young and flourishing profession. By the time of his resignation in 1900 from the strategic position of secretary the new profession was firmly established. In the intervening years the historical scholars of the new type had been in great demand.[13]

Adams was no exception and in the decade after 1883 received offer after offer. Among his papers is an envelope on which Adams wrote " Chances in Other Colleges " and underneath are listed twenty colleges and universities. The correspondence included shows that in several cases only tentative approaches were begun but in others persistent efforts were made to induce Adams to leave Baltimore. The offer which tempted Adams most was made in 1891, the same year he was promoted to a full professorship in the Johns Hopkins. It was to be professor of history in the new University of Chicago, head of that department and Dean of the Graduate School.[14] Apparently the presidency of a state university did not tempt him, for he gave serious consideration to none of the several invitations extended to him.[15]

These offers of administrative posts came to him because of his scholarly writing as well as because of his reputation as an organizer and promoter of research. The field in which he had worked chiefly in his first years at the Hopkins was American institutional history which meant the tracing of

---

[13] For Adams's description of the situation in 1886 see letter No. 39.

[14] The reasons which induced Adams to decline the offer are given in his letter, No. 88.

[15] The correspondence in the case of Ohio State University makes interesting reading for anyone wishing to understand the history of higher education in the United States. See No. 131 and its sequels.

various local political institutions back to Germanic origins. It was evident that he had brought back to America more than a knowledge of German historical methods. Although these articles and monographs won applause both in America and Europe, at least from exponents of the Anglo-Saxon school of historical thought, they represented a brief phase in his career as a scholar. None was published after 1883. From then until his death most of his writings were on the subject of higher education in the United States. Some of them were on the new "scientific" methods in history or on the history of the study of history at this or that university. Others were devoted to the history of particular universities. This work brought him into close association with the United States Bureau of Education in Washington which published a number of his monographs. In 1887 he began to edit for the Bureau a series of "Contributions to American Educational History" and especially a series of histories of higher education in the various states. Many of the twenty-nine monographs of this character which were published before his death were written by graduates of his department. In all of his own writing in this field, even the most scholarly, a strong promotional spirit is clearly evident. Some of his briefer articles especially on university extension, a movement in which he became greatly interested, were frankly propagandist.[16] The most extended piece of historical writing Adams produced was in the same general field. This was his two volume Life and Writings of Jared Sparks (Boston, 1893) which he wrote at the request of the Sparks family.[17]

It is a tribute to the scholarly ideals he instilled in his students that they never claimed, even in the memorial volume, that he was a great writer of scholarly history. He undoubtedly recognized his own limitations in that direction. Dr. Jameson, who was so closely associated with him, reported

---

[16] Anyone studying the history of university extension in the United States or of the Chautauqua movement can find helpful material in his letters.

[17] The most interesting provisions of the contract they signed are given in letter No. 38, n. 1.

a conversation with Adams in which he said he had once planned to write a large history on the relations of church and state but realizing he could not also devote himself to his students chose the latter alternative. It was a wise decision. He had in rare proportions some of the qualities most desirable in a teacher. He always took a personal and generous interest in his students. A natural enthusiast himself, he imparted to them his enthusiasm for scholarly work. He seemed to have the faculty of bringing out the best that was in them. The finest scholars among his students—and no professor of history in the United States has yet had better—repeatedly testified to that effect.

A LIST OF THE LETTERS BY DATE AND CORRESPONDENT

No.
1	April 16, 1876	To Daniel Coit Gilman
2	April 16, 1876	To The Trustees of the Hopkins University
a		From Emil Otto
b		From Johann K. Bluntschli
c		From Eduard A. Winkelmann
d		From Julius H. Seelye
3	May 21, 1876	To Daniel Coit Gilman
4	Dec. 13, 1877	From George Bancroft
5	Dec. 24, 1877	From Henry Adams
6	Jan. 2, 1878	From Johann K. Bluntschli
7	Jan. 20, 1878	From Hermann Eduard von Hols.
8	Dec. 6, 1878	To Hermann Eduard von Holst
9	Dec. 9, 1878	From Hermann Eduard von Holst
10	April 29, 1880	From Daniel Coit Gilman
11	April 14, 1881	To Daniel Coit Gilman
12	July 26, 1881	From William E. Foster
13	Sept. 7, 1881	From Daniel Coit Gilman
14	Oct. 1, 1881	From John T. Short
15	Oct. 22, 1881	From John T. Short
16	Oct. 26, 1881	From Edward Channing
17	Nov. 15, 1881	From James Bryce
18	Dec. 15, 1881	From John T. Short
19	June 18, 1882	From James Bryce
20	July 3, 1882	To Daniel Coit Gilman
21	July 22, 1882	From Daniel Coit Gilman
22	Sept. 3, 1882	From William E. Foster
23	Dec. 18, 1882	From G. Stanley Hall
24	April 5, 1883	From William E. Foster
25	April 10, 1883	From William E. Foster
26	May 30, 1883	From George E. Howard
27	June 6, 1883	From Albert S. Bolles
28	July 15, 1883	From Daniel Coit Gilman
29	Nov. 24, 1883	To Andrew D. White
30	Dec. 5, 1883	From James Bryce
31	Aug. 8, 1884	To Daniel Coit Gilman
32	Aug. 19, 1884	From Daniel Coit Gilman
33	Mar. 5, 1885	To Frederic Bancroft
34	Oct. 1, 1885	From Frederic Bancroft
35	Nov. 16, 1885	From Charles H. Levermore
36	Jan. 17, 1886	From Frederic Bancroft
37	Feb. 9, 1886	From Charles Kendall Adams

19

38	May 24, 1886	From William E. Sparks
39	May 29, 1886	To the President and Executive Committee of the Johns Hopkins University
40	Aug. 2, 1886	From William F. Allen
41	Nov. 27, 1886	From Woodrow Wilson
42	Dec. 5, 1886	From Woodrow Wilson
43	Jan. 21, 1887	From Woodrow Wilson
44	Jan. 29, 1887	From Charles H. Levermore
45	Feb. 11, 1887	D. N. Richardson
46	Mar. 29, 1887	From Woodrow Wilson
47	April 4, 1887	From James B. Angell
48	April 6, 1887	To Daniel Coit Gilman
49	April 6, 1887	To Frederic Bancroft
50	May 9, 1887	From George F. Hoar
51	May 11, 1887	From Lyon G. Tyler
52	May 16, 1887	From Woodrow Wilson
53	Aug. 9, 1887	From Inazo Ota [Nitobe]
54	Dec. 17, 1887	From Charles I. Stillé
55	Feb. 6, 1888	From James K. Hosmer
56	Mar. 7, 1888	From George W. Kirchwey
57	Mar. 14, 1888	From William J. Ashley
58	May 26, 1888	From Hannis Taylor
59	Jan. 10, 1889	From Anna E. Ticknor
60	June 21, 1889	From Frederick Jackson Turner
61	June 27, 1889	From Woodrow Wilson
62	Sept. 17, 1889	From Clarence W. Bowen
63	Nov. 7, 1889	From Theodore Roosevelt
64	Jan. 11, 1890	From Frederick Jackson Turner
65	Feb. 3, 1890	From William P. Trent
66	Feb. 4, 1890	To Andrew D. White
67	Feb. 21, 1890	From John Franklin Jameson
68	March 27, 1890	From Woodrow Wilson
69	May 25, 1890	From Daniel Coit Gilman
70	June 2, 1890	To Frederic Bancroft
71	June 13, 1890	From George D. Ferguson
72	July 2, 1890	From John Franklin Jameson
73	Sept. 27, 1890	From Frederick Jackson Turner
74	Oct. 13, 1890	From William R. Harper
75	Nov. 8, 1890	From Reuben G. Thwaites
76	Nov. 13, 1890	From William P. Trent
77	Dec. 8, 1890	From Frederick Jackson Turner
78	Dec. 22, 1890	To Daniel Coit Gilman
79	Feb. 23, 1891	From George W. Knight
80	Feb. 26, 1891	From Charles Kendall Adams
81	Mar. 5, 1891	To Frederic Bancroft

82	April 6, 1891	From Frank W. Blackmar
83	April 6, 1891	To Daniel Coit Gilman
84	April 8, 1891	From James A. James
85	April 13, 1891	To Daniel Coit Gilman
86	April 28, 1891	From Walter Hines Page
87	April 29, 1891	From George W. Knight
88	May 1, 1891	To William R. Harper
89	May 7, 1891	From Frederick Jackson Turner
90	May 17, 1891	From Frederick Jackson Turner
91	May 23, 1891	From Charles H. Haskins
92	Sept. 29, 1891	From Charles H. Haskins
93	Sept. 30, 1891	From Bernard C. Steiner
94	Oct. 4, 1891	From John H. T. McPherson
95	Oct. 19, 1891	From Frederick Jackson Turner
96	Nov. 11, 1891	From John H. T. McPherson
97	Nov. 12, 1891	From Barrett Wendell
98	Nov. 21, 1891	From Brooks Adams
99	Dec. 9, 1891	From Frederick Jackson Turner
100	Jan. 18, 1892	From Frederick Jackson Turner
101	Jan. 21, 1892	From Justin Winsor
102	Feb. 5, 1892	To Frederic Bancroft
103	Feb. 15, 1892	From John Martin Vincent
104	Feb. 16, 1892	From Michael D. Harter
105	Mar. 12, 1892	From John Martin Vincent
106	Mar. 18, 1892	From John Martin Vincent
107	April 7, 1892	From James Bryce
108	July 28, 1892	From James Bryce
109	Oct. 10, 1892	From James Bryce
110	Jan. 7, 1893	From Theodore Marburg
111	Feb. 24, 1893	From John W. Perrin
112	Mar. 4, 1893	From James A. Woodburn
113	Mar. 13, 1893	From James W. Black
114	Mar. 15, 1893	From A. Howard Clark
115	Mar. 21, 1893	From Herbert Friedenwald
116	Mar. 22, 1893	From Justin Winsor
117	April 10, 1893	From Lynn R. Meekins
118	May —, 1893	From Henry Adams
119	——, [1893]	From Newton D. Baker
120	July 9, 1893	From Shirley C. Hughson
121	Sept. 24, 1893	From Justin Winsor
122	Oct. 10, 1893	From Clarence W. Bowen
123	Nov. 12, 1893	From Edward P. Cheyney
124	Nov. 17, 1893	To Macmillan & Co.
125	Jan. 30, 1894	From William R. Harper
126	Feb. 5, 1894	From Frederick Jackson Turner

127	Feb. 19, 1894	From James W. Black
128	Mar. 13, 1894	From Woodrow Wilson
129	Mar. 26, 1894	To Macmillan & Co.
130	April 3, 1894	From William F. Willoughby
131	May 21, 1894	From W. I. Chamberlain
132	May 23, 1894	To W. I. Chamberlain
133	May 28, 1894	From W. I. Chamberlain
134	May 30, 1894	From William H. Scott
135	May 30, 1894	From William H. Scott
136	June 4, 1894	To W. I. Chamberlain
137	June 5, 1894	From Daniel Coit Gilman
138	June 5, 1894	From W. I. Chamberlain
139	June 9, 1894	To W. I. Chamberlain
140	June 13, 1894	From Walter Quincy Scott
141	June 16, 1894	From James A. Woodburn
142	June 16, 1894	From Frederic Bancroft
143	July 31, 1895	From John S. Bassett
144	Aug. 10, 1895	From John A. Fairlie
145	Jan. 16, 1896	From John S. Bassett
146	Sept. 20, 1897	From George B. Adams
147	Sept. 26, 1897	From John S. Bassett
148	Sept. 28, 1897	From James Schouler
149	Dec. 20, 1897	From Frank W. Blackmar
150	Jan. 8, 1898	From William P. Trent
151	Feb. 8, 1898	From J. B. Paton
152	April 8, 1898	From Sidney Webb
153	April 14, 1898	From Edward Eggleston
154	Sept. 22, 1898	From D. C. Heath
155	Oct. 11, 1898	From D. C. Heath
156	Nov. 15, 1898	From John S. Bassett
157	Nov. 21, 1898	From Berthold Fernow
158	Dec. 16, 1898	From John S. Bassett
159	Dec. 26, 1898	From James A. Woodburn
160	Feb. 13, 1899	From Samuel Macaulay Jackson
161	Feb. 18, 1899	From John S. Bassett
162	Mar. 6, 1899	From Elroy M. Avery
163	Mar. 21, 1899	From James Bryce
164	April 3, 1899	From John S. Bassett
165	April 18, 1899	From George W. Knight
166	April 22, 1899	From A. Howard Clark
167	April 28, 1899	From Reuben G. Thwaites
168	June 15, 1899	From James Schouler
169	Jan. 2, 1900	From Albert Bushnell Hart
170	May 17, 1900	From A. Howard Clark
171	May 22, 1900	From A. Howard Clark

172	July 26, 1900	From Frederick Bancroft
173	Oct. 25, 1900	From Albert Bushnell Hart
174	Nov. 10, 1900	From Albert Bushnell Hart
175	Nov. 24, 1900	From Clarence W. Bowen
176	Dec. 1, 1900	From James Schouler
177	Dec. 7, 1900	From John S. Bassett
178	Dec. 18, 1900	From John S. Bassett
179	Jan. 2, 1901	From John H. Finley
180	Jan. 6, 1901	From James Schouler
181	Feb. 16, 1901	From David Kinley

A LIST OF THE LETTERS BY AUTHOR

Letter Number

Adams, Brooks..............98
Adams, Charles Kendall......37, 80
Adams, George Burton........146
Adams, Henry...............5, 118
Adams, Herbert B...........1, 2, 3, 8, 11, 20, 29, 31, 33, 39, 48, 49,
66, 70, 78, 81, 83, 85, 88, 102, 124,
129, 132, 136, 139
Allen, William F.............40
Angell, James B.............47
Ashley, W. J................57
Avery, Elroy M.............162
Baker, Newton D...........119
Bancroft, Frederic..........34, 36, 142, 172
Bancroft, George............4
Bassett, John S.............143, 145, 147, 156, 158, 161, 164, 177,
178
Black, J. W................113, 127
Blackmar, Frank W.........82, 149
Bluntschli, J. K.............6
Bolles, Albert S.............27
Bowen, Clarence W..........62, 122, 175
Bryce, James...............17, 19, 30, 107, 108, 109, 163
Chamberlain, W. I..........131, 133, 138
Channing, Edward 16
Cheyney, Edward P.........123
Clark, A. Howard...........114, 166, 170, 171
Eggleston, Edward..........153
Fairlie, John A.............144
Ferguson, George D.........71
Fernow, Berthold 157
Finley, John H. 179
Foster, W. E. 12, 22, 24, 25
Friedenwald, Herbert 115
Gilman, D. C. 10, 13, 21, 28, 32, 69, 137
Hall, G. Stanley 23
Harper, W. R. 74, 125
Hart, Albert Bushnell 169, 173, 174
Harter, Michael 104
Haskins, Charles H. 91, 92
Heath, D. C. 154, 155
Hoar, George F. 50

von Holst, H. 7, 9
Hosmer, James K. 55
Howard, George E. 26
Hughson, Shirley C. 120
Jackson, Samuel Macauley 160
James, James A. 84
Jameson, J. Franklin 67, 72
Kinley, David 181
Kirchwey, George W. 56
Knight, George W. 79, 87, 165
Levermore, Charles H.........35, 44
McPherson, J. H. T. 94, 96
Marburg, Theodore 110
Meekins, Lynn R. 117
(Nitobe) Ota, Inazo 53
Page, Walter Hines..........86
Paton, J. B.................151
Perrin, John W.............111
Richardson, D. N............45
Roosevelt, Theodore.........63
Schouler, James 148, 168, 176, 180
Scott, Walter Quincy.........140
Scott, W. H................134, 135
Short, John T...............14, 15, 18
Sparks, William E. 38
Steiner, Bernard C...........93
Stillé, C. I.................54
Taylor, Hannis 58
Thwaites, Reuben G..........75, 167
Ticknor, Anna E.............59
Trent, W. P.................65, 76, 150
Turner, Frederick J........... 00, 04, 73, 77, 10, 00, 08, 00, 100, 100
Tyler, Lyon G...............51
Vincent, John Martin.........103, 105, 106
Webb, Sidney 152
Wendell, Barrett 97
Willoughby, W. F...........130
Wilson, Woodrow 41, 42, 43, 46, 52, 61, 68, 128
Winsor, Justin 101, 116, 121
Woodburn, James A..........112, 141, 159

1 — To Daniel Coit Gilman

Heidelberg, Apr. 16, 1876.

Professor D. C. Gilman,
President of the Hopkins University,—

Dear Sir,—

An item in the New York Tribune was the immediate occasion of my addressing the enclosed application to the Trustees of the Johns Hopkins University. I pray that you will make such disposition of the document as facts and circumstances may justify. I should be extremely obliged if you would send me the prospectus of Hopkins University and also the regulations in regard to the habilitation of Privat-Docenten. Next July I shall have concluded a three years' course of study in Europe. History has been my principal field of work, but the questions of State and Politics have also interested me greatly. I began Political Science under Treitschke, in Berlin, in the winter of 1874 and last summer I heard a similar course here under Geheimerath Bluntschli, Pres. of the last European Conference on International Law. I shall hear the same Professor this semester on *Völkerrecht* and he is to be my chief examiner in the Science of State.

If you desire American testimonials in regard to my character and scholarship, allow me to refer you especially to Prof. W. S. Tyler of Amherst College, and to Prof. J. H. Seelye, M. C.

Very Respectfully,

H. B. Adams

2 — To the Trustees of the Hopkins University

Heidelberg, Baden, April 16, 1876.

To
The Trustees of the Hopkins University:

Gentlemen,—

The announcement of your intention to establish fellowships at the Johns Hopkins University for young men en-

27

gaged in certain departments of special study prompts me to present an application for the fellowship in History.

My name is Herbert B. Adams, of Amherst, Massachusetts. I graduated at Phillips Exeter Academy in the class of 1868 and at Amherst College, Mass., in the class of 1872. The following year, I taught the Middle Classical class at Williston Seminary, East Hampton, Mass., substituting for the regular teacher who was traveling abroad. In July, 1873, I came to Europe and proceeded to Lausanne, Switzerland, where I passed four months studying French with Professor Thébault, of the Cantonal College. The following winter I spent in Rome, and early in 1874 I came to Heidelberg.

The special studies which I have pursued in Germany and in which I purpose undergoing an examination at this University next July, for the degree of Ph. D., group themselves as follows:

I.
Science of *State* and of *Politics*

II.	III.
Constitutional History	Political History
/	/
International Law.	History of Civilization.

In the last mentioned rubric, *Culturgeschichte* has claimed my special attention. I have attended several courses in Art History under Professor Stark of Heidelberg, and the winter of 1874-5 I passed at Berlin, under Professors Ernst Curtius, the archaeologist, and Hermann Grimm, the art-historian.

It is my aim to become a professor of historical and political science in America: I should be glad, however, for the present, to continue my studies in Baltimore according to the plan indicated in the above schedule. I shall return to America very soon after my examination here.

For my work and character at Exeter, I beg leave to refer you to Professor Cilley, of that Academy: at Amherst College, to Professor J. H. Seelye, M. C.: at Williston Seminary, to Professor W. S. Tyler, of Amherst College, one of the Trus-

tees of the above mentioned school.   I enclose herewith a few
certificates from Heidelberg Professors in regard to my course
of study at this University.

With great respect,

Herbert B. Adams

Per Adr.

Dr. Emil Otto, 105 Hauptstrasse.

2a — From Emil Otto

Mr. Herbert B. Adams has studied in Heidelberg most of
the time since February 1874.   Living in my family for several semesters, he is perfectly well known to me, and I can
confidently recommend him as a young man of good character and excellent qualities of mind and heart.   I have instructed him personally in German and I believe he has
perfectly mastered it.   He has also attended my French class
at the University with great regularity and best success.   His
studies here às well as in Berlin have been mainly historical.
Last winter he read an original article (dissertation) in the
Museum before the " Staatswissenschaftlichen Gesellschaft "
of professors and students and won from the former great
praise.   He intends to go up for examination this summer in
" Staats= & Geschichtswissenschafften for the degree of Dr.
phil., and I have no doubt he will succeed.

I have great pleasure in giving him this testimonial.

Dr. Emil Otto,

Lecturer of Modern Languages at the
University

Heidelberg April 14th 1876

2b — From Johann K. Bluntschli

Herr Herbert B. Adams aus Massachusetts hat im Winter-
semester 1875/76 bei mir die Vorträge über allgemeine
Staatslehre und Staatsrecht mit ausgezeichnetem Fleisse

besucht & an den Arbeiten des staatswissenschaftlichen Seminars & der staatswissenschaftlichen Gesellschaft einen hervorragenden Antheil genommen.

Heidelberg 10 April 1876   Dr Bluntschli, Professor
                                          Geheimerath

2c — From Eduard A. Winkelmann

Herr Herbert Adams aus Massachusetts hat im vorigen Winter meine beiden Vorlesungen über 1) Encyclopaedie und Methodologie der historischen Wissenschaften, und 2) Historiographie des Mittelalters mit grosser Regelmässigkeit und dauerndem Interesse besucht und für den Sommer sich zu der Vorlesung über Allgemeine Geschichte des Mittelalters angemeldet. Ich hege das Vertrauen, dass er einst Tüchtiges leisten wird.

                              Dr Winkelmann
                ord. Prof. d. Geschichte an d. Univ. Heidelberg

Heidelberg 15. April 1876.

2d — From Julius H. Seelye

House of Representatives
Washington, D. C., May 31, 1876

President D. C. Gilman,

Dear Sir,

Learning that Mr. Herbert B. Adams is an applicant for one of the Fellowships in History of the Johns Hopkins University, permit me to say in furtherance of this application that Mr. Adams was graduated at Amherst College, 1872, and, after teaching one year in Williston Seminary, Easthampton, has spent the succeeding three years in Germany, chiefly at Heidelberg in the thorough and comprehensive study of History and Political Science under the instruction of Professors Bluntschli and Knies, to which study and instruction therein he purposes devoting his life. He is also a young man of most excellent character. I have pleasure in highly and heartily commending him, and am, with high respect,

Very truly yrs

J. H. Seelye

3 — To Daniel Coit Gilman

Heidelberg, May 21, 1876.

President D. C. Gilman,
Johns Hopkins University,
Baltimore, Md.,—

Dear Sir:

Your letter of May 3 is here. In regard to essays or disquisitions, I must confess that I have nothing on hand that is in condition to offer a committee as a specimen of my original work. Whatever I have done in the way of research has been in the Historical and Political *Seminar*. The work of the former consists in *Quellenstudien*, the comparison of original sources of history, under the direction of one of the Professors. We have held chiefly to Pertz's *Monumenta Germaniae Historica*, and the only opportunity for display lies in the grouping of fresh points of fact in regard to some given subject. For example, I worked up last winter, from Latin sources, "Arnoldo da Brescia and his place in Italian History." I presented my points orally in connection with text from Otto of Freising, and occupied thus two sessions of the *Seminar*.

In Dr. Bluntschli's Private Class we have compared the constitutions and development of European States, discussing freely together on points of constitutional law. My only rhetorical performance in Heidelberg has been a *Vortrag* in German, of one hour, held last winter in the *Museum*, on "Universal Suffrage," but I hardly think the effort would tend to enhance my claims as a student of History.

I am very busy now preparing for my examination, which

occurs in the middle of July. I intend to take a short trip
through Belgium and Holland on my way to Glasgow, from
which port I shall embark for New York towards the 15th
of August.

If you would drop a line to Dr. Tyler, Prof. of Greek at
Amherst College and to Prof. J. H. Seelye, M. C., I think
you would receive testimonials in my favor, which would have
some weight with the Committee. I did considerable literary
work at Amherst College and obtained the first prize for English composition in my Senior year.

It is my aim to pursue historical researches and to contribute something to Political Science. I would like to write
the History of American Political Literature and to help
organize the Sources of American History. The treasures of
the Congressional Library and the nearness of Baltimore to
Washington makes me especially desirous of an appointment
as *Privat-docent* to the Johns Hopkins University.

Very respectfully,

H. B. Adams

4 — From George Bancroft

1623, H Street
Washington, D. C.
13 Dec. 1877

My dear Sir,

Let me present to you my best thanks for your monograph
on the cession of lands to the United States.[1] I find it equally
interesting & instructive, & am delighted to see the true
spirit of historical inquiry infusing itself into the generation
which is soon to take the places of those of us whose end is at
hand.

Very truly,

Again greatly obliged,

Geo. Bancroft

---

[1] *Maryland's Influence in Founding a National Commonwealth, or
the History of the Accession of Public Lands.* Maryland Historical
Society, Fund Publication, No. 11, 1877.

5 — From Henry Adams

1501 H St. Washington
24 Dec[r]. 1877.

My dear Sir

I should sooner have acknowledged the receipt of your very excellent monograph if I had not waited to make a return in kind. I send you herewith a volume of my own which appears today, and which, although it will teach you nothing about public lands, may perhaps interest you in some other ways.

By the way, I had occasion last week to look up that Diary of Washington's during his journey of 1784 to the Mononga-hela. Not being able to find it in print, I hunted up the original. I am a little surprised that it has not been printed. To you it would be interesting.

I am, with great sympathy in your historical labors,

Very sincerely Yrs

Henry Adams

Herbert B. Adams Esq Ph. D.

6 — From Johann K. Bluntschli

Heidelberg 2. Jan. 1878.

Lieber Doctor.

Besten Dank für Ihre Zusendung der interessanten Schrift über Marylands Einfluss auf die Union. Die grosse Bedeutung des amerikanischen Colonialsystems im Westen für die nationale Entwicklung der Union ist mir daraus zuerst klar geworden, ebenso wie ich von Washingtons Landspeculationen zuerst durch Sie hörte.

Wenn die particularistischen Studien der Geschichte einzelner Staaten zugleich die nationale Entwicklung der ganzen Union fördern, so sind sie doppelt willkommen & auch für weitere Kreise werthvoll.

Es freut mich, dass Sie unsers Heidelberg mit Liebe geden-

3

ken. An Ihren glücklichen Fortschritten bei der Universität Baltimore nehme ich innigen Antheil.

Mir versicherte ein Deutscher, Kapp, der viele Jahre in Amerika gelebt hatte, dass mein populares Buch (in Einem Bande) deutsche Staatslehre sich, wenn die nöthigen Modificationen & Ergänzung[en] durch Darstellung der nordamerikan Verfassungszustände [vorgenommen würden], sehr zu einem politischen Buch für Amerika eignen, & dort wohl grössere Verbreitung erfahren würde, als in Deutschland, wo das politische Denken noch nicht in Übung ist. Er forderte mich auf, darüber an Bancroft zu schreiben, damit dieser sich der Sache annehme. Ich habe es bisher noch unterlassen. Aber es wäre mir lieb Ihre Ansicht darüber zu vernehmen. Überlegen Sie sich die Sache & schreiben Sie mir, was Sie davon halten.

Wir sind gegenwärtig noch durch den russisch-türkischen Krieg in eine Spannung versetzt, die viele Arbeit hemmt. Ich hoffe aber, dass bis zum Frühjahr, vielleicht noch früher, der Friede kommt & dass die Versuche Englands, die Türkei zum Widerstand zu reizen, & gelegentlich für sich eine Beute wegzuschnappen, scheitern werden.

Die deutsche Kneipe bitte ich auch zu grüssen

Ganz

Ihr

Bluntschli

7 — From Hermann Eduard von Holst

Freiburg, Jan 20, '78

Dear Sir,

I have delayed thanking you for your treatise, because I did not want to do so before I had found time to read it. It has not only interested me very highly, but I have learned much from it and sincerely wish that you will continue these studies and present us, after some years, with a thorough monograph on this so very important land question. That this is not a polite phrase, but my honest opinion, you will see by the review of the treatise which I have written for Sybel's Historische Zeitschrift.

So far as the American historians and writers on political and constitutional questions think my work of any value and worthy of some consideration, they would do a good work in imitating your kind example. They, perhaps, would do it a little more frequently if they had any idea how *very* hard it is in Germany to get hold of the most necessary materials for such an undertaking. "International ignorance," as the Nation terms it, is with us as yet in a most flourishing condition with regard to the United States. Whoever does not believe that need only consult the catalogues of our best public libraries, and half an hour will be more than sufficient to convince him. I sometimes feel as if I could hardly keep up my courage, because I can't take a single step ahead without missing this or that; to a very great extent it is even absolutely impossible to learn what has been written and published. You will excuse these complaints, as they are made in the interest of science and not of my person. I have uttered them very emphatically in the preface to the second volume, which is to be given to the public in a few weeks. May they have some effect, at least in stirring up a little the administrations of our libraries.

Please to give my very best regards to President Gilman. Whenever a report is published about the progress of the University, I would be much pleased to get it.

Very respectfully and Truly

Yours

H. Holst

8 — *To Hermann Eduard von Holst*

Johns Hopkins Univ.

Dr. Von Holst: Baltimore, Dec. 6, 1878

Dear Sir,

I have been consulted by one or two newspapermen for information concerning your course of lectures at this university and concerning your past career. It is deemed advisable by Mr. Gilman that a few facts of a biographical character be presented to the public through the medium of our city press and I have been requested to address you for authentic data.

If you have not time to write out an autobiographical sketch, you will perhaps be so good as to fill out the following blanks and to add a few details which I can insert in a more extended notice:

Dr. Von Holst is professor of history in Freiburg, South Germany, to which university he was called from Strasburg in the year 1874. He is now visiting this country under the auspices of the Berlin Academy of Sciences in order to obtain further materials for his work on American constitutional history. This is Von Holst's second visit to the United States, his first sojourn having been from 1867 to 1872, during which time he made a careful study of our institutions and collected materials for his history. The first volume appeared in German in 1873 and the second in 1878. The first volume was translated into English by Messrs. Lalor and Mason and was published by Callaghan & Co. of Chicago in 1876. The work of Dr. Von Holst has been reviewed by

and is now very generally recognized among American scholars as the most critical and, at the same time, as the most impartial and thoroughly scientific treatment to which the constitutional and political history of the U. S. has hitherto been subjected. Dr. Von Holst is a frequent contributor to Sybel's *Historische Zeitschrift,* the leading historical magazine of Germany, and he is also the principal reviewer, for this magazine, of American historical works. One object of Dr. Von Holst's visit to Baltimore and to the state of Maryland is to obtain access to the archives of the Maryland Historical Society and to the unpublished collections at Annapolis, as well as to be within easy reach of the congressional library at Washington.

This rough sketch of your relation to this country I have ventured to draft from the imperfect data at my command and would respectfully solicit any further details that you may see fit to impart.

Hochachtungs voll,

Herbert B. Adams

9 — From Hermann Eduard von Holst

N. Y. Dec. 9. '78.

226 W. 36th.

Dr. H. B. Adams.

Dear Sir

In spite of all my good intentions I have not been able to answer your kind letter of the 6th inst. already yesterday. I would greatly prefer it, if you would have the kindness to write the desired sketch of my past career. I add a few details, neither expecting nor desiring that they should be mentioned,—just only for your information, leaving every thing else entirely to your own judgment.

In 1867 I *emigrated* to the U. St., because, on account of a semi-political pamphlet, I could not risk to return from Germany to Russia, which—though I am a German, is my native country. To myself this fact has always in so far appeared as not quite indifferent, as I looked upon the people in a way which was calculated to exercise a considerable influence on my opinions. I was satisfied that my lot was for ever cast with them, and so in 4½ years I acquired something of a natural American feeling, so far as that can be developed in an adopted citizen. The call to the University of Strasbourg determined me to return to Germany.

My larger essays—(Charles Sumner, Toussaint L'Ouverture, The Centennial of the U. St., Parkman's Jesuits in America, John Brown, the silver bill, etc. all based upon careful original researches)—are published in the Preussische Jahrbücher.

I am told that the translation of the second volume—by Mr. Lalor, will be given in a few weeks to the public. The first volume has been reviewed in the U. St. by Mr. Lawson and Henry Adams in the North American, Mr. Horace White and Judge Cooley. By whom the reviews in the Nation, N. Y. Tribune, World etc, etc. are, I do not know. About the German reviews, I suppose, you won't care. For safety's sake I shall mention a few prominent names: R. Gneist, R. Pauli, R. Schleiden, Fr. Kapp, Prof. Haenal, Oppenheim.

Whether I shall go to Annapolis, I do not know as yet. The time I have to spend in the U. St., is so very short, that I have to confine my investigations to the time from the annexation of Texas, i. e. I have to work for the 3d and 4th volume, and leave, for the present, the 1st and 2d to take care of themselves.

It would be a great relief to me, if it could be mentioned in some way, that I had only very reluctantly and with important reservations accepted the invitation of the Trustees of Johns Hopkins University. I expressly declared that my knowledge of the English language was too limited to play myself off, under any circumstances, as an English lecturer. And besides I stated, that I had neither the material nor the time—because I had first and above all to attend to my duties here—to write anything that would deserve to be written. If I accepted the invitation, it was only because I thought, educated Americans might feel some curiosity to see and hear a foreigner, who had made the study of their history and their institutions the principal task of his life as a scholar and writer. Please speak with Pres. Gilman about this request. I think that not only I, but also the Trustees and the audience will fare much better, if it is known from the first that not a series of thorough and elaborate treatises is to be expected, but a more or less rambling and off-hand discussion of a theme which is of general interest. If Pres. Gilman should think otherwise, I would request that at least the press might be privately informed of what I have written to him and now briefly stated to you. I come in an armor of blotting paper, so that the weakest critical shaft would stick fast in my flesh and I would have to leave the stage as a porcupine.

Hoping that I shall have soon the pleasure of making your personal acquaintance

I am

Truly yours

H. Holst

10 — From Daniel Coit Gilman

My dear Adams,

I thank you for your note. The word from Pres. Seelye is quite enough. I only wanted to be sure that he approved the nominations, & of course I am glad to know that he suggested it. Holst's letter is very suggestive. I think he still wants to come among us,—& if he should, I don't know what would happen. This is certain that you have won by steady, varied, & excellent work a strong hold upon our confidence & respect, —& that we want you to remain in J. H. U; but if an older man like Holst or Diman should consent to join us, it might delay your advancement,—or alter your work;—so I should not dare to dissuade you from listening to overtures at N. if they seem to you pleasant. Does " not ready to die yet "— mean that Northampton is Heaven?

Personally I should be very sorry indeed to have you choose N. in place of B.,—but if you are considering the whole matter, I think you ought to bear in mind, that now as a year ago, some of our Trustees are very desirous of bringing here one of the two professors named. I have no new light on their attitude, & I do not think that any name but theirs is under consideration for the post of Prof. of History.

Yours sincerely

Dr H B Adams

D C Gilman

I will return H's letter

B. Ap. 29. 80

11 — To Daniel Coit Gilman

P.S. Harvard is likely to give a Ph.D. in Hist. to Miss Morris.

Smith College, Northampton, April 14, 1881.

Dear Mr. Gilman:

The Baltimore oriole has come again and once more the noise of the Type Writer is heard in the land. Smith College putteth forth her hands for the green dates of History and the Biological vine is climbing over the wall.

My trip to Virginia was most enjoyable. At the University of Virginia, our first objective point beyond Washington, Mr. Williams and I called first upon Dr. Miner, the best representative of the old school of courtly Virginia gentlemen. He was quite delighted to learn that one of our men (Brinton) was coming to study Law under his direction. He accompanied us to Dr. Cabell's and to Prof. Holmes', and then invited us to dinner the next day. We called upon Prof. Mallett, who was lecturing when we first arrived and he showed us his laboratory, the library, and museums, and took us home to tea. In the evening I called upon Mrs. Prof. Price, to whom Mrs. Lee had given me a letter. I saw the professor, who reminded me in some ways of his former master, Prof. Gildersleeve. Prof. Price invited me to breakfast with his family the next day and told me to bring my friend.

That same evening we called upon Col. Venable, who lives in the town of Charlottesville and were received most kindly. He called upon us the next forenoon and left cards for admission to Monticello and letters of introduction to prominent people in Richmond, among others to Gov. Holliday. The prospect from Monticello reminded me somewhat of the view over the Conn. Valley from Pelham Hills, only the former is much finer. Returning from Monticello, we visited the County Court House and met Col. Venable again and inquired to some extent into the County system of Virginia. Afterwards, at the hotel, I became acquainted with the government revenue collector (an old Confederate) and saw the County of Albermarle from a Mahone standpoint.

Starting for Richmond that evening (Wednesday) I luckily made the acquaintance of a Mr. Ficklin, for many years member of the Virginia House of Delegates from Buckingham, and through him I got a Bourbon view of State and County politics. He talked five hours, with hardly a break! Arriving in Richmond, he took us to his hotel, demanded for us the best rooms in the house, and introduced me to several prominent public men, among others to Attorney Gen. Field, a one-legged man of more bonhommie than elegance.

Next day, Mr. Ficklin took us over the State House, introduced us to more officials and public men, and—best of all for my purpose—to Col. McRea, the state librarian, and to Dr. Wm. Palmer, a very scholarly, charming man, editor of the Calendar of Virginia State Papers. Mr. Ficklin also took us over to the Governor's mansion, where we had a pleasant talk and where, of course, I broached my Local Government hobby. The Gov. appeared interested and invited us to breakfast the next morning,—much to my astonishment. And, now that I am upon the subject, I may as well say, it proved the most enjoyable breakfast I ever sat down to, although I *have* eaten better shad in New England and have seen neater table-cloths, with fewer holes (The Governor is a widower, and I fear his " niggers," as he calls them do not take very good care of him). Dr. Curry was present and a representative young Virginian named Lyons, formerly in the Univ. of Virginia. We discussed the old-time rural civilization of that State, which Gov. Holliday was disposed to rank higher than municipal civilization. The Gov. also praised most highly the old Virginia system of County Judges, the " finest type the world ever saw." He and Dr. Curry both encouraged my project of studying up the Local Institutions of the U. S., from the comparative standpoint; indeed, Dr. Curry promised to find me some young men in the South, who would aid us in investigating the subject of local government in Georgia and Alabama. We also talked of Universities. Gov. Holliday inquired very particularly about you and commissioned me to extend you a most cordial invitation to visit him in Richmond. He impressed me as a very cultivated, scholarly, but somewhat disappointed man. He is certainly the best type of the aristocratic Bourbon democrat. He believes in paying the debt to the last dollar, and deplores such a break-up of " the solid South " as Republican combinations with Mahone, " the readjuster," and with the worst elements in Virginia politics, are likely to effect. Mahone stands for repudiation, abolition of the poll-tax, and for demagogue measures in general. It is impossible not to sympathize with the high-minded, property-holding class in this Virginia struggle. I heard Johnston speak in the U. S. Senate and think he stands for more virtue than Mahone.

Dr. Curry, whom I called upon and who afterward called upon me, interested me almost as much as did Gov. Holliday. The Doctor explained the practical workings of the Peabody Education Fund and its influence in fostering the local spirit, —a point in which I was especially interested. Dr. Curry appears to me to be a very frank, earnest, sincere man, with a sufficient sense of the honor and responsibility of his position as the successor of Dr. Sears (whom he cannot extol too highly). The Doctor seems disposed to recognize Northern ideas, but is clearly influenced by Southern prejudices. Without possessing much originality, he will prove, I think, a mediator between the two sections of country and carry out Dr. Sears' plan even more perfectly than could have Dr. Sears himself. Although mildly dogmatic, he does not seem especially opinionated in any rigid sense, or very much biassed towards sect or religion. One of the Professors in the Baptist College with which Dr. Curry was formerly connected, said the Doctor was better adapted for politics than for Church connections, and that he regarded his D.D. as a kind of damper upon political aspirations. I don't believe that exactly, but I think Dr. Curry is a kind of secular priest, disposed to plant schools rather than churches, and fonder of influencing legislation than of engaging in Baptist propaganda. There is a good deal of the priestly diplomatist in his composition. He combs his hair straight back from his forehead, like Dr. Hodges, and he doesn't look at you when he talks, which he does blandly and well. He said he had received several letters from you in reference to the attitude of the Peabody Fund towards the J. H. U. He asked if the University would not be adapted for advanced or college teachers rather than for normal school teachers. I said that would naturally be the case, but enlarged in general terms about the need of a better grade of teachers even in the Common Schools and instanced the Quincy case (which I had just read up) and Charles Francis Adams, Jr., i. e. his article in Harpers. Dr. Curry said he should come over to Baltimore about the second week in June. I of course said nothing about the Southern scheme, but I sincerely hope you will push it. It seems to me the most pregnant idea ever conceived within the Johns Hopkins.

I might write you about many other people and things I saw, for my two days in Richmond were exceedingly crowded with experiences. I visited the Iron Works, the Tobacco Exchange, various Tobacco manufacturies, heard four hundred darkies sing in one shop, was treated with the greatest politeness by many business men, was shown over the Haxall Flouring Mills by the proprietor in person, was taken to the Westmoreland Club (where I saw the Library of the Va. Hist. Soc.), saw Libby Prison, and drove all over the city.

Socially my visit was most delightful. I carried Easter cards to Mrs. Haxall (whom I once met in Baltimore) from Mrs. Lee. Mrs. H. is a famous beauty; she is one of three sisters, all blondes, and curiously enough their family name was Triplet! One married Prof. Price, of the Univ. of Va.; another captured the Flouring Mills of Philip Haxall (after two fellows had fought a duel over her); and the third is still in the market. Well, Mrs. Haxall, upon whom we called insisted upon getting up a little evening party for us, and it proved a very pleasant affair. I saw something of the beauty and chivalry of Virginia, and came away happy.

So all things considered, my trip of four days in the Old Dominion was a great success. I saw good types of the social, the economic, the educational, the " Historical and Political " interests of a war-worn but rapidly reviving State.

In conclusion, allow me to recommend (for the encouragement of McIlwaine's research into the County System of Virginia) that Dr. Browne be requested to order from Col. McRea, State Librarian of Va., one copy of Dr. Wm. Palmer's Calendar of the State Papers of Virginia (price $3.50) and one set of Hening's Statutes of Va. Both works will prove mines of historical material, and Hening I am sure, cannot be found, even in the Law Library at Baltimore. I had to send to Washington for one of Mr. Bancroft's set, when I was using Hening two years ago. The work is now very scarce and very valuable. Col. McRea told me the Library had two or three duplicate sets, one of which he said he would sell us at circa $2. a vol. There are about 16 vols. in the set. Yours

Adams

12 — From William E. Foster

Providence Public Library,
57 Snow Street.

Providence, R. I., July 26, 1881

My dear Sir,

Yours of July 25, with the reference lists enclosed, at hand. Say nothing about any obligation on your part. I am very glad if I have been of any service to you in this matter. Is it too much to hope that you will sometime embody your researches on *the town,* in a volume, and thus make them generally accessible?

It is a matter which has interested me very much, although my own knowledge of the subject is confined to the treatment

of it by such general and " popular " writers as Green, in his
" History of the English people," (book 3, ch. 1.)

I am glad to know the authorship of the *Nation's* review
of Lodge. I had read it with interest; with so much interest,
in fact, that I was on the point of saying to you in my last
letter that I " trusted you had not failed to notice some rather
striking remarks on the early parish organization of Virginia
in the *Nation*, May 26 " (!). That would have been amusing,
would it not?[1]

By the way, it is an interesting feature of the subject, that
this marked difference in the local organizations of the northern and southern colonies at the start, has, perhaps, while
they have both equally developed the principle of local self-
government, had some effect in determining whether that
principle should take the form of emphasized state-allegiance
or the reverse. It is mainly a difference as to what is regarded
as the " unit " of local interest. In Virginia and the south
generally, there was little, when you passed below the state
organization, that offered sufficient compactness and tan-
gibility for such a sentiment. How different it is with the
towns of New England any one who has been born and brought
up in a Massachusetts town, with all its separate local tra-
ditions and interests can well understand. The writer of the
work entitled " The republic of republics," (whoever he may
be, for " P.C. Centz," is alleged to stand for J. P. Benjamin),
professes himself shocked at President Lincoln's query whether, as against the " national " government, there was any
more basis for the sentiment of state sovereignty than of
county sovereignty. If you carry it a step farther and compare
the town sentiment with the state sentiment, there is not so
much absurdity in the query.

Do not understand me as claiming that the difference thus

---

[1] Henry Cabot Lodge, *A Short History of the English Colonies in
America* (New York, 1881). In the last paragraph of this unsigned
review Adams wrote " The history of the local institutions of the
South is yet to be written. It is a good field of investigation for
the rising generation of students in that section of the country. . . .
this subject, which assumes an ever-increasing interest as constitutional history works downwards to the protoplasm of state-life."

indicated has been anything like a hard and fast line in the actual history of American politics. No one who has read history can have failed to notice that the " national and state authority " controversy has only too often impartially located itself on opposite sides of Mason and Dixon's line, according as self-interest dictated at the time.

I was only pointing out what may have been one of the governing and perhaps unobserved tendencies which has had some influence in the matter.

I am glad also that you find the *Monthly Reference Lists* practically useful. I have sometimes wished I could supply our subscribers with my own annotated copy of the lists, containing my additions to the printed sheets of the articles, etc., which appear afterwards. But I have no doubt, if the person would only bear this in mind, we would find it as easy to keep up these annotations as I do. Suppose you suggest this to your " History Club."

Yours most truly,

W. E. Foster.

13 — From Daniel Coit Gilman

Princeton, Mass
Sept. 7. 81.

My dear Adams

Your note of Sept. 3 found me yesterday in Boston,—& such a dark day as it was never has been equalled since the colonial days, when " lights " were called for in anticipation of the last Day.

I am delighted to hear of your good vacation work, from one end of Massachusetts to the other. I think there can be no doubt that you are tilling a fruitful field; & I long to see your monograph completed before others run away with your ideas. You will be interested to know that Prof. Bryce, (" Holy R. Empire ") is in this country & will come to Balt. & give us two or three lectures. I have also asked

Freeman to give us some private talks while his public course
is in progress at the Peabody. You may tell mathematicians,
in confidence, (I dont want it to leak out in the papers quite
yet) that we expect Prof. Cayley, of the Univ. of Cambridge,
Eng. to spend much of next winter & spring with us, as
lecturer. I am turned homeward.

Ever truly yours

D. C. Gilman

14 — From John T. Short

Ohio State University,
Columbus, O.
1st Oct. 1881.

Professor H. B. Adams, Ph. D.
Johns Hopkins University.

Dear Sir:

I am considering the feasibility of starting a Journal of
Historical and Political Science, to serve as the medium of
publication for the most advanced thought and thorough
investigation in our field. If Historical Journals have had
poor success in this country it has been in great part due to
the fact that no truly scientific work has been attempted.
I take the liberty of conferring with you briefly. What would
be your opinion of the probable success of such a journal as
I have in mind, if published in New York, say monthly or
bi-monthly, in some such form as the Library Journal but
of double its thickness and in better print? Will you be
kind enough to indicate to me your view of how it could be
published, by whom, on what terms, etc, etc? Would you also
please state whether you would to some extent unite in the
undertaking by becoming a contributing editor and upon what
conditions? It seems to me that such an organ for the historical departments of our various colleges need not be begun
upon any large scale in order to give it character and a
position. By making it very select, very choice, very critical

and marking out for it a plane on a level with the German Journals of the same character it seems to me that it would find recognition and have a mission—not in money-making—but in furthering historical studies throuout the whole country. It would be my idea to receive contributions of the highest merit only, and for a time only from writers of established reputation. Whether such contributions could be obtained gratis for the purpose of starting the Journal, until it could pay for them you can say better than I can.

I have not addressed any one else upon the subject as yet, and would be pleased to hear from you before taking further steps. Though I have never had the pleasure of a personal acquaintance with you I have ventured to broach this matter to you with the confidence that you would be heartily in favor of any step in the direction indicated. I beg to refer you, as to myself, to my friend Hon. George Bancroft, and to Hon. A. R. Spofford. I have a slight acquaintance with President Gilman, but only slight. Please give me your valuable advice and assure me of your active cooperation in case I should engage in the undertaking.

With Great Respect

I am, dear Sir,

Yours truly

John T. Short
Prof. of History.

15 — From John T. Short

Columbus, O. Oct. 22, 1881

My dear Sir:

I beg your pardon for my delay in answering your favor of the 10th inst. I addressed a letter to Professor C. K. Adams of Ann Arbor, on this subject, without referring to your letter, and have waited in vain for a letter in reply. You have my thanks for the cordiality you manifest and for valuable suggestions. I had, in fact, wondered more than once why the Johns Hopkins University had not initiated such an enterprise as we contemplate. I cannot now see why it would not enter upon it; and I sincerely trust that at an early day President Gilman will see the way clear. You are right in saying that a College or University subsidy would give independence to the Journal and it may be best to wait for one. I have no personal advantage to seek, nor personal ends to further by any interest I have taken or may take in the movement. I want to see a Journal of Historical & Political Science founded by the right men, before inferior & incompetent persons pre-occupy the field. My plan for publication is as follows: That an editorial corps be selected and organized into a company—the editorial company in fact; the constitution of the company to be some such one as you suggest with your own name at the head of the list. The members of the company should enter into a contract with each other to be responsible for the contributions to their respective departments; and to furnish each his proportionate share of matter. The editorial company should sign a contract to furnish one half the matter for each issue. They should further elect one of their number a Managing editor, who should, by the way, be an eastern gentleman—yourself for instance.

With such an arrangement on paper, namely, an editorial corps such as you have named, with the addition of your name at its head, and an agreement signed binding the editorial company to furnish half the matter for a Journal of such a character as such gentlemen would consent to be connected with, I think there would be no trouble in obtaining a contract from one of the leading publishers, in which he would bind himself 1st to bear all expenses of publication & circulation; 2nd to provide funds for paying for one half the matter used in each issue, such matter to be from the pens of Historical & Political writers of the best reputation in this country & in Europe, & to be paid for liberally; 3rd to give the editorial company and its representative—the

4

Managing editor, unlimited control both of the matter and advertisements (if any were allowed) that might appear; 4th to further agree to pay to the editorial company at the close of each year or at the termination of every half year, one half the profits of the Journal. Profits there would doubtless be, after the first year, if the purchased articles were written with some attractiveness of style—I say *some,* for barrenness and historical accuracy are not necessarily inseparable. My idea would be to make the Journal so choice, so far in advance of any American Journal or Review that it would inevitably win its way, would find its place in all libraries & into the hands of leading members of the Bar and of educated persons who take an interest in Politics.

The editorial company ought to set apart one fourth of the proceeds accruing to them, as compensation for the Managing editor, and should divide the remainder in proportion to service rendered.

I am assured by persons who are familiar with the publishing interests of certain New York houses that I would have little trouble in making the arrangements I have indicated.

However, I am not particular about pushing the matter and would cheerfully wait for the subsidy, if you think it best. Suppose you correspond with some of the gentlemen named in your letter and secure an expression from them.

Yours very sincerely

John T. Short

Professor H. B. Adams,
    Johns Hopkins University.

16 — From Edward Channing

Harvard College
Oct 26th 1881.

My dear Dr. Adams:—

Here are about 400 words on the maps. I hope you will add your remarks as to the proper way of teaching history.

My course is in full blast. We meet in the college library just over the table where you consulted Jaquinot's articles. The subjects so far chosen are (1) The Fisheries, (2) The Civil Service (3) The rights & Duties of an American Citizen at home and abroad & (4) The Bulwer-Clayton Treaty. Their roots are so deeply laid in the past that I hope to get some good historical essays.

Very truly,

Edward Channing.

17 — From James Bryce

Telegrams or letters will find me at this address.

115 East 25th Street
Nov. 15 [1881] New York

Dear Mr. Adams,

It seems to me that the best plan would be to omit Ireland altogether from the four or five lectures which you wish me to give, and to substitute another subject. There will then be no such risk as I feared. There are unhappily plenty of other political problems on our side [of] the ocean. I give on the opposite page a list of what would probably do.[1] But if you and the other authorities would prefer something more specifically scholastic, I could take " Five Classical Spots," and give five lectures on Troy, Ithaca, Athens, Constantinople, and Mount Ararat—all of which I have visited. I have named five of the " Problems " and of these classical-historical: but perhaps may not be able to stop longer than for four days: as to that I can scarcely tell yet. But I think I may probably venture to say that I can come on Monday and begin to lecture that day—if that day is still a convenient one for you in Baltimore. Of course the sooner will probably be the better for me,—as I may be more pressed for time later on.

---

[1] In the *Johns Hopkins University Circulars* for Dec., 1881 (p. 169), a sixth lecture on the Relations of Law and History is reported.

Probably I shall hear from you: I trust to have good news of Mr. Gilman's progress—Yours very truly

J. Bryce

Some English Problems

The Crown and the House of Lords
The Suffrage and the Distribution of Seats
The Land the Poor
The Church and the Universities
Foreign and Colonial Policy

18 — From John T. Short

Ohio State University
Department of History and English

Columbus,
15 Dec. 1881

My dear Sir:

Your esteemed favor of the 5th inst. interests me greatly. I believe you are on the right track, and will secure precisely the organ that the workers in Historical & Political Science need,—along the line that you indicate. I sincerely trust that you may speedily accomplish your project for the Anglo-American journal, under the editorship of Green; and will add that you must allow me to enlarge your plan to the extent of insisting that you become the American editor. This I can do, and shall take occasion to do in the most efficient way of which I am capable, by writing to our English friends and to the publishers when the proper time arrives.

Please then, my dear Sir, go forward without delay, and inform me of what I can do to further your excellent plan.

Yours very sincerely

John T. Short

Professor H. B. Adams
Baltimore.

19 — From James Bryce

London
June 18/82

Dear Mr. Adams,

I hope I acknowledged the third paper, that on New York Local Government, when it reached me, but am not quite certain, and so wish to make sure. John Morley, editor of Fortnightly, to whom I sent the two former papers, proposed to print them both, thinking them—one particularly of course, as it was decidedly the better—interesting and valuable.[1] They have not yet appeared. I suppose his space has been occupied by more pressing things.

I am heartily glad to hear that Gilman is quite himself again, & also that you have got your Archives Bill through. That ought to be a useful example to other states. It is wonderful how much that is good still remains unprinted here.

Have you made any further enquiries or calculations as to the prospects which a Historical Review would have in America? What circulation could you guarantee for a journal appearing 4 (or 5) times a year—price $1, as big or bigger than our XIXth Century or Fortnightly? and would it be necessary to have a considerable space allotted to American history? A. W. Ward of Manchester has been again discussing the subject with me: the key of the position seems to me to be with your side; for I doubt whether our sale alone would be sufficient to enable us to pay all we ought to pay our Editor & contributors.

Freeman is in good health & cheery—fiercer than ever

---

[1] In the margin Adams wrote " Shaw's and Gould's " and " Shaw's " where Bryce referred to the better of the two articles he had sent Morley. In *The Fortnightly Review* of October, 1882 (CXC, 485-495) Albert Shaw's article entitled " Local Government in America " was printed. The article on New York was undoubtedly that of John Franklin Jameson which appeared in *The Magazine of American History* in May and September, 1882 (VIII, 315-330, 598-611), under the title " The Origin and Development of the Municipal Government of New York City. I. The Dutch Period. II. The English and American Period."

against "Francis Joseph." He does not seem to me to have been quite so much influenced by America or brought back quite so many new ideas from it as I should have expected, but those he has brought back are mostly just.

Any information you can ever give me regarding the progress of historical studies & University matters generally on your side will be welcome. As you have seen, our political horizon continues very cloudy.

Kindest remembrances to the Gilmans, Martins, Sylvester, Morris, and all other friends at J. H. U.

Always truly yours

J. Bryce

20 — To Daniel Coit Gilman

Amherst, Massachusetts, July 3, 1882.

Dear Mr. Gilman:

I wrote you the other day, addressing my letter "Princeton, Mass.," supposing that you had gone there for the summer. Your note from Lake Mohonk afterward came to hand. I have written Yager, suggesting that free tuition might be afforded him and recommending him to make the acquaintance of Lee Sale in Louisville, who would give him information touching the methods and work of the University. You know Sale belongs to our graduate workers. I also recommended a course of reading for Yager during this vacation.

Wilhelm has written me a note of apology for his querulous tone regarding Gould's appointment. Wilhelm has been out among the mountains of the Blue Ridge and feels better. He will make the Eastern Shore trip with Ingle, according to our original plan, and finish up his paper on the Old Town Institutions of Maryland for the Historical Society in the Fall. Wilhelm was overworked and nervous. I was sorry for him, for really he represented a year's more graduate work than did Gould and is, moreover, a graduate of the Johns Hopkins, a fact which, as Wilhelm very justly said, ought *per se* to count more than graduation from an obscure Canadian College with backing from a wandering Russian! But Wil-

helm now understands, I think, the circumstances which influenced the appointment of Gould, viz., *finished, published,
recognized* work; and Wilhelm will proceed to accomplish the
same and through the Maryland Historical Society. I want
to see each candidate for Ph. D. in History obtain some corporate recognition of his work, some local reputation which
will help him on in his future career.

It will be a good thing for the University if we can ally
with us the Historical Societies and *quasi* historians in all
the seaboard States. Gould did well for us in Philadelphia.
Jameson is pretty well established with the New York set. I
have now a good chance in Rhode Island, for Foster wants me
to read a paper before that State Society. Wisconsin has
treated us very kindly, presenting books, making me a member of their Society; and Wilhelm and John Johnson have
just been taken into the Maryland Historical. Ingle is on
the Md. Epis. Libr. Committee and will hold that little
cloister-fort, with the forces it represents. I have never
begun to realize until this year the importance of corporate
influences, of associations of men and money. That Peabody connection is going to be a great thing for the University when the Pratt Library shall have drawn off every
spring of Library popularity from the great foundation.

I send you a letter from Mr. Bryce, which I received this
morning and which suggests a feasible plan of cooperation
between friends of History in the Old Country and the
New. To my mind there is a peculiar propriety in *united
English effort* in the direction of historical science; for the
history of the two countries is one. The whole tenor of our
researches at the J. H. U. is to show the continuity of English institutions in American. Mr. Freeman has struck for
me that key-note in his Introduction.[1] Now my idea is this:
supposing you write to Mr. Bryce slightly encouraging the
main idea of an English journal of History, in a broad sense,

---

[1] The first numbers of *The Johns Hopkins University Studies in
Historical and Political Science* appeared in the fall of 1882. Edward
A. Freeman gave the project his blessing by writing a prefatory
article entitled " An Introduction to American Institutional History."

including American contributions, which shall be subject to an American sub-editorship. Taxation without representation is a bad principle. *Generous cooperation* must be the principle of the magazine. It should be English, *with American assistance.* It should be published through Macmillan in England and America, and through the cooperation of the Johns Hopkins University. A prospectus sent out by the J. H. U. to all our American Historical Societies, establishing a channel for reports, would secure many subscriptions at once, and accomplish the end we have been working towards in another way. All good libraries might be enlisted, thus accomplishing another cooperative work, with the Johns Hopkins ahead. All ambitious specialists in Historical and Political Science would look favorably upon a published list of patrons of such a magazine and would be inclined to subscribe. I think it not improbable that 300 names might be secured, through the agency of the Johns Hopkins; then if the Trustees would vote an annual subsidy, as they do in the case of the Physiological Journal, the work could go forward as a Johns Hopkins undertaking, with Johns Hopkins support and partial control as regards contributions and American management. The thing would be a scientific tentacle reaching over England and drawing life to our little Baltimore centre from the best intellectual resources of the old world. Such a journal we never could institute by ourselves alone. But this project will give us all the strength of an American journal, without the responsibility and odium of managing editorship, without distracting bother, but with free scope for our best work and a free lance among the American Indians—our valued contemporaries.

The little scheme of "University Studies in Historical and Political Science" can in the mean time, pending negotiations, go on at a trifling expense, but as a scheme of cooperation with State Historical Societies which will seem naturally to evolve into this larger and more satisfactory historical representation for England, Old and New.

Respectfully submitted,

H. B. Adams

21 — From Daniel Coit Gilman

Princeton, Mass

July 22. 1882

Dear Adams,

I like the idea of cooperating with Bryce in the matter of his historical publication,—but I don't think we can commit ourselves till we reassemble in Oct. I think I will write to him. Your work is already attracting much attention and respect. Several persons have spoken to me of it,—among others Pres. Andrews of Marietta, & Mr. Mowry of a school in Providence complimented your *Md. Hist. Soc.* monograph, and Prof. Lyman at New Haven said that Freeman, again and again, spoke of your good work. Press on. The proposed series of papers, if they prove as good as they promise, will bring your work into notice, & will have weight doubtless, with the Trustees, in the question of cooperating with Bryce. Are you to be in Boston? I expect to spend a few days there, about August first & should like to meet you. I am well under way with Monroe.[1] Would Jameson like, for compensation,—to read my proofs, & verify in a library, all questions of dates. I am working under great disadvantages, —but I have with me abundant original manuscript matter from the Gouverneur papers.

Ever truly yours,

D. C. Gilman

Thanks for " Constables "—& for the newspapers.[2]

Dr. H. B. Adams

---

[1] The biography of Monroe in the American Statesmen series.
[2] Adams published two articles under the title " Constables " in the *New England Historical and Genealogical Register* for April and for July, 1882. They were later reprinted in the first volume of the *Studies.*

22 — *From William E. Foster*

Providence Public Library,
57 Snow Street.

Providence, R. I., Sept. 3, 1882

My dear Adams,

*   *   *   *

I am exceedingly glad that you have been able to visit Rhode Island. There are three things that I particularly want to see done. (1) The actual ensuring of the preparation and publication of the " Memorial history of Rhode Island," in season for 1886; (2) an adequate treatment of Stephen Hopkins, and his influence in state and national affairs; (3) the completion and publication of your series of studies.

To my mind the development of the Providence of today out of the beginnings of 1636 is one of the most interesting studies that I know of. To see how the operation of natural causes crystallized the original settlement here into an isolated, homogeneous, narrow-minded community, and how the operation of natural causes again had been gradually and steadily converting it into a city in which these characteristics are absent. How the situation of the town, on a constantly travelled thoroughfare between Boston and New York laid it open to the most wide and varied outside influences; how its situation as a natural center for local trade for a circle of 25 miles around drew it involuntarily into close and constant communication with the old Plymouth colony settlements, with Massachusetts towns in Norfolk and Worcester counties; how the growth of its foreign commerce sent its own citizens into all parts of the world and opened their eyes to what there was outside of its limits; how the accumulation of large fortunes still farther stimulated the tendency to travel and set up at home institutions which had been found attractive abroad; how the accession of the Massachusetts strip of Territory in 1746 was a most important contribution to the liberalizing of Rhode Island sentiment, by introducing into it an element which had been allied in all its sympathies and associations for more than one hundred years with Plymouth and Massachusetts; how the establishment of the college, in 1767, added an element heretofore unknown, but whose influence in the direction of cosmopolitan, unrestricted, world-culture was to be as potent as any other; how the revolutionary movement, including the preliminary years, 1763-75, served to fuse the separate colonies in one common spirit; how the intelligent public spirit of Stephen Hopkins developed and intensified this influence;—and here perhaps some one would say " And how all this progress and development was neutralized and overthrown by the course of Rhode Island in refusing to adopt the constitution and enter the union, 1787-90. But an examination of the interior history of that period will show that Providence and Newport realized the importance of this step from the outset and acted in this direction to the extent of their power and influence. The country members of the general assembly, however, succeeded in overbalancing this influence until May, 1790.

You will find interesting material on this matter in Staples's " Rhode Island in the Continental Congress,"—a book which I will lend you if you have not access to it.

Since 1790, the town and city of Providence has more than kept pace with the liberalizing influences which have been active in the country. The development of her manufactures, the increase of her capital, her public improvements, the accumulation of articles of value in the departments of art and and literature, (some of which you had an opportunity of seeing), the growth of the great body of alumni of the college, representing and identified with the interests of every state in the union, the extension and very great improvement of her public school system, the writings and influence of men like Professor Diman and Col. Higginson,—these have had an influence the full extent of which is not yet seen.

But if I do not stop here, you will be suggesting that—

" I have leave to print."

And so I will stop.

Yours as ever,

Foster.

23 — From G. Stanley Hall

Dr. H. B. Adams,

My Dear Sir:

Messrs Ginn & Heath are to publish in January a translation of Diesterweg's chapter (from his Wegweiser) on teaching history.[1] It was written as you know for teachers of history in grades corresponding to our Grammar & High Schools only, or at least was in no sense designed to be of service for University work. Professor Allen of Madison, with whom Ginn & Heath are on intimate terms is preparing a somewhat extended list of books in English on the history of different countries to take the place in some sense of the extended bibliography wh. Diesterweg gives. I think the publishers will try to bring the book eventually into the hands of most teachers of history in grades corresponding to Gymnasial in Germany. This is the first of a series of translations on methods of teaching which I have selected & assigned to the best translators I could find who wd undertake it at six to eight percent of wholesale rates, my own work & that of Professor Allen being entirely gratuitous.

Now, to state my fond hope boldly, I am very anxious to incorporate somehow some account of your methods of work at B. especially so far as adaptable in any sense to High School work or even to the regulation course of the [small?] college. So

I. have you written or could you write any hints to teachers how to study or how to teach the historic material right about them. My hope that you might be interested in the scheme to this extent rests on the query whether such teachers might not eventually be thus made tributary in some way to your comprehensive plan of gathering information of local institutions.

---

[1] *Methods of Teaching History* (Boston, 1883). Part I, which occupied more than half the volume, consisted of translated portions of Diesterweg's *Wegweiser zur Bildung für Deutsche Lehrer*. Part II included six chapters by "Eminent American Teachers of History." The first, by Adams, was entitled "Special Methods of Historical Study." Part III contained the long bibliography prepared by Professor W. F. Allen.

II. If however you have no time for this, may I refer to whatever expositions of your own work have yet been made public, & will you kindly tell me what to refer to.

From the slight knowledge I have of your ways of getting men to work in history, it seems to me they might be adapted to high school work with great success.

Yours respectfully

G. Stanley Hall

N. Somerville Mass

Dec 18 [1882]

24 — From William E. Foster

Providence Public Library,
57 Snow Street.

Providence, R. I., April 5, 1883

My dear Adams,

*   *   *   *

I shall read the review of Doyle tonight with interest. The *Nation's* review of McMaster is by Johnston, as I happen to know from a letter of his. You ask whether I have read McMaster. No, much to my regret. I was away from the city, on the week of its publication, and since my return have been steadily working up to an opportunity to read this and Morse's "Jefferson." I have thus far been unsuccessful.[1]

As you say, American history *is* booming. Have you interested yourself at all in the "Rhode Island history" of the last 6 or 8 weeks? Interesting, I assure you. Like a "little pot, soon hot," the "Plantations" have really been boiling hot. I must say, though I am a Massachusetts man, that

---

[1] Under the date of April 17, Foster wrote, "Morse's 'Jefferson' I am happy to say that I have digested;—a very rich thing it is. McMaster I am about half way through. I wonder exceedingly at some things in it, but it is a more interesting book than Macaulay's 'England.' "

I can never forgive the Massachusetts people for putting their most disreputable citizen into the governorship last fall. To that directly is to be traced the trouble of the last few weeks. Sprague is nobody;—not even a " Little-tin-Butler-on-wheels," as the *Springfield Republican* called him. Bankrupt in character, reputation, business, politics, everything, you cannot conceive of such a creature being picked up by any party, except under the influence of the Butler craze. If the election yesterday had resulted differently, Sprague would only nominally have been governor of Rhode Island. The real governor would have been Butler himself, who would be only too happy to run two states—into the ground.

But it is enough to stagger any man to see how absolutely *for nothing* arguments or logic count with the adherents of Butler or Sprague. It is the Jackson experience over again. Prove to your man that the candidate is disreputable, dishonest, tricky. His only answer is " Hurrah for Jackson !," or Butler, or Sprague, as the case may be.

One unforeseen result of the last campaign will apparently be to put a quietus for a long time on the movement for an extension of the suffrage in R. I., which had really gained important headway. The inference being that if there are so many voters in the state who under present conditions would vote for an object like Sprague it would be the height of imprudence to let the bars down any farther.

This view of the case would rather ruffle the spirit of the late Thomas Jefferson, I am well aware. (I am waiting not very patiently to see what Morse says of him.) But I am free to confess that on looking back over the " political development " of my own views for the last ten years, it is not by any means in the direction of Jefferson, but of Hamilton.

*   *   *   *

Truly yours,

W. E. Foster

25 — From William E. Foster

Providence Public Library,
57 Snow Street.

Providence, R. I., April 16, 1883

My dear Adams,

" Parish institutions of Maryland " rec'd.[1] It is literally built on Bacon, is it not? From your revised prospectus I notice that Shaw's article was read before your Assoc., as a paper, a fact which had escaped my notice before.

Why not send a set of the " Johns Hopkins University Studies " to Herr Professor Erdmannsdörffer, (Heidelberg) ?, or rather to the Universitäts-Bibliothek.

My friend, Wheeler, (now at Heidelberg), writes me that Professor Erdmannsdörffer borrowed his copy of the " Germanic origin of New England towns," (I had sent Wheeler a copy), and afterwards wanted to keep it. He (Professor E.) says: " Adams ought to send them his publications."

Wheeler adds: " Professor Erdmannsdörffer always speaks in the kindest way of Adams. He said to me the other day: ' I always remember with pleasure his participation in my Seminar. It was a pleasure to have him present.' " But I will spare your blushes, and change the subject.

Professor William P. Atkinson, of the Massachusetts Institute of Technology, Boston, writes me that he is " hoping to establish in the new building " " a sort of working historical laboratory for (his) students, that shall correspond to (their) chemical and physical laboratories, and where the process of learning shall be much the same,—not memorizing a text-book, but, so to speak, manipulating literary, political, and historical apparatus."

I do not need to be informed, of course, that you are up to your eyes in work, and have not much time for writing. Still, if you could drop him a line, briefly explaining your own

---

[1] Edward Ingle, a graduate student in the Johns Hopkins, was the author of this article which was published in the *Magazine of American History* of April, 1883 and reprinted in the first volume of the *Studies*.

" laboratory " method, I should esteem it a personal favor. Please say to him that you write at my request.

I mail you a Prov. *Journal*, with report of historical address on the Jesuits in Maryland. Some of my subscribers asked me to treat this 250th anniversary in the *Monthly Reference Lists*. But I fear I should find difficulty in treating such a topic so as to escape somebody's charging " lack of impartiality," and I am not going to attempt it.

By the way, has Leypoldt sent you the proof of " John Adams's administration " yet?

Hastily yours,

William E. Foster.

(Wheeler says : " Adams's paper was most intensely interesting to me. I hope to be able to verify his observations in a Pfingsten trip which Professor Osthoff and I have planned for the Odenwald.")

26 — *From George E. Howard*

State University,
Lincoln, Nebr. 5-30-'83.

Dr. H. B. Adams
Johns Hopkins University
Dear Sir:—

It has been my intention for some months to write you a letter expressive of the interest felt, even in this remote corner of the vineyard, in the great work which you are accomplishing at Johns Hopkins.

I have observed with keen interest and with great hope for the future of historic science in this country, what seems to me to be the first rational and successful effort to elevate the study of institutions to the place which it is destined to occupy in the University course, both as a means of discipline and as the basis of general culture. This sympathy with your work, augmented by the many good things which I have heard in regard thereto from my friend Caldwell, together with the kind notice of the beginning in historic study already made in Nebraska, to which I am under obligations to you, seems already almost to warrant the claim of acquaintance.

I wish particularly to express my appreciation of the "Johns Hopkins Historic Studies." They are accomplishing more real good for the advancement of the study of history, than anything before undertaken in this country. They possess the merit of being at once a model for higher academic study, in thorough keeping with the most advanced thought and method, and are also most valuable products of original investigation. I see no reason why they may not be taken as suggestive models for the more advanced work of our higher institutions throughout the land. It would immediately transform the study from the condition of dry routine to that of productiveness. While but a small portion of the work produced might be worthy of publication, it would gradually develop among us the habit of drinking at the *Quellen* and of fruitful study so peculiar to academic life in Germany. It is painful to realize the condition of historic study in the multitude of so-called colleges and universities in the United States, particularly in the west, though some of the western state schools are vitalized by the spirit of modern ideas. When a Chair of History was established here, grave professors, educated under the old order of things, regarded it as an unwarranted expenditure of time and money. History should, they thought, be made auxiliary to some other department. This feeling prevails very widely among certain classes of educators. Nevertheless it is *the* study of this age. I am glad to report that we are making progress here. Already the department is popular, drawing a larger number of elective students, and gradually winning the acknowledgment that it offers a larger share of practical knowledge and real mental discipline than any other department. Hitherto I have been overladen with tutorial work—eighteen to twenty-five hours a week in the classroom

—leaving, as you can imagine, little time for composition or investigation. But a strong effort is now being made to take a step in advance. We hope to open a seminary for advanced students and graduates with the beginning of the next academic year.

You certainly have great cause for satisfaction. Johns Hopkins, and not Ann Arbor, Cornell, or even Harvard, is now regarded by the more intelligent, as the best conception of the University for America which has yet appeared. In the Department of History and Political Science we of the west are looking constantly to Baltimore as our guide.

If it is your desire to widen the circle of cooperation, I should be very glad to profit by a direct connection with you in this work. Just at present I am using all my spare time in preparing a manual on English institutions, in the hope of doing something to make the study according to the comparative method practicable in a greater number of schools. The *textbook* is the symbol of the radical evil of the routine school. The comparison of many books is absolutely essential to the application of the comparative method. To economize time in the mechanical part of this labor is one portion of the task I have set myself, while I hope to complete my preparatory education by a more thorough study of the authorities and sources. When this work is completed, I should be glad to prepare something for your inspection and criticism with a view to publication. The West offers many facilities for the study of institutions, though, of course, society here is far more conglomerate and artificial than in New England or the South.

In conclusion I venture to ask of you two favors: If your leisure permits, be so kind as to send me a testimonial as to Mr. H. W. Caldwell's qualification for the position of Assistant in the department of history.[1] I desire to secure his appointment by the Board of Regents. I wish to obtain the assistance of someone who can work in the seminary, and,

---

[1] Howard W. Caldwell was a graduate student in the Johns Hopkins during the year 1882-1883.

in general, someone who is thoroughly imbued with the spirit of modern ideas and methods. The second favor is one which, I fear, I cannot very modestly ask, but necessity compels me to throw myself on your generosity:—I should like to obtain through Mr. Caldwell from your library a few books of which I stand greatly in need. I will be responsible for their safe return. If they can be spared even for a few days, it will be a great accommodation, and will be most gratefully acknowledged.

Pardon this long trespass on your time, and believe me

Very sincerely yours,

Geo. E. Howard.

27 — From Albert S. Bolles

Philadelphia June 6 1883.

Dear Mr. Adams,

Yesterday on my return from Reutgers and Princeton Mr. Barker showed me your letter and desired me to reply. I went to those places at his request to see Dr. Scott and Mr. McMaster.[1] Both, in my judgment, are well qualified for the work wanted of them here. I have no doubt of Dr. Scott's wide attainments in American history; and his knowledge of our constitutional history is especially valuable. I much admired his courtesy, his frankness and his deep conscientious-noss. He certainly is a rare man. If I had not seen Mr. McMaster I am quite sure that Mr. Barker would have been content without going further.

---

[1] On May 15, 1883, Professor R. E. Thompson of the University of Pennsylvania wrote to Adams asking if he would consider a call to a new professorship in that institution. In a letter to Wharton Barker, dated June 6, Adams said, " only the strongest inducements held out to me by President Gilman, could have induced me to decline it, as I did in a telegram to Provost Pepper." He went on to recommend Austin Scott at that time professor in Rutgers College. Adams did not mention McMaster. For the contents of the letter to Barker, which is in the archives of the University of Pennsylvania, I am indebted to Dr. Eric F. Goldman.

On the other hand, it is doubtful if we could draw him away from Reutgers. He said that he would probably be offered a chair and a salary of $2250, while we could offer only $250 more. If the slight addition were any inducement to leave doubtless Reutgers would increase the amount to our figure. Besides, he is near Newark. He told me that Dr. Stearns would cheerfully acquiesce in his going wherever his best interests seemed to lie, but I think that we both can comprehend how difficult would be the parting with one so dear to us as Dr. S. is to them. On the other side may be put the facts that his work here would be more concentrated, that there would be less of it, and a richer field for study and outside cultivation.

With respect to Mr. McMaster the way is perfectly clear for us. His range of attainments is narrower than that of Dr. Scott's, but his knowledge of history in general and American history in particular is truly wonderful. He has read enormously and remembered everything. He began reading history when very young, and his devotion to the subject is as rare as it is beautiful. He is a quiet gentle sort of man; but underneath is a deep genuine enthusiasm which I am sure would be felt by every student who came under the shadow of his teaching. Then, too, his wide and just reputation is of no little worth to a collegiate institution. He has taught very efficiently at Princeton. This, in brief, is the situation. It is by no means easy to decide what to do. Both are excellent men. I think, however, that the tide among those who are the most deeply interested is setting toward Mr. McMaster. I can assure [you] that whatever may be the result Mr. Barker is grateful for the kindly interest you have shown in the matter.

Yours sincerely,

Albert S. Bolles.

28 — From Daniel Coit Gilman

Oxford
July 15. 83

Dear Adams

I have seen Prof Stubbs today & told him of your work in which he seems to be much interested. I have promised him some of your *tracts*. *Will you send them*; also the diagram &c of your historical laboratory.[1] Sir H. Maine was also very appreciative.

Yours very truly

D C Gilman

29 — To Andrew D. White

Johns Hopkins University, Nov. 24, 1883

Dear Sir:

By a curious chance Dr Charles Gross dropped in upon us only a day or two after I wrote you. He has been here for some little time and I have become well acquainted with him. Last Friday evening by request he read at our Historical Seminary an abstract of his paper upon the Guild Merchant, a study introductory to the English Municipality. He made a strong impression upon the minds of our men. I think Gross has struck a very rich vein of historical inquiry, for the whole subject of English Colonisation in America is manifestly the outgrowth of mercantile associations like those of Plymouth and London. One has only to read the charters of the Virginia Company to see that; but we have even found

---

[1] The desire to be " scientific " undoubtedly was responsible for the great emphasis Adams gave to the physical arrangement of the historical seminar room. He had a diagram made showing the exact location of the seminar table, the various offices, the alcoves containing different kinds of periodicals and documents, etc., etc. He published it frequently: in the *Studies*, II, 137; in *Methods of Teaching History*, G. Stanley Hall, ed. (1885 edition), p. 147; in *The Study of History in American Colleges and Universities* (U. S. Bureau of Education, Circular of Information No. 2, 1887). " The Baltimore seminaries," he wrote, " are laboratories where books are treated like mineralogical specimens, passed from hand to hand, examined, and tested." *Ibid.*, p. 175.

a perpetuation of the Guild spirit in our Colonial Companies. I have urged Gross to go back to England and continue his work until he can lay the foundation for a study of American States and Cities. He has promised me a paper on " The English Municipality. An Introduction to the Study of American Cities." I have also urged him to prepare a course of twenty lectures on English Self Government, with reference to the City, the County, and the Parish. I shall urge Mr. Gilman most strongly to invite Gross to give this course at the Johns Hopkins next year, and I wish you would allow him to repeat it at Cornell. The man will have a success as a lecturer and as an original investigator; but I fancy it will be very difficult for him to get a start as a regular instructor in an American College, on account of his Jewish connections. A University position must be created for him in some way, for he is really too brilliant and too well-trained for any subordinate kind of work. With Gross as contributor, the Studies in American Institutional History would rapidly advance.

Very Truly

H B Adams [1]

President A. D. White
Cornell University.

30 — From James Bryce

77, Mount Vernon St.,
Boston Mass.

Dec. 5 [1883]

My dear Adams

Enclosed I send you a short sketch of our De Tocqueville discussion in the Seminar meeting; you may enlarge or abridge it as you think fit—it is meant only as a basis.

Will you please ask Prof. Ely to send me the pamphlet by Wm. Rathbone which I shewed him if he has quite done with it, & will you ask him to append any criticism or illustra-

---

[1] The original of this letter is in the Andrew D. White Papers in the Cornell University library.

tion that occurs to him, in case he has time to do so? I must write to Rathbone about it, and am waiting to do so.

This place is in some excitement over the "Greek question" as they call it: & it looks as if the Trojans were to win. There is talk of establishing a historical seminary like yours. They have got a capital law school, indeed when I see that, and when I see your organization for historical & Staatswissenschaftlich studies I blush for the motherland which with all her vast endowments has nothing so satisfactory. "Having many other things to write unto thee, I will rather come and speak face to face," and when I take my journey unto (or from) Washington, shall try to do so.

Yours always truly, with sincere thanks

for your courtesies in Baltimore,

J. Bryce

31 — To Daniel Coit Gilman

Amherst, Mass. August 8, 1884

Dear Mr. Gilman:

I have just received your letter and have written President White, urging him to be present at our Saratoga convention of teachers and friends of History, and to read his article on the Ethical Value of Historical Studies. I presume it is the chapter that he proposes to contribute to Dr. Hall's new volume.

The convention will be a success in a quiet way. Mr. Winsor, whom I visited in Cambridge last week, and young Channing (Professor Torrey's protégé) will represent Harvard in the flesh. Emerton is coming with his newly imported German Professor, who is to represent German Literature as German History at Harvard College. He has worked on the *Monumenta* with Waitz and will strengthen historical work at Harvard by the double advantage of *German* lectures on German *literature*. Besides the new blood of Harvard, we shall have at the convention Levermore to represent *young*

Yale and the Johns Hopkins. I am very proud of this delegate. Dr. Austin Scott has offered a "constitutional" paper. C. K. Adams, Moses Coit Tyler, and their disciples will be on hand. Young Columbia, I think, is well disposed, although Burgess was thinking of a convention in New York City. But Saratoga will win. C. K. Adams has been asked to give the "send-off," but I have no doubt he would like to see President White preside at the meetings. Would not that course permit an ethical "inaugural?" We shall form a very happy family and have a very good time.

* * *, *

Very Truly,

H. B. Adams

32 — From Daniel Coit Gilman

Boston, Aug 19 1884

My dear Adams,

At Houghton's, Mr. Scudder asked me about W. Wilson, as a possible writer of "N. Carolina" for the State histories. I commended him strongly & advised him to ask your opinion. He wants to know Wilson's ancestral and domestic ties—whether or not they are of the Old North State. You will know, I presume, & I hope will be asked. Tillinghast of the Public State Library told me that your Hist. Studies were in constant demand. He thinks you will have to reprint Vol. I., & ought to stereotype in future.

Yrs truly,

D. C. Gilman

33 — To Frederic Bancroft

Johns Hopkins University,
Seminary of History and Politics.
Baltimore, Mar. 5 1885

Dear Mr. Bancroft:

The newspaper clippings came to hand this morning and I have read with great interest your contribution to The

[NY Evening] Post. The entire lot has now been filed & indexed.

We shall be very glad to have you come in May & if you will fix the date I will reserve the time. In fact, I think I can arrange a series of Slave & Negro Studies for that month:

Slavery in Md.
What became of the Northern Slave
The Last Fugitive Slave
The Negro in Politics
(is that it?)
The order is immaterial. Set your own time.

Very truly

H. B. Adams

34 — From Frederic Bancroft

Charlottenburg b/Berlin,
Fasanenstr. 12
Oct. 1. 1885.

Dear Doctor Adams:

Your kind letter of introduction to Von Holst was received a few hours before I left New York. As I could not acknowledge its receipt from N. Y., I concluded to wait until Aug. when I then intended to visit Freiburg: and hoped to then write my acknowledgments and a few lines about my future plans.

Both because I found that I had not accomplished as much as I hoped to during the summer and because the courses for the next semester are especially inviting, I have decided to remain here till spring, and then go southward.

In accordance with your advice I shall give special attention to the lectures by Gneist and Weizsäcker, although I heard the former last semester.

The following are the courses which I shall probably hear:—

Gneist " Preuss. Verfass.— u. Verwaltungsrecht "

Weizsäcker " Allgemeine Verfassungsgeschichte "
Wagner " Finanzwissenschaft "
Von Treitschke " Politik "
Aegidi " Verfassungsgeschichte Deutschlands im 19ten
   Jahrhundert "

I don't know much about Treitschke or his course, but
he seems to be one of the most brilliant and interesting of the
lecturers here.

Remembering with much pleasure my long conversation
with you in Baltimore and your generous and brotherly interest in students of political science I will presume that a
few lines in the spring will not be a bore after I get settled
in Freiburg or Paris.

> Very respectfully and gratefully yours,
>
> > Frederic A. Bancroft

P.S. The wording of the letter of introduction—as it was
so complimentary—made me tremble, because I feared lest his
" scholarly appreciation " would fail to find anything appreciable in my study. But as I have since received a good
many words of praise and encouragement from several prominent men (such as Carl Schurz, who wrote me enthusiasti-
cally about it, said I must publish it, and invited me to
come and see him), I think I shall venture to send him
[von Holst] a copy shortly.   F. A. B.

35 — From Charles H. Levermore

> Branch Office, New Haven, Conn.
>
> Nov. 16, 1885.

Dear Doctor Adams—

Last Saturday I shipped off the Magnum Opus to Henry
Holt & to H. M. & Co. I feel like Christian when his pack
rolled off. The natural buoyancy of my disposition is once
more reasserting itself in all manner of freaks and fantastic
ideas. Perhaps one of the craziest whims of all is that I

should like to obtain a position in South America, where I might hope to work up the history of the S. A. Republics, as Motley did the Dutch story of old.[1] Buenos Ayres and Santiago have both become objects of longing to my fevered fancy,—and do you suppose that anything short of actual experience can cure me? I should think that the educational systems of Chili or of the Argentine might be in need of me, and that a successful campaign ought to be conducted thro Washington or New York. I wrote to the N. Y. Consul, but I receive no answer as yet. Is all this an air-bubble? I understand from Dewey that there is a chance for an instructor in European History in the Univ. of California. Dewey is prospecting it some, but seems to think that he doesn't want to go there unless he is forced to. He recommends me to look it up. Apart from the alluring field of the Pampas & the Southern Alps, our Pacific Coast would suit me well enough. Do you think well of that institution? If you had not known of Dewey's researches in that direction, please do not mention this to him. It may be that his remarks were confidential altho I have no reason to think so.

Things are already waxing hot here at Yale over the Presidency & all that follows in its train. It is said that Sumner and Father Noah haven't spoken to each other in a year. So far things seem to be shaping themselves in the direction of a tremendous spanking for the Rehoboam party. Meanwhile Timotheus Dwight stoops more than ever in anticipation of the approaching honors. Kingsley printed my discourse on ye horrid witcherie, and now forsooth he thinks I am a mine & is trying to work me for more gratuitous contributions.[2] I shall resist the coy tempter. I am now beginning anew to struggle with my books for the exams.

Yours Sincerely
Charles H. Levermore [3]

---

[1] Adams wrote in the margin opposite this sentence "Not half bad."

[2] "Witchcraft in Connecticut, 1647-1697," in the *New Englander* of Nov., 1885.

[3] Levermore received a Ph. D. degree from the Johns Hopkins in 1885.

36 — From Frederic Bancroft

Charlottenburg—Berlin, Jan. 17, 1886
Fasanenstr. 12.

Dear Doctor Adams:

Since receiving your very kind and interesting letter some two months ago I have postponed writing to you, from Sunday to Sunday, partly because I had nothing especial to write about and partly because I didn't feel like infringing upon so much of your time.

I ought to have acknowledged the receipt of " The City of Washington " some time ago, for I have read it with no little pleasure.

The semester is now about one-half ended and I can judge of what I am getting. Weizsäcker has left no stone unturned between Rome and the 13th Century, where he is now leading us into all the dusty corners of France. If he can manage to continue this thoroughness and still bring us into the light of the 19th Century before Mar. 15, I shall be more than pleased with him.

I heard v. Treitschke's *Politik* a few times, and it was so painful for me to see and hear him that I gave it up and used the hour in hearing Bresslau on 17th and 18th century history. I think v. T. must have grown much worse since you heard him, as now he cannot hear his own voice, runs all sentences together, has no inflection according to sense, but his talk is most distressing sobbing. I shall try to read a friend's notes on the lectures—which will be much better than any I could have taken under the circumstances.

While I find Bresslau neither grand nor very striking, he impresses me as a very clever historian, and has the rare faculty of wasting no words, making every sentence produce an impression of something real to his hearers, and was, almost from the first lecture, as easy to understand as if he spoke English.

Gneist is about as concise and Wagner as verbose (especially in his books) as one can easily imagine. As yet Wagner seems to me far below what I expected.

With a half dozen others I work two hours every Saturday
in the Statistical Bureau under Böckh, the professor of Statistics here. He is taking us into a few interesting original investigations of the Berliners.

Aegidi did not begin his German Constitutional History
of the 19th Century until the second week in Nov., and
then actually spent three weeks in the 17th Century, about
ten days on the 18th, and has now been screeching himself
hoarse about the French wickedness in this century for only
two or three weeks. He makes so much noise that I cannot
appreciate what he is saying. From his lectures and from
those of Bresslau on the 19th Century which I mean to have
copied from another's notes I hope to get a good idea of the
opinion of the professors on the German history of this
century.

Living as I do "in the country" as my friends here all
name my abode, I have been able to make good use of my
time by keeping away from the Americans; and as both
the *Herr u. Frau,* with whom alone I board, are always
ready to read aloud to me or hear me read, I have managed
to get through a large number of German books, both literary and scholarly. The *Frau* "schwärms" for Goethe and
Schiller, Freitag and Heyse, and the *Herr* especially for
Prussian or German history and politics (especially such keen
books as "Bismarck Nach dem Kriege"), so that "between
them both" and myself we lick *two* platters. We are now
in the midst of no less serious recreation than that famous
and charming work of Pertz's "Aus Stein's Leben"—which
as you probably know comprises nearly 2000 closely printed
pages. Therefore aside, even, from my regular studies I
have found my six or seven months here very profitable.

I don't know when I have had anything please me so
much as a very cordial note from Von Holst which, I received a few weeks ago. He generously offered me the use
of his library, to guide and assist my studies in any way possible if I should come to Freiburg. Of course, therefore,
I shall go to Freiburg. I hope to be in the harness by Apr. 1
for seven months of hard work before going to Paris. For

his kind offer and for whatever flows therefrom, I shall not forget that I am indebted to you. By the way, the historian's brother—a very wealthy architect with as bright a family as I have ever known—lives but a short distance from here. As I became quite well acquainted with them two and a half years ago (Clifford Bateman's sister was then living with them, whom I knew very well at home) I have often enjoyed their hospitality, the pretty daughters and the sparkling German.

I see that our Columbia School is about to fall in line with your good example of political science studies. I judge from a recent letter that "Roman Law" Smith will be editor. My "Negro" has been again invited to put on a new coat and come before the public, but I fear to appear before so profound a scholar as Von Holst except as the most penitent and unassuming of beginners in United States history. If von Holst thinks best I shall work up something in U. S. history during my stay there.

But I have written a dreadfully windy letter! I hope it is not altogether unpardonable in its countless I's and may at least help recall your student days in *Deutschland* and thus result in one pleasing phase.

If you come in the neighborhood of Freiburg next summer I hope you will let me know and give me an opportunity to have another as profitable and interesting a talk with you as that in Baltimore in May last.

Very gratefully and respectfully

Frederic A. Bancroft

37 — From Charles Kendall Adams

President's Rooms,   Dictated.
Cornell University,

Ithaca, N. Y., Feb. 9 1886

Dear Professor Adams:

I approve of the nomination of Professor W. M. Pottle-thwaite, D. D., of West Point, for membership. At the suggestion of Professor Tyler I also send the name of Chas. H. Hull, who has been doing some special work on the pre-historic history of Washington. That is to say, he has found some material in Washington and elsewhere on the secret negotiations which led to the establishment of the capitol at that place. Tyler thinks it is really new material and that he will be able to present a paper should it be wished at the spring meeting that will be new and creditable. He will make this paper his graduating thesis and Tyler thinks it is well worthy of a place on our programme. So you may regard this as in part an answer to your second question. I have not yet seen all of our men, and so cannot quite yet tell you what we shall be able to do. Even whether I can go is not altogether certain, though of course I could pull away if it seemed to be necessary. I regret to think that I shall not be able to prepare anything for the occasion. If such meetings had to rely upon college presidents, the association would soon go to the dogs.

Now to your third question I have to say that so far as I know nothing has ever been written in reference to the history of the historical department at the University of Michigan. The department has a history, however, that is very interesting, and that I think is of some importance. President White in 1857 brought an enthusiasm to his new chair that sent a sort of historical glow through all the veins and arteries of the University. This was done mainly through his lectures, which combined instruction and inspiration in a very remarkable degree. This enthusiasm was perhaps fairly well kept up, but no very great change was made in the historical work until in 1869 I introduced the seminary method, bringing it from Germany, and putting my classes into the work of investigation. So far as I know this was about the first, if not absolutely the first establishment of what could be called a historical seminary in the United States. For a considerable number of years the work was still rather elementary. Within the last five or six years, since we have been able to bring materials together for the use of students, the work, I think, has been highly creditable.

You will allow me to add, perhaps, that since, within the last year, I have observed more largely, I have come to have an increasing respect for the work done at the University of Michigan. The people at the East generally have a very inadequate idea of the general excellence of that institution.

I wish to refer to another matter. Mr. James Fraser Gluck, an alumnus and Trustee of this University has suggested to me that he would be willing to write a paper for your municipal series on the government of Buffalo. He is familiar with all the details of the great struggle which brought Mr. Cleveland forward as the representative in New York of municipal reform. As to Mr. Gluck's characteristics and ability to do this work well, you may perhaps infer from the enclosed slip from the Albany Argus. I can give it any endorsement you might feel inclined to ask. He has literary gifts that are unmistakable, and I think would do the work well.

I will try to get more definite information within a very few days as to what we can do at the April meeting, and report to you without delay.

Very heartily yours,

C. K. Adams

Professor H. B. Adams,
Johns Hopkins University,
Baltimore, Md.

38 — From William E. Sparks

Boston, May 24 1886

Prof. H. B. Adams,
Johns Hopkins University,
Baltimore, Md.

My dear Sir,

Two boxes of papers,—one large box & one small,—will probably be shipped tomorrow, to your address as above, by Adams Ex. Co., prepaid. I have put therein everything my Mother considered necessary or useful to you, and as called for by section 2 of contract.[1] The Mss. of Articles in the No. American Review were omitted, knowing that you had them in printed form in the library of the University; they are all given in Poole's last Index to that Review, since, at his request, I furnished him with a list of them. The Mss. of the larger works have not been sent, as it was thought that

---

[1] Under date of May 20, 1886, an agreement was signed by Adams and Mary C. Sparks, the widow of Jared Sparks. The most interesting provisions are as follows:

1. That, in consideraton of the sum of two thousand dollars, to be paid as hereinafter stated, the said Adams has agreed and does hereby agree with the said Sparks to write, collate and prepare, between the date hereof and the first day of January, 1890, a Manuscript, (with Index), of "THE LIFE AND WRITINGS OF JARED SPARKS," for publication, in two octavo volumes of not less than five hundred pages each, small pica type; to make, on behalf of the said Mary C. Sparks and for her account, a contract, on as favorable terms as possible, with some publisher or publishers to be selected or approved by her, or her legal representative, for the printing and publication of five hundred copies of said Manuscript; to correct the proofs thereof, when printed, and to supervise the said publication.

2. That, in consideration of such literary work, so to be done, the said Mary C. Sparks has agreed and does hereby agree with the said Adams to forthwith loan and deliver to him, at the Johns Hopkins University, in the said City of Baltimore, for his use in said work, all the private letters, manuscripts and papers of the said Jared Sparks, deceased, all obituary notices of him, and all other written or printed material, now in her possession, necessary for, or serviceable in, the preparation of said work, including the sketch of the early life of the said Jared Sparks heretofore commenced by her; . . .

3. It is mutually understood and agreed that the said Adams shall be at liberty to make such extracts, as he may see fit, from any letters, papers or material entrusted to him as hereinbefore provided, and to incorporate such extracts in his said work, but none of such letters, papers or material shall be used by or shown to any other person, or referred to for any purpose other than the work aforesaid, and that upon the completion of said work, all such letters, papers and material shall be returned to the said Mary C. Sparks, or held subject to her order.

*   *   *   *

5. It is further understood and agreed that the said Mary C. Sparks, her son William E. Sparks, of Boston, Massachusetts, her son-in-law Benjamin P. Moore, of the said City of Baltimore, and Lizzie Sparks Pickering, of Cambridge, Mass., and each of them, if they desire, may see and read said work, when ready for the printer and before publication, and may alter or expunge therefrom any matter which any two of them, if living, or any one of them, if the other two be dead, may, after perusal, deem objectionable.

*   *   *   *

6

you would prefer to consult them as printed. The one point on which they might be desirable for you seems to be to judge of the care taken in writing them by a study of corrections made in style or language before finally sending to the printer, & this is a point on which my Father exercised great care. I will only say that such corrections are few & apparently of no great importance. Very possibly he may have written them twice over.

I presume you are aware of the fact that Guizot's Washington is a translation of that of Sparks, although not so credited on title page. Mr. Guizot received great praise & various public & civic honors for this work, but only mentions obscurely the name of my Father somewhere in the preface. Mr. Sparks himself had selected Guizot for this purpose & had arranged with him to undertake the work.

The contract is being copied & will probably be mailed to you tomorrow.

I remain, Dear Sir,

Very sincerely yours,

Wm. E. Sparks.

39 — To the President and Executive Committee

To the President and Executive Committee of the Johns Hopkins University.

A Plea for the Organization of the Department of Historical and Political Science.

Gentlemen:

It is now nearly ten years since the beginning of historical and political studies in this institution. In 1876 there was but one instructor in this field and only one exercise a week. Now there are three regular instructors and one tutor, giving altogether twenty-eight exercises a week. At the outset there were two Fellows in Political Science and one in History, but no regular graduate students in this department. Now there are twenty graduate students and only one fellowship. The first year there was no provision for undergraduate instruction in History as a part of the A. B. course. Such work was begun upon the voluntary system by the Fellow in History with a class of two. At the present time, History and Historical Geography are required three hours a week, for one year, on the part of all undergraduate students. There are, moreover, at least thirty undergraduates who have elected History and Political Science each for a two years' course. Altogether there are at present in this department 94 students. Without instituting any comparisons, it is obvious that historical and political studies have won a place in the curriculum of this University. A full report of the work of the past year is herewith presented in printed form:

An earnest plea for the recognition of the results of the past decade and for the organization of this growing department upon a professorial basis, with representation in the Academic Council, is made upon the following special grounds:

1. The study of Historical and Political Science should be distinctly and honorably recognized in every American University as a means of training American youth to good citizenship and American teachers to a knowledge of constitutional government, political history, the science of administration, and political economy. While fostering science of every kind, Universities should especially foster *Scientia pro Patria*.

2. These studies of History, Politics, and Economics occupy in European Universities and Gymnasia a distinguished place. They have been recognized by distinct professorships in every American institution of academic fame, except the Johns Hopkins University. Harvard has three professors (Torrey, Gurney, and Emerton); two Assistant Professors (McVane and Young); three instructors (Hart, Channing, and Weaver),—all in the department of History. Harvard has one Professor and two Assistant Professors in Political Economy. Yale has just organized a School of Political Science, with two Professors of Political Economy (Sumner and Hadley) and three young instructors,—all working upon

the Seminary plan. Yale has also two Professors of History. Cornell University has had two presidents who were at the same time Professors of History. She has also a distinct professorship of American History, two Associate Professors of Political Science, three Lecturers, and one historical instructor. Columbia College has three Professors of History and Political Science and four resident Lecturers taken from her own graduates. The University of Pennsylvania has two Professors of History, two Professors of Political Economy, and one instructor in History. Princeton College has two Professors in Historical and Political Science. In fact, there is scarcely a reputable *College* in the country which has not recognized these studies upon terms of equality with the Classics, Mathematics, and Natural Sciences. The experience of the old world and of the new alike proves that the study of Man and Society is coming to the front.

3. In the face of superior facilities for historical and political study elsewhere, in spite of these many and growing combinations at Harvard, Yale, Columbia, Cornell, Michigan, Philadelphia, our small department in Baltimore has made some headway. We have more and better graduate students, and they have done more original work, than can be found elsewhere in this country. This original work has made itself felt in other institutions which are now following our example. Harvard has just received a gift of $15,000 to encourage monographic publication in our field. The Faculty of the Columbia School of Political Science have just begun to publish a Political Science Quarterly, which the Editor privately avows to me is in imitation of our methods of publication. The University of Pennsylvania is now publishing her Annals of Political Science. Amherst College and the University of Michigan have caught the idea of our monographic series and have applied it to published papers in Philosophy. So well known in America are our Baltimore Studies that they now pay their own way.

But our work has received more appreciative recognition in Europe than in this country. Not to speak of the cordial letters of Sir Henry Maine, Professors Freeman, Laveleye, Frédéricq, Winkelmann (Rector of Heidelberg, 1885), Cossa, and many others, it may be mentioned that the work of our department has been favorably reviewed in the most critical European journals representing our field, notably by the Revue des Deux Mondes, Journal des Economistes, the Revue Historique, the Historische Zeitschrift, the English Historical Review, etc. Last week I received a letter from M. Monod, of Paris, asking me to become the American representative of the Revue Historique which he edits. Dr Ely's forthcoming work on the Labor Movement in America is forthwith to be translated into German and the work of our pupil Dr Shaw is already translated into that language.

4. While such evidence of appreciation abroad is more or less gratifying, what the University needs and what our department needs is appreciation *at home*. Certain it is that without more earnest support by the University the two leaders in this field of History and Politics are likely to lose both heart and interest in their present work. In this connection it seems proper to state, although I do it with reluctance, that within the past few years I have received calls to three distinct professorships of History: (1) in Smith College, Northampton, Massachusetts, with $2,500 salary; (2) in the University of Pennsylvania with $2,750, the place which John Bach McMaster now holds, to which I should certainly have gone, if the Johns Hopkins had not made an equal offer; (3) in the University of Michigan, of which last offer I shall further speak. I have also had overtures relating to two college presidencies: one in Iowa College, Des Moines, with $3,000 salary and a house; and another in the University of Nebraska, with $4,000 salary. While I have no confidence in my ability to become a College President, I may be forced into a Western College in sheer despair.

Last summer I was invited by President Angell to accept the professorship of History in the University of Michigan in place of Charles Kendall Adams, President-elect of Cornell University. The prospect of leadership, with the added salary of Deanship, in that flourishing School of Political Science, where History was emancipated as long ago as Andrew D. White was made Professor in that department; where $5,000 have lately been expended upon the Seminary Library by authority of Professor Adams,—this prospect was not without its attractions. In June I was on the point of accepting. In July I was calmer, and decided to decline the offer, without any consultation with Baltimore authorities, hoping that they would do me justice when the facts should become known. After my declination, the professorship of History in Ann Arbor was urged upon Judge T. M. Cooley, who consented to hold it until a younger man could be found. I am informed that the place is still open.

5. Inasmuch as Judge Cooley was once called to the position which I now crave in Baltimore, that is, headship of a department of Historical and Political Science, it seems to me that the logic of the present situation is somewhat in my favor.

6. My promotion in Baltimore would facilitate the immediate organization of the entire department of History, Politics, and Economics. It would at once clear the way to a recognition of Dr Ely as Associate Professor of Political Economy and Administration (often companion subjects in German Universities). He justly deserves this honor and, considering his present leading position among the economists of the country, I think it highly inexpedient to withhold it longer. I know positively that overtures as to the Professorship of Political Economy in the University of Pennsylvania, which E. J. James now holds, were first made to Dr. Ely and that James owes his present position to Ely's influence. In this connection I may say that, during the past year alone, four Hopkins graduates have secured academic positions in either History or Political Science through my instrumentality: (1) Wilson at Bryn Mawr; (2) Dewey in the Mass. Institute of Technology; (3) Bemis at Amherst; and (4) Levermore in the Univ. of California.

7. The question at issue is not so much a matter of money

as a point of personal honor and of just recognition. I shall be content with such gradual economic advancement as the University may consider fair and reasonable in view of its growing economic embarrassment. Dr Ely, I am quite sure, is content with his present salary, if only his title is made that of an " Associate Professor." Dr. Jameson, a scholarly and meritorious man, would be satisfied with such extra compensation as would naturally fall to him if he should again be intrusted with the work of the late Professor Morris in Classical Historians (through translations). He has done this work since the Professor's death with entire satisfaction. In addition to the above force, I ask only that a tutor, possibly Mr Vincent, be appointed in place of Mr. Holcomb, at $250 salary, to aid in the undergraduate work in History; and that Woodrow Wilson, of Bryn Mawr, be invited to give our department a course of five or ten lectures on American Administration, perhaps exchanging lectures with me for a short period.

Respectfully and earnestly submitted,

H. B. Adams

Baltimore, May 29, 1886

40 — From William F. Allen

Madison, Wis., 228 Langdon St., Aug. 2 1886

My dear Mr. Adams,

I do not think that the department of History had any history before my day—not from any inferiority on the part of the instructors, or want of estimate of the value of the department, but from the smallness of the instructional force. When I came here we had a Faculty of eight, and my work included Latin, Greek, History and Political Economy. History was confined to a term of Guizot in the Senior year, and of Taylor's Handbook in the Junior. The latter I was relieved of by one of the other professors. Soon I was relieved of Greek & Political Economy, and began to experiment in history. I tried a good many methods with greater or generally less success, and by looking over the catalogues I could write out a chronology of my experiments if you desired. But I don't think they would be edifying. About ten years ago I was able, in a revision of our courses, to work into the outline which I have sketched in Dr. Hall's book,[1] and which I find very satisfactory. Here too there was considerable experimenting in detail, which is of questionable interest. I have finally settled upon the topical method, where the subject admits of it, and elsewhere (as in institutional history) familiar lectures, so far as possible consisting of commentary, conversation and elaboration of material like that in Stubbs' Select Charters. I use that book in one term of the Senior year. For the rest I find my selections where I can, & print them off for the use of the class—as specimen enclosed.

I believe I was one of the first who made American History a required study, which it is for the Junior class of the Classical courses. A great many others elect it, so that my classes in it average between 40 and 50. This was introduced in the academic year 1879-80.

I am going away for about a fortnight in the country, after which I will do anything I can for you. But I don't think I can get hold of all material before the term opens, the first week of September. Let me know how detailed you would like the information. At the same time I doubt very much whether there is material here for any elaborate treatment.

Yours very truly,

William F. Allen.

41 — From Woodrow Wilson

Bryn Mawr, Pa.,

27 Nov., 1886.

Dear Dr. Adams,

I received your kind letter of Nov. 25 yesterday, and I hasten to reply. I had not forgotten my response to your

---

[1] G. Diesterweg, *Methods of Teaching History*, ed. G. Stanley Hall (Boston, 1883).

suggestion that I should present in Balto. the results of my
studies, now in progress, in comparative politics and administration; but, you remember, I coupled an " if " with
my assent: " if I got my material into shape to be presented
this winter,"—and there's the trouble. I worked diligently
all summer, and I am taking advantage of every scrap of
leisure afforded by my duties here to push my special studies,
which just now, unfortunately, cannot be made to come in
in class; but I have not yet gone over, with even a first survey,
the whole field; and the habit of my mind is such that until
I see my *whole* subject I can't write on a part of it anything
that I would like to put forth in public as *results*. I am,
therefore, so to say, *waiting on myself,* waiting on the slow-
ness of my thought,—expecting the time when, all the in-
gredients of the *entire* substance of my studies being mixed
in, the several portions of my treatment may crystalize
symmetrically. I am writing of course when I can; but I have
written nothing safe to be promulgated. I have only made
sketches.

You will see, therefore, just how I must feel with reference to a possible invitation to lecture a portion of the year
in Balto.,—or all the year in Ithaca (I read a paper *about*
the study of administration, not long ago, to the Hist. Association of Cornell, by the way, which may have killed my
chances there!) A division of my time between Bryn Mawr
and Balto. would, however, commend itself most strongly to
me, so far as I can see at present: and I see no reason to
think that I would not, by the second half of the next University year at any rate, have something confident to say in
a course of lectures on governmental methods. I think, too,
that such an arrangement could be effected. The authorities
here seem generously desirous to meet my wishes in most
things.

What I have said is, I believe, the most definite thing I
can say at present,—and is as definite as your question calls
for. I have several schemes in head for next year; but none

of them are final as yet; and any proposition from Balto. would be apt to give them pause.

[Woodrow Wilson] [1]

---

[1] The rest of this letter is missing.

Wilson had been a graduate student at the Hopkins during the academic years 1883-1884 and 1884-1885, and had returned for examinations and the Ph. D. degree in 1886.

The relations between Adams and Wilson are an interesting subject of speculation. The letters of Wilson to Adams seem to indicate a lack of close community of thought or of soul between the two men. They were usually devoted almost solely to the business details concerning the series of lectures which Wilson delivered annually at the Hopkins for ten years. With one exception (No. 42) they contain neither full expressions of Wilson's ideas on his field of study such as might be expected in letters to a recognized authority and his former teacher, nor accounts of his hopes, plans or acts such as he wrote to intimate friends.

Wilson's opinion of Adams has been variously recorded. During his first year as a graduate student Wilson was severely critical. He objected to the subjects that Adams particularly favored. "These professors," he complained—incorrectly as he was soon to learn in his own case—"wanted to set everybody under their authority to working on what they called 'institutional history,' to digging, that is, into the dusty records of old settlements and colonial cities, to rehabilitating in authentic form the stories, now almost mythical, of the struggles, the ups and the downs, of the first colonists here there and everywhere on this then interesting continent." (Ray Stannard Baker, *Woodrow Wilson*, I, 174.) He objected even more to the quality of instruction offered. Adams, he wrote, "skipped too lightly . . . over too many subjects," "was too much of a showman to be a thorough scholar," permitted "his pupils to starve 'on a very meagre diet of ill-served lectures.'" (*Ibid.*, 178-179.) After hearing Bryce lecture at the University he wrote, "A taste of the instruction of such a man makes me all the more conscious of the insipidity of the lectures I hear daily in the classroom." (*Ibid.*, 196.)

Time was to soften these judgments. Toward the end of his second year of graduate study Wilson confessed that he had "expected too much at first, neglecting the principle . . . that everything of progress comes from one's private reading—not from lectures; that professors can give you always copious bibliographies and sometimes inspiration or suggestion, but never learning." (*Ibid.*, 179.) Many years later when writing a memorial sketch Wilson, either because the occasion demanded it or more likely because he had then a better perspective, paid high tribute to Adams. He then wrote, "His head was a veritable clearing house of ideas in the field of historical study, and no one ever seriously studied under him who did not get, in its most serviceable form, the modern ideals of work upon the sources; and not the ideals merely, but also a very definite principle of concrete application in daily study. The thesis work done under him may fairly be said to have set the pace for university work throughout the United States." (*Ibid.*, 179.)

What Adams thought of Wilson cannot be stated in his own words.

42 — From Woodrow Wilson

Bryn Mawr, Pa.,
5 Dec., 1886.

Dear Dr. Adams,

Thank you very much for your kind letter of Nov. 30.[1]
Things are moving rather fast with me nowadays, and, although, as you say, there is no need for haste in my plans

---

On various occasions people wrote to him asking his opinion but in spite of search and inquiry none of his replies has been found. That he set a high value on Wilson's abilities is decisively proven by the fact that he brought Wilson back to the Hopkins to lecture to the graduate students. Beginning in the academic year 1887-1888 Wilson lectured regularly at the Hopkins during the succeeding ten years.

Indeed Adams could hardly have failed to form a favorable opinion of Wilson if he were influenced at all by the evidence he received in numerous letters. When reading his correspondence I was immediately struck by the remarkable impression Wilson made on the people with whom he associated. In the case of no other graduate of the Department were there so many letters containing praise and a recognition of power. Evidently Gilman shared the general view, for after Adams died he offered Wilson the position of head of the Department. Under the date of March 18, 1901, Wilson replied as follows:

My dear Mr. Gilman,

I need not tell you how deeply your letter about the filling of Dr. Adams's place has gratified me, or how sorry I am to be obliged to say that I cannot consider the matter. The fact is, that I am under obligations here which I do not feel at liberty to turn away from or disregard. The Princeton people have so bound me to the place by every kindness and favour and honour, and have on several recent occasions made such a point of my staying here that I should really be ashamed to leave, as if I had not found my interests sufficiently advanced by them or were weary of their service. There would be points of delicacy for me about accepting a chair elsewhere which I confess I should not know how to meet.

This letter of yours will always be a gratification for me to think of, as a very substantial proof of your confidence in me as a scholar and as a man; and I thank you for it most heartily. It is no easy matter to return this sort of answer to it.

I am sure you know how irreparable I think the loss of the University in losing you. Your work and your individuality cannot be duplicated. With warmest regard,

Loyally and sincerely Yours,

Woodrow Wilson

[1] Written along the left-hand margin of the letter is this note: I will get the photo. of the library for you the next time I go in to Phila.

so far as the development of my work is concerned, I feel
that I should like to know what chances there are for the
sort of work in comparative politics I want to do in order
that I may see the whole field and so make no false move.

Amongst other things, I am thinking very seriously of
going to Europe next summer to stay two, or it might be
three, years and see the constitutions of the Continent *alive*.
Of course, as you know, I have long *wanted* to go abroad;
but it is only within the past few weeks that I have come
within sight of probable means of realizing the wish. Now
that new places such as I want are about opening to me,—
now is the time to go, if by doing so I shall not be cutting
myself off from advantageous engagements, but shall, as I
believe, be only making myself surer of them, because better
qualified for them. I *must* learn German as it cannot be
learned from books, and I must see European politics and
administration as no library can show them to me, even if
these objects may be attained only piece-meal during suc-
cessive *summers* spent abroad. It would be vastly better to
give two or three unbroken years to the purpose; and that is
what I am rapidly coming to the determination to do. As you
know, what I " go in for " is the *life*, not the texts, of constitutions, the practise not the laws of administration: and I
can get at these things only by cross-questioning systems at
their homes.[1] I have learned, for instance, all that is necessary to be known about what that autocratic person, the
French *Prefect*, *may* do, and what the law has to say about
his appointment:—*anybody* can find such things out and
make long-headed remarks about them. What I want to
know is, what the Prefect *does* do and under what influence
he is appointed. I must know the live prefect before I can
feel that I know anything about French administration. And
this will serve as an instance of what I am going to Europe
to study. I can't believe that I am mistaken in thinking that
such study would be the making of any courses I might after-

---

[1] He had written *Congressional Government* during his residence
as a graduate student in the Johns Hopkins but had never once
visited Congress. Baker, I, 218.

wards be called on to deliver on comparative politics and administration. And, since positions such as I want are *ripening* rather than yet *ripe*, this seems the nick of time for my preparation. For, besides, *I* am riper than I was two or three years ago.[1]

Very cordially yrs.

Woodrow Wilson

43 — *From Woodrow Wilson*

Bryn Mawr, Pa.,
21 Jany., 1887.

My dear Dr. Adams,

Your letter of Jany. 18 came promptly to hand. I thank you very much for having urged the matter forward so promptly. Considering the traveling expenses I would be put to in going down to Baltimore every week for twelve or thirteen weeks, the offer is rather less than I expected: but I see the advantages which it offers, provided ' prospects ' are beyond it. Before giving any definite judgment about it, however, I want to see whether or not we have in mind the same *subject-matter* for the lectures. I understand the field to be *comparative public law*: i. e. administration, but administration put in its proper *constitutional* relations and seen in its proper constitutional perspective: in a word, the way in which the functions of government are performed in the various states of most importance. Am I, right there?

I am negotiating with the authorities here as to what modifications it will be possible to make in my work next year with a view to letting in work once a week at the Hopkins. I could not afford, pecuniarily, to give up any of my salary here for a diminution of class duties; and, on the other hand, I could not afford, mentally, to *add* lectures such as I should

---

[1] Wilson discussed his plans for studying in Europe in a letter to his intimate friend Heath Dabney. Baker, I, 276-278. Fate intervened. Very soon after the letter to Adams was written the Wilsons knew that they were to have a second child. Jessie Wilson was born on Aug. 28, 1887. At this time Wilson's regular salary was $1500 a year.

expect to write for the Hopkins to the sum of full duties here.
The only chance lies in the direction of making room for
the same course—in its rudiments at least—here;—or in
getting an assistant. Of the latter I fear there is small chance
till year after next.—But of course I shall let you know
results, and shall make up the elements for a decision in the
matter as soon as possible. With sincere regard,

Very truly Yours,

Woodrow Wilson

Dr. H. B. Adams,
Baltimore, Md.

44 — From Charles H. Levermore

Univ. of California
Berkeley. Cal. Jan. 29 1887.

My dear Doctor Adams—

So I am a Margrave, am I?[1] Here then the Margrave
sends in his report of his dealings with the Huns and Slavs.
A full report of my relations with the brethern of Genghiz,
Kublai, Timour, et al. would include a description of the
daily chafferings at my back-door over lettuce, onions, cauli-
flower, peas et cetera, but my interest is just now especially
excited in a little Jap who has become my wife's attendant
demon. He knows about fifty English words, grins horribly,
and is as polite as tho he owed us something. I showed him
Sato's picture, which he recognized and I understand that
another Sato is in the High School in Oakland. He is not
a brother, but is a relative of the great Shosuke Khan.

I rejoice to hear of the prosperity at St. John's shrine. I

---

[1] "Upon a map of the United States, . . . the writer has caused
to be ticketed, and labelled with individual names, the various
institutions of learning which have employed the services of graduate students from the Johns Hopkins University. . . . The application
of this novel idea to the graphical illustration of what the writer
is inclined to call the colonial system of the Johns Hopkins University . . ." Herbert B. Adams, *The College of William and Mary*,
pp. 73-74. U. S. Bureau of Education, Circulars of Information, No.
1, 1887.

look back into my memory and recall the swift rush of life
in that institution, the varied program of attractions, the
rich possibilities of suggestion at every turn—and I sometimes think that I know what it is to fly with Uranus away
from the sun. But I have been so steadily occupied in the
endeavor to keep my mental equipment bright for the daily
encounter, that I have not felt the lack of reading-matter,
of music & lectures, of vigorous society. I have only seen it.
In coming years, if I stay here, the disconnected nature of
our society here will plainly be the greatest drawback—the
river of current thought & opinion does not pour thro this
University. We are still digging the channels for it.

There is no University Exchange here. Prest. Holden &
several others of the Faculty live in San Francisco—still
others, in Oakland. Few of the older Professors who live
here in Berkeley, feel able to gather company around them.
Prof. Howison, whose tilts with Professor Palmer you have
probably noticed, is a man who likes to put the Universe in
his pocket, & I try to pick his pocket occasionally.

My own chief, Prof. Moses, is a hardworking student, who
lives the life of a hermit, as it seems to me. His wife is now
in Germany, so that there is very little to call him out of
his seclusion. He is making an exhaustive study of Mexican
politics. I have given four hours a week, thru the term that
is just closing, to the study of English History with a class
numbering 58. We used the first two volumes of Bright's
Hist. as a guide. During the coming term we shall read the
Hist. of Eng. in the 18th Cent. by Lecky. A class in European Hist. has also taken four hours a week, reading Johnson's " Normans in Europe " Bryce's " Holy Roman Empire "
& Lodge's " Modern History " as guides. I have lectured to
this class on " The Migrations " & on " Hist of the Church."
The climate here is almost perfect. The curving hills have
fairly commanded my admiration—

Sincerely Yours

C. H. Levermore

45 — From D. N. Richardson

State University of Iowa.
Business Department.
Iowa City, Iowa, Feby 11 1887.

Prof Herbert B. Adams,
Johns Hopkins Univ.
Baltimore.

Dear Sir—

As President Pickard is about to lay aside school work, we are looking over the field for a suitable man for his chair.

I hardly need try to tell you what manner of man we want, only that the incumbent is not expected to do much if any teaching.

The Univ is fully equipped as to Departments, has an income of about 73.000$: has about 575 students, and should be in line with the very best schools of the land. The High Schools of Iowa graduate into the Univ.; there is no trouble in our school; there is need of reorganization—more vitality; there will be vacancies provided in several prof. chairs—the filling of which the new incumbent is expected to have a voice: The salary is what we may have to pay—The best workmen command high wages—

In short if you will entertain a proposition from us, kindly write me at once, Care Parker House, Boston, Mass, and I will see you personally on my return trip to the west.

Awaiting your reply I am

Yours Truly

D. N. Richardson

Ch. E. Com.

S. U. I.

It is fair to say that Pr J. W. Burgess recommends you to our attention—

46 — From Woodrow Wilson

Bryn Mawr, Pa.,
29 March, 1887.

My dear Dr. Adams,

I write to ask that you will be kind enough either to tell me yourself or to put me in the way of finding out something about the life and studies of Dr. v. Holst in this country, when 'getting up' our constitutional history, as well as about the rest of his career. I am about to write a review of Mason's translation of his monograph in Marquardsen's 'Handbuch,' and the review must needs be interesting rather than learned or critical—about the book and its author rather than about the intimate points of its contents. You will greatly oblige me if you will put me in possession of materials for such uses which I may appropriate on short notice.

You have heard of no one yet who could serve us as an assistant in history? I was 'a little previous,' it turns out, in claiming to have secured Hodder. I could not get him after all; and now I am all at sea again—and, having accepted the lectureship with you, I am a little concerned lest I should miss getting an assistant altogether and be left with a quite overwhelming lot of work on my hands next year. It ought not to be hard to fill the place satisfactorily inasmuch as whoever took it would have the immediate prospect of having the whole of the history work handed over to him, with corresponding increase of pay, in case he did good service— and I suppose also the chance to have my place should I go elsewhere. At any rate I *wish* that the place *might* seem attractive to some such man as we need.

Very sincerely Yours,

Woodrow Wilson

P.S. I hope the B. & O. ' deal ' has brought in some wealth to the Univ. that may be made to work great advantage to the ' school of administration ' wh. Gould and I are to inaugurate?   Yrs.

W. W.

47 — From James B. Angell

President's Office.　　　　　　　University of Michigan
　　　　　　　　　　　　　　Ann Arbor, April 4 1887
My dear Sir,

Judge Cooley, as you know, has been drafted into public service and so has dropped his work in American History and Pol. Science here.

I venture therefore to ask whether at present you are any more disposed than you were, when I approached you before, to consider the question of succeeding him here. I am not authorized at this moment to offer a Chair absolutely to any one. So you can write hypothetically, if you prefer. The title could be modified, if desired. If a man like you were to come, he would be expected to take the general charge of our historical work. Dr. Hudson, an excellent man for his place, is Assistant Professor. The salary of a Professor is now $2200, but it is not unlikely that it will be raised for the coming year to $2500, which is worth here nearly or quite $3000 in the East. The field is simply boundless. The classes are large, and under our flexible system the opportunity for specializing is great & is eagerly seized.

Could you drop me a line so that it would reach me by the end of the week, indicating whether you can give any consideration to the subject. If you can, possibly we might arrange for an interview in Phila next week, as I now expect to attend the Columbia Centennial on the 13th. Possibly you are to be there also.

If it is clear that you cannot consider the subject at all, can you suggest any good man who is available? Is Woodrow Wilson up to the mark, and, if so, can he be had? Do you know his age?

An early answer will greatly help.

　　　　　　　　　　　　　　Yours very truly

　　　　　　　　　　　　　　James B. Angell

Professor H. B. Adams
Baltimore.

48 — To Daniel Coit Gilman

Johns Hopkins University,
Seminary of History and Politics.
Baltimore, Apr. 6 1887

President Gilman:

Mr. Woodrow Wilson has definitely accepted the overtures
made to him with regard to a three years' lectureship in
Administration and Comparative Public Law. The arrangement is for 25 lectures each year, without repetition. The
lectures are to be given Friday P. M. and Saturday A. M.,
second half year. This plan suits us all and will enable Mr.
Wilson to attend and strengthen our Seminary of History
and Politics. Hoping that this arrangement will receive the
approbation of the Executive Committee and that $500 a
year will be appropriated for its fulfilment, I have the honor
to remain

Very respectfully,

H. B. Adams

49 — To Frederic Bancroft

Johns Hopkins University,
Seminary of History and Politics
Baltimore, Apr. 6 1887

Dear Mr. Bancroft:

Accept my best thanks for your valuable list of authorities
upon Administration. They are just what we need. I am
glad you are enjoying so much your sojourn in Paris. M.
Boutmy, the director of the École Libre, has just accorded
to me the privilege of sending two Hopkins men gratis to his
institution. I have long cherished the notion that our American students devote too exclusive attention to Germany in
their foreign study. I was cheated out of my original plan
of first studying in Paris by the persuasions of an older and
newly-married brother, who thought the French capital an
unsafe place for a young man! Accordingly, to gratify his

sense of prudence and virtue, I packed off to Heidelberg, where 35 per cent of the births are illegitimate. A virtuous people those Germans! Nevertheless I am fond of them.

I am looking forward to the time when you will begin to write and lecture in America. If nothing turns up, you would do well, I think, to settle down here and prepare something for publication in my series, either in the Studies or Extra Volumes. I have a great scheme afoot for fostering historical and political studies in America and I think you will find Baltimore and Washington the best vantage-ground for public and private good.

Very cordially,

H. B. Adams.

Last night I thought of suggesting a good chance for you next year and this morning the chance seems brilliant. What do you say to my nominating you for the associateship in History at the new and best college for women at Bryn Mawr, close by Philadelphia and all those fine libraries? Woodrow Wilson is chief but we have just engaged him here for 25 lectures the second half year. He will need assistance therefore in History and doubtless his assistant will inherit all the History, while he will devote himself exclusively to political science. The work next year will be very light, circa five hours a week in classical history, and the pay will be equally light, $850, I believe. The second year if the incumbent is satisfactory the salary will be $1,000. Please write me at once whether you will accept this position if offered. *I should strongly advise it,* for the work will be pleasant and easy and will give you free scope for original study in Philadelphia libraries, besides being very near Baltimore and Washington. It is great fun teaching girls. I tried it at Smith College. Moreover Bryn Mawr has a superb faculty of well trained men, including at least four Hopkinsians. There is nothing official about this, but *if you will make up your mind at once I think you will do a good thing.*

Very cordially,

H. B. A.

50 — From George F. Hoar

Worcester May 9 /87

My dear Sir,

I was much gratified by the paper on Wm & Mary.[1] I should wish to give careful study to the detail of the plan and be quite sure of the wisdom of the managers before giving my adhesion to a scheme for an institution for instruction in modern politics or in contemporary history to be established at Washington. I know of nothing so unscholarly and so unscientific as the contributions of some of our scholars and men of science to these things. Perhaps the responsibility of teaching would secure better results.

I am

faithfully yours

Geo F Hoar

51 — From Lyon G. Tyler

Richmond Va
May 11. 1887

Dear Sir:

Let me thank you for your volume on old William and Mary College. I wish that something would be done to get it on its legs again, but we are too poor in Virginia to accomplish much. The part of the country in which the College is located was in slavery days the richest portion of the State, but now I do not believe that there is hardly a solvent person in the Peninsula—certainly not over a very few. The

---

[1] *The College of William and Mary: a Contribution to the History of Higher Education, with Suggestions for Its National Promotion.* U. S. Bureau of Education, Circulars of Information, No. 1, 1887. In this monograph Adams urged the establishment of a civil academy or national university in Washington, which might do for the civil service what West Point and Annapolis did for the army and navy. There is among the Adams letters a considerable number from persons interested in promoting such a project and especially from John W. Hoyt who headed a committee created for that purpose.

Eastern counties suffered much more from the war than the Northern. And yet no people have ever exhibited more true character or heroism in struggling against adverse influences.

As my ancestors lived from the 17th Century immediately in the neighborhood of William & Mary; and many of my relations were educated within its walls, I would indeed like to see something grow out of your noble work, of a substantial character.

As I am writing, I call to mind your account of the attempted removal of William and Mary to Richmond in 1824-5. I remember in writing the life of my father a very full estimate by years (in a document appended to the Journal of House of Del.) of the attendance at the College both before and after the Revolution. My father who was then a member of the board of visitors (he was afterwards rector and chancellor) opposed the proposition of the majority of the visitors and faculty in a speech which is still to be found in the *Enquirer* and which I have often heard stated settled the mind of the Legislature. Judge James Semple, the dissenting member of the faculty was Mr. Tyler's brother-in-law and to them probably more than any others the defeat of the scheme was due. There was no collusion with Mr. Jefferson on this subject, but the fact is the *people* of the Peninsula were opposed to the removal and Mr. Tyler thought that William and Mary College, without its environment, would be like the Egyptian obelisk in modern New York—a curiosity it might be but that was all. At the same time he was a warm friend of the University of Virginia. He was indeed a man singularly free from any unworthy jealousies.

As to your commendation of Washington's suggestion of a National University, I appreciate what is so well stated, but we of the South are more interested in popular education at present. If we could only secure the passage of the Blair bill of which I am an ardent advocate, the good could not be estimated. The trouble with our education has been that we have worked too much from the top downward instead of from the bottom upward. We must educate the masses. I know that in this age very little regard would be paid to the fact that the Federal Convention of 1787 expressly voted down Washington's idea of a national university. With me constitutional restrictions have very little weight, believing that the " *general welfare* " doctrine was *settled* by the war and I go in for what the South can get. At the same time I am the ardent advocate of any measure that consults the interest of both sections of the Union.

I remain

Truly yrs

Lyon G. Tyler

52 — *From Woodrow Wilson*

Bryn Mawr, Pa.,

16 May, 1887.

Dear Dr. Adams,

I enclose the statement for which you ask. I hope it will prove what you want.

A very unexpected resolution has been taken concerning the tutorship in history here. So few of the students now in college have offered ancient history (the course that would be given next year) that it has been determined to make them, and any new ones who may offer, wait a year, and *make no appointment* till the year '88-'89, when a larger salary can be given and a man such as we want probably secured

I at last return the extract about von Holst which you were kind enough to lend me. Many thanks for it: it served my purpose excellently.

The William and Mary report came to hand, and I am delighted with ' the idea.' It is brought out with great force (to which the official endorsement in the prefatory letter adds a valuable element) and ought to tell: would certainly tell if we had an integrate instead of a disintegrate govt: *may* tell anyhow. Fortune speed it!

Very truly Yours,

Woodrow Wilson

53 — From Inazo Ota [Nitobe]

Bonn am Rhein
VIII 9. 1887.

Dr. Herbert B. Adams,

Dear Sir:

Your kind letter of the 28th ult. found me this morning in the enjoyment of that peculiar German institution to which I am not yet perfectly reconciled, viz.—das Frühstück. Otherwise I find most things in German life very agreeable: in fact, I find myself here more in my element than I did in the States, and you can easily see why. As I am going to write pretty plainly what features in American life are not enjoyable to a Japanese, in my last chapter—"Japanese in Am."—I will not now write to you some of the contrasts between Am. & German life.

I send by this mail Chapt. III.[1] I am afraid that the whole thing may become too long for a monograph. I wish you would take full liberty to cut off what you think is *cuttable*. I am at work on my IV and V. I hope to complete them during the summer. Plenty to do, as usual. I must learn German better; also I want to see something of the Rhine region. All the Japanese here besides myself—six in number—are going tomorrow to Switzerland with Professor Rein. But I am left alone to wander in the valleys of the German language and often to ascend steep hills of conjugation and sometimes fall headlong down the precipices of horrible declension. Before I feast my eyes on the summit of Mt. Rigi or glide over the deep and clear waters of Lake Maggiore, must I take a glimpse of the sublime light of Goethe's mind and feel at least a ripple of the serene depth of Schiller's heart. When I become tired with my thesis and German, I am reading Bryce's Holy Roman Empire and Seeley's Stein. I never knew before that the former was

---

[1] *The Intercourse between the United States and Japan* ("Johns Hopkins University Studies in Historical and Political Science," Extra Volume VIII, Baltimore, 1891).

such a clever book: his bold, statesmanlike interpretations of History are delightful.

By the way, speaking of Stein's Life and Times, I must tell you that a few hundred feet from the main University buildings is an elevated little place (still called Alte Zoll, though it is only a kind of a little park) on the bank of the Rhine and overlooking the noble river and its valley for miles along. Here on this eminence, stands a bronze statue of Arndt in a standing posture, his left hand resting on a stub of oak and his right hand pointing gently to the stream below, and on one side of the pedestal is carved—"Der Rhein Deutschlands Strom, nicht Deutschlands Grenze," and on another side—"Der Gott der Eisen Wachsen liess, der wollte keine Knechte." The monument was erected by "the German People." Perhaps you may be interested in having a picture of it, when you lecture on the Rise of Prussia. So I send you one.

Another thing. On this self same spot are a pair of large cannon captured from the French in the late war and presented by the Kaiser, perhaps as a tribute to the poet. And what is significant of the time, I see that they were within the last three or four weeks polished!

A few hundred yards from the Alte Zoll, along the Rhine stands a plain two story house, where the poet lived for eleven years. It is still known as Arndt-Haus, but is now occupied by a gymnastic teacher. I understand that the property belongs to the City.

I have not learned and probably will never learn beer-drinking. The other day some twenty students with Prof. Rein and a Director of Gymnasium in Frankfurt, made a scientific excursion to Lacher See in which I also joined. We had dinner and of course beer. Being asked by two or three fellows whether I would not learn to drink it: I answered loud enough to be heard by all,—"I have *many other* things to learn." Did they think that a Mongolian Batu had resuscitated to repeat the episode of 1241, to fight against the time-honored institution of the German race? Possibly some did, for they looked grim, but I found the

Frankfurt Director and the Professor as well as many students on my side. Afterwards several students came up to me—not indeed to challenge me to a duel for so great an insult to their national custom—but to ask whether there is "kein Bier" drunk in Japan. I assured them that there are many "Brauerei," at which they actually seemed gratified. I dare say that were you to see me now, you will find me appreciably changed already. Am I so easily Germanized? No, indeed, I am too much of a Japanese to be so easily affected by foreign influences. Nevertheless I am not what I was in U. S. I feel more at home here and I behave accordingly. Speak we may of the freedom of a Republic, I felt in America tyranny of custom.

Now, doctor, with best wishes for your health.

I remain as ever

Yours truly,

Inazo Ota [Nitobe] [1]

54 — From Charles I. Stillé

Philada Dec 17, '87
2201 St. James Place

Dear Dr. Adams,

I find that you have been led into some strange error by your informant concerning the history instruction in the Univ. of Penna. as given in the Report to the Bureau of Education, which you have been kind enough to send me.[2]

The "Wharton School" is a mere offshoot of the University and a very unsatisfactory provision for a want which I begged for more than fourteen years the Trustees to supply. I urged the establishment of a *post-graduate* school of History

---

[1] Ota had been a student at the Hopkins during the years 1884-1887. Soon after going to Germany the death of his brother made him the heir of the Nitobe family and he assumed that name to which he was to bring such distinction in later years.

[2] Herbert B. Adams, *The Study of History in American Colleges and Universities*, U. S. Bureau of Education, Circular of Information, No. 2, 1887.

and Political Science which would give instruction to young men *& women* of a higher kind. The founder of the school sought to make it a means of preparing young men for *business & commercial life,* & those young men at an age when their minds were not sufficiently matured to receive & profit by systematic advanced instruction. The Professors have done their best with the material provided for them, but I cannot help feeling that the system for the reason I have given is a vicious one. One of the Professors has resigned (Prof. Bolles) and this, of course, adds to the difficulty.

But what I complain of is the statement that history is taught in that University only in the Wharton School. No history is taught there save *American* history, you can judge how completely the students must be at sea when their instruction is so confined.

But historical instruction and that of the most advanced kind has been given in the Depts of Arts & the Towne Scientific School for more than twenty years before the Wharton School existed. I held the chair of history there for fourteen years, & during those years I gave the following courses extending through the year.

1. General colonial history & that of the American colonies
2. Guizot with illustrations
3. Gibbon. Decline & Fall &c.
4. Medieval history
5. Europe in the age of Louis XIV
6. Europe in the 18th century
7. Relations of English history to English literature.

My assistant did the preliminary work in the Freshman & Soph. classes.

My successor is John Foster Kirk, the author of Charles the Bold, and I am told, follows the example which I set in the hope that some day we would have a true school of History & Political Science—as at Columbia and Michigan—

Very sincerely,

C. I. Stillé

Dr. H. B. Adams

55 — From James K. Hosmer

Washington University,
Saint Louis, Mo.
Feb. 6, 1888

My dear Professor Adams,

Ever since the government documents came to hand with your accounts of historical instruction, and of old " William & Mary," I have intended to write to you, to express to you my sense of what great things you are doing for history here in America. You not only write yourself what is of great value, but you stir up everywhere investigation, and there is no corner of the country, I suppose, which does not feel your influence. In England summer before last Mr. Freeman, whom I visited at Somerleaze, expressed to me in the strongest terms his sense of your energy, and of the value of the work you are doing. Multitudes feel it, and I have no doubt you often have an expression similar to that which I am making to you now of warm appreciation for what you are accomplishing.

When I was in Berlin in 1870, Mommsen whom I had the privilege of meeting suggested to me something similar to your Historical & Political Studies, and when I came to St. Louis, in 1874, I made a proposition to our Chancellor and Faculty, looking toward some such activity for our institution, as has marked so honorably Johns Hopkins, in the way of publishing in various lines the work of scholars whom we could induce to thorough study. Lack of means, lack of time, too, on the part of the teachers of a half-manned institution like ours, brought my proposition to nought. I have been delighted, however, that Johns Hopkins has had the disposition and ability to take it up, and was greatly pleased four years ago, when you asked me for my " Sam Adams " monograph.

I feel, too, that the Historical Association may be regarded as your creation. Its influence I have no doubt is very important, and I hope the coming meeting at Columbus will wake up the West.

Now that I am writing to you I may venture to refer to my own work. For some years, ever since I finished my "Samuel Adams" in fact, I have been writing a life of "Young Sir Henry Vane." I investigated here and in the Boston libraries, reading what I could find, then spent the summer of '86 in London, where I worked in the British Museum and Public Record Office. Masson's "Milton" had given me the impression that I might come upon much of interest about Vane, in the old order books of the "Committee of the Two Kingdoms" and of the "Council of State," the executive bodies during the Commonwealth and just before, of which Vane was a leading figure. I was not disappointed. I was treated with great courtesy, and allowed to make large researches in the unprinted documents, the manuscript archives, and the great collection of "Thomasson Tracts," some 4000 volumes, comprising all the fugitive literature of the age of the Commonwealth, sermons, pamphlets, news-sheets, broadsides, ballads, and what not.

I received help from various gentlemen, among others from Mr. Bryce, but particularly from Mr. Samuel Rawson Gardiner, regarded in England as the highest living authority upon the 17th century. I worked side by side with Mr. Gardiner, visited him at Bromley, talked with him at length, and received from him all sorts of valuable hints as to books, manuscripts, and lines of research. The Duke of Cleveland, also, Vane's descendant, gave me permission to visit Raby Castle in Durham, Vane's seat, and I also went to Edgehill, Naseby, Marston Moor, &c., places interesting as more or less closely connected with Vane, and the struggle in which he was a leader.

I have not called my book finished until recently. It is now in the hands of Houghton, Mifflin, & Co., and will I suppose before long go to press. They propose to make a handsome octavo of some 400 pages. It will contain a fine portrait of Vane, and perhaps heads of others of the great Commonwealthsmen, after Houbraken. My hope is it will seem a piece of respectable historical work. So far as I know no American student has gone any more deeply into that time than I have: I have tried to make a good presentment of what I have found.

The interesting thing about Vane is that, while so thoroughly an Englishman, he was as thoroughly an American, believing as much as Lincoln, in government of, by, and for the people. I think of having for a title-page something like this: "The Life of Young Sir H. V., with an account of the English Commonwealth as an anticipation of the American Idea." Really Vane, Cromwell, and their fellows would have made, in all substantial respects, an America of England in the 17th century, and what they tried to bring about is in our time fast becoming a reality. I write my book in the interest of a closer interdependence among the great branches of the English-speaking race. The motto is a sentence from John Bright's letter to the committee for the centennial of the Constitution last summer. "As you enter upon a new century of your constitution, cannot something be done toward making our two nations one people."

I had several articles in the *Nation* last spring and summer, which, modified, will be parts of my book,—Two papers called "After the Ironsides on a Tricycle," giving accounts of visits to Marston Moor, and Naseby, a paper on Admiral Blake, and one on the "Constitutional Idea," Sept. 1st. Possibly you may have seen them. I also enclose to you an article from the Pall Mall Gazette which gives my idea.

I fear you will think I have written you at an unconscionable length, and I beg pardon for thus imposing on you. The fact is, we are coming to look on you as a sort of director and superintendent of historical work, and to feel that you ought to know what is going on.

I sincerely hope my account of my work will not be quite without interest to you.

Hoping that you are very well and that all goes well with your useful enterprises, I am

Very truly yours,

James K. Hosmer

56 — From George W. Kirchwey

University of the State of New York

Office of the Regents,
Albany, March 7, 1888.

Dr. Herbert B. Adams,

My dear Sir:

* * * *

I beg that you will set me down as a member of the Historical Association. If you will inform me how to acquire "good & regular standing," I will cheerfully & promptly comply.

Mr. Fernow and I have for some time been considering the advisability of starting an American Hist. Review, devoted to American (N. & S.) history, with special reference to the earlier period. It is not to be popular (and so will not conflict with the Mag. of Am. Hist.), nor will it trench upon the field so admirably filled by the J. H. U. Studies, etc. It is to be solid, giving the results of original investigation, and to present only the highest grade of historical work. We have received encouragement and promise of help from high sources—Justin Winsor, John Bigelow, *et al,* and are reaching out for Von Holst, Doyle, and other European students of our history and institutions. Of course, if we once get it under way we shall lean heavily on the group of able men who have been trained by you at the Johns Hopkins, and we count not a little on your sympathy and coöperation. What do you think of the feasibility of our scheme? Perhaps it might be managed in some way to make our *magazine* (which we intend to launch in the modest form of a quarterly) the organ of the Hist. Assn.—but I do not fail to notice that this is a bold suggestion to emanate from this quarter.

Trusting to hear from you soon, I am,

Very sincerely yours,

Geo. W. Kirchwey

57 — From William J. Ashley

Lincoln College,
Oxford.
March 14, 1888

Dear Prof. Adams,

I didn't in the least mind your publishing my paper—tho' I should have liked to append some sort of note, saying that the article represented a frame of mind in which I idealized to myself the Oxford tutorial system, which every month's experience teaches me more & more to dislike. The main difference between our condition & that of American universities is that we have to drive men, of whom two out of every three, do not wish to study.

Freeman mentioned to me your writing to him—I am grateful to you. But Rogers is pretty sure to be elected—& tho' he won't be a good professor, it is a fitting reward, & on the whole the best thing. I am standing for a Professorship of Political Science at Toronto—including History, Economics, Comparative Politics, Internl Law. My emoluments here are greater—but

(1) I want to marry—& tho I can do it with my fellowship, if I wait long enough, it will then be subject to irksome conditions.

(2) I dislike tutorial work, & want to get more time for my own research.

Will you, kindly, within a day or so after the receipt of this, send me a few lines of testimonial, mentioning what bits of my writing you have seen, & saying something about my possible fitness for teaching Pol. Science. I should be much obliged to you.

Sincerely yours,

W. J. Ashley

58 — From Hannis Taylor

28 St. Michael St.

Mobile, Ala., May 26th 1888.

Prof. H. B. Adams,

Johns Hopkins University,

Baltimore, Md;

My dear Sir;

I have read with great interest and attention your kind and instructive letter of the 22d inst. When I consider its contents, in connection with the paper sent me through Mrs. Lay, I realize the fact that you are the only person with whom I have had the good fortune to come into contact who comprehends at once the real ends I have in view, and the difficulties that stand in the way of their execution. After mature consideration I can not dissent from a single conclusion that you have reached as to my undertaking. The wonder to me is that you should be able to take in at a glance all that I have been able to see after so many years of special study and reflection. When I take your views of my project, as a whole, I gather great hope from them, for the reason that you admit that there is at least one path to success, and, unless I greatly deceive myself, I have been pursuing that path from the beginning. To use your own language:— " In my judgment the strength and hope of such a project as yours (which can never rival Stubbs and the great original masters) lie in the possibility of tracing the great stream of American democracy to its earliest English source. Hegel somewhere says that the passing over of the world-spirit from one nation to another is the chief content of the world's history. In this transitional process, from the spirit of Anglican to American liberty, lies your grand opportunity. An American interpretation of English history in its relation to the rise of this great federal republic, the lineal descendant of those early Germanic tribal federations—this, I take it is the dominant idea of your proposed work." When you read my Introduction you will see how I have concentrated what-

8

ever of force I may possess into the expression and elaboration
of that idea. I have tried to bring home the fact to the
student of our federal constitution that until he gains a clear
insight into that marvelous process of historic development
which binds the little group of Teutonic states as originally
established in Britain to the group of English states planted
ten centuries later upon the eastern coast of what is now
the U. S., our constitutional history must ever remain a sealed
book to him. A very clever young lady who read a few weeks
ago my two opening chapters, outlining the primitive Teutonic constitution, said to me—" You don't say so in so many
words, but I can see through what you do say the beginnings
of our American democracy." I can't agree with your Baltimore judge that the tendency of American lawyers of the
better class is to turn away from English constitutional history. The *craving* is there, but the difficulty is to gain access
to the knowledge in a practical form and within reasonable
limits. If the average American lawyer were to ask you for
a history of the English constitution, and you were to give
him Stubbs,—I believe he would say, after he had put his
teeth into it, that you had given him a stone. I say that in
the light of the belief that the Bishop's work is the greatest
constitutional history ever written. And yet it can never be
of much practical value to the general reader, it must ever
remain as a great quarry out of which other builders must
obtain their very best material. If I felt that I had to come
into competition with the Bishop in any way, I would abandon
my task. But upon the contrary I feel that he is a help to
me. Such a work as his makes such a work as mine possible.
He has expanded into three volumes one part of my subject.
I believe, after years of assimilation, I can condense the
essence of the three into one, and then apply the result to
the illustration of the constitutional history of the U. S. I
was sorry, after writing my last letter, that I had made the
request as to the examination of my work, chapter by chapter.
I am satisfied that such an examination would impose great
labor upon your students, with but little corresponding benefit
to me. I have resolved, if I can make satisfactory arrange-

ments, to publish my first volume this fall. It brings the story down to the accession of Henry VII, and completes the formative period of the constitution. The first, and perhaps the most pleasant, impression my book will make, will be through the Introduction, which I shall expand into nearly fifty printed pages. I must spare no pains upon that part of my work, for through the Introduction I must illustrate the "transitional process from the spirit of Anglican to American liberty" in which you so truly say lies my "grand opportunity." In the language of the street, I will "pool all my issues" with you, if you will only help me with your critical judgment as to my Preface and Introduction.

*   *   *   *

Very truly yours

Hannis Taylor

59 — From Anna E. Ticknor

41 Marlborough Street
Boston. Jan 10. 1889

Dear Mr Adams

I fancy you were the cause of my receiving lately, from the Bureau of Education, a copy of your monograph on Jefferson & the University of Virginia, and I wish to thank you for it personally.[1] It is an interesting record of Mr. Jefferson's work, of the activity of his intellect, applying itself at one & the same time to such different interests.

You have given several pages to a notice of my father's acquaintance with Mr. Jefferson & his plans, which is, of course, the part of your paper that draws my attention peculiarly. One or two of your questions, thrown out by way of pointing your suggestions, I am going to answer as if they were bona fide questions, doing it in some detail, because I think the details will interest you.

---

[1] Herbert B. Adams, *Thomas Jefferson and the University of Virginia*, U. S. Bureau of Education, Circulars of Information, No. 1, 1888.

You ask "where did George Ticknor get all these advanced ideas?" &c.—I answer, unhesitatingly, at the German Universities. Mme de Stael's account of these Universities drew him there in 1815—he pursued his studies at Göttingen for two semesters, giving extreme attention to the history & character of that University & writing out his observations on it very fully; but beside this, in his summer holidays, as he wrote to a friend in Nov. 1816— " My great object was to see the Universities & schools, and, in two months, with the letters I had, this was very easily accomplished. I saw Leipzig, Berlin, Halle & Jena; the great schools at Meissen & at [?] & twenty smaller ones, and all the considerable men who teach in them; & if I were to write you a letter now, on the comparative state of education in Europe & America, in the same unlicensed tone I did last winter, it would probably be even less to the liking of the fautores literarum among us than the first was. But enough of this, for it is a subject on which I am much more likely to grow excited & extravagant than that of battles & campaigns " (he had of course seen the fields of Leipzig & Jena &c) " & if I ever come home again I shall be much more likely to take the Latin Primer or Greek Collectanea & try to show how boys are drilled to know something, than to shoulder my musket & show how fields were won."

I have heard him talk so much of these matters & the German Universities that I have no doubts on the subject, & others will sustain me in my recollections.

You ask " Did Ticknor devise that entire group of advanced ideas independently of the personal influence of Thomas Jefferson, who had been writing to him for ten years? " &c. I answer, distinctly, yes—for Mr. Jefferson's letters to my father contain nothing at all calculated to exercise any influence whatever on the subject. I possess the letters, sixteen in number; written between March 19, 1815 and April 1, 1825; & as, in each, Mr. Jefferson mentions the date of the previous letter or the length of time since it was written, I am satisfied I have them all.

Ten of these letters contain no reference at all to University or other education. The first eight are wholly concerned with the purchase in Europe of books for Mr. Jefferson's private library, closing with remarks on public affairs. These come down to June 6, 1817 inclusive. The 9th and 10th letters are given in the memoir of my father; & the only passage omitted—in that of Oct 25, 1818—consists of ten lines about the numbers & the salaries of the Professors. The next,—Dec 26, '19—after a description of the comforts to be provided for his Professors, is filled with inquiries about procuring such Professors; a reference to recommendations of Blaettermann, received from my father; & questions about Edinburgh as a place for finding teachers. Two letters in 1821 are wholly on other matters. That of July (not June) 16, 1823—acknowledging the receipt of my father's Syllabus, contains the following sentences. " I have considered this [Syllabus] with great interest & satisfaction, as it gives me a model of the course I wish to see pursued in the different branches of instruction in our University, that is to say, a methodical critical & profound explanation, by way of praelection, of every science we propose to teach "—and " There is no person from whose information of the European institutions, & especially of their discipline I should expect so much aid in this difficult work. Come then, dear Sir, & give to our institution the benefit of your counsel." This is not the tone of one conveying advanced ideas to another—The next is Aug 15, 1824 when Mr. Jefferson says " I am sorry to hear of a schism within the walls of Harvard. Yet I do not wonder at it. You have a good deal among you of ecclesiastical leaven." and six lines more of that sort; the rest is about the proposed visit of my parents, news about new Professors, & disappointment about money from the legislature.

Finally, after my father's second & last visit to Monticello, Mr. Jefferson writes in April 1825—to announce the opening of the University giving 9 lines to his elective system.

My father in writing from Göttingen, where he was so deeply interested in university education, seems not to have associated Mr. Jefferson at all in his mind with that subject, for in four letters of which I have press copies he does not refer to it, but fills his pages with literary items & details about the purchase of books—

When he says to Mr. Harrison that he had "no misgivings" he does not mean that he believed the system good at Harvard, but he had confidence in the wisdom of the men who constituted "the organization & management" & their readiness to adopt new ideas.

The phrase you italicize in the letter to Mr. Prescott suggests no flattering meaning to me, for the praise seems to be given outright & criticism held back for private discourse.

This letter is long enough already but I want to touch on that last visit to Monticello. My father's account of his deciding to go in 1824 is given in his own words in Curtis's Life of Webster "I told him [Mr. Webster] that Jefferson had invited me to meet Genl. Lafayette at Monticello, but that I did not think I should be able to do it. I thought, however, that in the event of my going to Washington, I should endeavor, as Mrs. Ticknor would be with me, to take her to Jefferson's. He said he should like to be of the party." My parents passed two months in Washington, for social purposes. To see Mr. Madison & Mr. Jefferson was of interest enough for a pilgrimage, life in Virginia was worth seeing, my mother had special reasons for wishing to see Mrs. Randolph & her daughters, all this must be taken into the account. People were not spoiled by modern facilities for traveling, & having got as far as Washington, they would not be deterred by a few more days discomfort from seeking such unusual & interesting experiences. The University was a great point of interest, its buildings were visited & its affairs talked of, but it did not take precedence of all else.

My father often spoke of Mr. Jefferson's project for his University, much as he did in his letter to Mr. Prescott, but not in the manner he would if it had been to him a source of inspiration. His work for reform was in the same direction, but it was built on his own studies & observations—

This correspondence, which you have led me to look over anew, is interesting, & it is one of many that my father left, which will some day furnish materials for pleasant pictures of men & life in past days.

I am glad to hear from Miss Hayes that you still cherish kindly purposes towards " Studies at Home," & I shall feel proud & pleased if I find you can maintain your friendly views of us in the new monograph we are expecting from you on Higher Education in the U. S.

I need not say that this is strictly a private letter; nor that I shall always be happy to hear from you—

Truly yours

Anna E. Ticknor

60 — From Frederick Jackson Turner

Portage Wisconsin
June 21, 1889

My dear Dr Adams:

I have just learned of a new United States history of which it is possible you have not heard, as you never mentioned the matter. The publishers of the Epoch Series have in hand a three volume history of this country on the scale and plan of the Epoch Series—The first volume reaches 1750, second to Washingtons Adm. (I believe) and third to present. My friend Thwaites of the Wis. Hist. Society is likely to do the first, and the others fall to Dr Woodrow Wilson, and Dr Hart. The work is to be out in a year. It is not yet announced and probably you would better not use my information, but it will be of interest if you have not yet heard of it.

I have recently conversed with a friend of mine Prof Olson, who teaches Norse etc at Wisconsin University, and who is fully up on the literature of Norwegian exploration. He says that some able monographs have recently appeared by Norwegian scholars on the Lief Erickson matter, and particularly in relation to the location and date of the visits to America. If you would like to use a paper by him on this subject I do not doubt I could get him to give you the benefit of his studies, for he is interested in having this feature of our history placed in the best way before American readers. There has been much unscientific writing about the matter.

Prof. Allen was pleased to hear from you. His Roman history is well along and may get to press before October.

Very truly yours

Fredk J Turner.[1]

61 — From Woodrow Wilson

106 High St.,
Middletown, Conn.,
27 June '89

My dear Dr. Adams,

Everybody in this little town has to entertain visitors as well as attend all exercises during the Commencement season, and I have not had a moment's time to answer your note of June 21 until now.

I enclose the outlines you want. Hope they are all right.

We had the pleasure of having Dr. Learned with us for a couple of days. I have never met him before and Mrs. Wilson and I enjoyed his stay with us immensely. He's famously good company, and certainly in every way worth knowing.

I have been indiscreet enough to consent to prepare one of the three ' Epochs of American History' which Prof. Hart of Harvard is to edit for Longmans, Green, & Co. I am to have the third, 1829-1889. The role of historian will be a new one for me, but I trust that my newness will not stick out in the result. It's a period concerning which I have some ideas of my own—and I shall enjoy the opportunity to work them out.

---

[1] Frederick Jackson Turner spent the year 1888-1889 as a graduate student in the Hopkins and received the Ph. D. degree in 1890.

The year here has been quite prosperous, but I am just now not a little tired.

As ever,

Sincerely Yours,

Dr. H. B. Adams   Woodrow Wilson

62 — From Clarence W. Bowen

The Independent.
251 Broadway
New York
Sept. 17, 1889.

My dear Adams:—

In reply to your letter regarding an American historical review, it of course is a new idea to me and I do not wish to write that I approve or disapprove until I know more fully what your views on the subject are. Would the American Historical Association be required to pay the expense of publishing this? If it should be started and published for one or two numbers it would be unfortunate to stop at the end of that time. We can go along first rate in the way we are now going and meet all our expenses, but publishing a review is, as I know from experience, a pretty expensive affair.

Let me hear from you more fully at your leisure on this subject.

Paul Ford is expected home from Europe in a few days. I think it will be well for him to take hold of the Bibliograph matter as you suggest and I trust you will write him within a few days on the subject. Is there anything you want me to say to him? I live very near to him and can easily see him if you would like to have me do so.

Very truly yours,

Clarence W. Bowen

63 — *From Theodore Roosevelt*

United States
Civil Service Commission
Washington, D. C.

Nov. 7th, 1889

Prof. H. B. Adams
Secy. Am. Hist. Assn.

My dear Sir:

I enclose herewith the sum of three dollars for the initiation fee; and have the pleasure to accept the election with which I have been honored.[1]

I will be glad to speak on " Certain Phases of the Westward Movement during the Revolutionary War," (you can change this title if you wish) as you request; subject only to the proviso that my official duties *may* call me away at that time. I could speak on the 30th of December could I not?

I welcomed Dr. Poole's criticism, for he evidently knew the subject; some of what he said I disagreed with of course; but he made one or two good points. I think I will take him as a text for the concluding portion of my remarks, simply to speak of the advantage of good historical criticism —and incidentally of the limitations of such criticism.

Very truly yours

Theodore Roosevelt

---

[1] Writing to Sir George Otto Trevelyan on January 23, 1904, Roosevelt said, " In a very small way I have been waging war with their kind (pedants) on this side of the water for a number of years. We have a preposterous little historical organization which, when I was just out of Harvard and very ignorant, I joined." Joseph Bucklin Bishop, *Theodore Roosevelt and His Time* (New York, 1920), II, 139-140.

64 — From Frederick Jackson Turner

> Department of History,
> University of Wisconsin,
> Madison, Wis.
> January 11, 1890

My dear Dr. Adams:

As you know, probably, Prest. Chamberlin followed your suggestions in the matter of the history department, and recalled Mr. Spencer to assist me "for the year." I owe you my thanks for your good advise [*sic*] and for your friendly offices with the president. While I have of course a strong ambition to have an independent chair, and while I should have a special pride in growing into the place that Prof Allen filled here, it was not so much a fear that I was to be left aside, as it was a repugnance to working under some man whom I could not respect and like; and there were some good reasons for apprehending such an outcome. I am not entirely sure that there are not such reasons yet. Of course I did not, (and did not *intend* to), urge my own cause upon Pres. C.—My friends had already been doing that when I wrote to you—I was debating what course I ought to take in the matter. My words to Pres. C. were, that if he wished to reorganize the department with a man of established reputation he should try to get Woodrow Wilson, or Dr. Emerton; if he wished to get a young man, to recall Spencer, or to get Mr. Haskins. He was very glad that he went to Washington—and throughout seems to have depended on your advise [*sic*].

I am now carrying courses in French Revolution, Primitive Society, Dynastic and Territorial History of Middle Ages, (freshman course), Constitutional History of U. S., and a seminary in History of the Northwest. My courses are all so nearly new, that I am finding my hands full. Are there any more developments regarding the project of a J. H. U. American History?

I hope to be able to come to Baltimore to take the degree examinations. It is a plan that I should not abandon unless my pressure of work and my finances make it impossible, and I don't intend to let this happen.

Very sincerely yours,

Frederick J. Turner.

65 — From William P. Trent

601 East Grace Street,
Richmond, Virginia.
Feb. 3rd, 1890.

My dear Dr. Adams,

I was very glad to get your kind letter a few days since. I am working "Society" for all it is worth & I hope the work will bear its fruit in due season. In the meantime from a talk I had with Hodgson a few days since I think the University of the South will hold on its legs until I can get something else to do.[1]

I want now to tell you something about the Josiah Phillips case & to ask your help & advice.

Josiah Phillips was a labourer in Princess Anne Co. who in 1777 & 78 headed a band of outlaws whom the Militia were powerless to put down. At last in desperation the then Governor Patrick Henry recommended that the Legislature should attaint Phillips & his comrades. This was done in a great hurry—Mr. *Thomas Jefferson* drawing up the bill of attainder. After some months Phillips was captured but, according to Judge Tucker, the Judges of the General Court refused to act upon the Bill of Attainder & had him tried for robbery (for which he was executed). If this account be true this case is the first on record in this country in which a bench of judges refused to consider an act of the legislature binding because they regarded the principle laid

---

[1] William P. Trent had been a graduate student in history at the Hopkins during 1887-1888. From then until 1900, when he became professor of English literature at Columbia University, he taught in the University of the South. Most but not all of the points mentioned in this letter are included in his article "The Case of Josiah Philips," *American Historical Review* (April 1896) I, 444-454.

down as dangerous to justice i. e. unconstitutional. This is
enough to make the case one of great importance. But there
is more to come.

In 1788 in the Va. Convention for ratifying the Constitution Edmund Randolph made a bitter assault on Patrick
Henry for his conduct in this very case claiming that under a
mere state government there was no security against such
acts of attainder &c. Randolph made the plain black & white
statement that Phillips was executed under the act of attainder—which was plainly not so—although he, Randolph,
had been *Clerk* of the *House when the* bill passed & *prosecut-
ing attorney in the case.* What is still stranger neither Henry
nor Marshall nor Mason, nor any who discussed the question,
seem to have remembered that Phillips was executed after a
regular indictment for robbery and not in consequence of
the bill of attainder. It is the most colossal case of forget-
fulness I ever heard of. You see at once how interesting the
case is; but it only leads up to a wider question which I have
not seen thoroughly discussed anywhere viz—the origin of
the clause in our constitution prohibiting the States from
passing bills of attainder. This is what I am now working
on. Do you not think it would make a good thesis? I am
using the Law Library here; but I fear that I shall have to
get assistance elsewhere. I propose to examine the laws &
Constitutions of the 13 colonies up to 1789 & note all instances of bills of attainder or of pains & penalties & so show
what spirit was abroad against them. The Mass. Constitution
declares against them in principal but not in name & there
were various acts during the Revolution which must have
showed men how dangerous they were; but I believe that this
Virginia case is the most typical of all and it is a curious
evidence of how English customs survived in Virginia—for
if I recollect the English Parliament had given over its use
of such bills for many years.

I should like to have your opinion about the case and any
suggestions you may make. If I can't get all the books
necessary here, could you set some Seminarian at work look-

ing some of the information up? It would be an interesting and not tedious work and I could easily explain to him by letter how to proceed & would give him due credit should the thesis be published.

I am yours very sincerely

W. P. Trent.

66 — To Andrew D. White

February 4 1890.

My dear Mr White:

I thank you for your suggestion with regard to the improvement of our circular letter to the State Historical Societies. I have shown the document to the Smithsonian authorities and they cordially approve it. It will doubtless accomplish the object that we have in view and head off that convention of historical societies in Philadelphia, proposed by Mr. Stephens of the Southern California Historical Society.

The Secretary of the Smithsonian has agreed to every point submitted in my letter and we can now regard our association as truly established in the national capital. We are to have a room there for our collections and our chosen curator is recognized as the representative of the Smithsonian in the promotion of our interests.

While we are now at liberty to submit all our papers to the Secretary for publication in connection with his report, we are warned that the printing is likely to be long delayed. I have only just received the Smithsonian Report containing the *Record of Science for 1886*! If our papers should be delayed longer than at present, I am afraid our membership would rebel. The idea has occurred to me that we might try an experiment with our new friends and give them, Pres. A's address, my general report, with the two long bibliographies, and reserve our regular proceedings for publication in *quarterly instalmt's* through the Putnams. In that way I could bring out the first part of our papers very quickly.

President Adams' address and other papers are already on hand. The first that come might be first served with printer's ink. I find the Modern Language Association publish their papers in quarterly parts, forming a volume each year. The example strikes me as excellent. We are now in position to begin the development of an *American Historical Review,* as The Nation, after the appearance of our last annual report, recommended us to do. What do you think of the idea? If you like it please send on your paper and I will put it into the first part of our proceedings. There is no immediate haste in the matter. I have talked it over with Dr. Goode, and he thinks the project commendable.

Very respectfully yours

H. B. Adams [1]

67 — From John Franklin Jameson

1 College Court,
Providence, February 21, 1890.

My dear Dr. Adams:

I ought to have made earlier acknowledgment of your kindness in sending me the proposed circular.[2] I doubt not the movement will have important results, and probably enough they may be beneficial in the main. As you know, I do not entertain a high opinion of our local historical societies, with two or three exceptions. The new movement is, in my opinion, likely to widen the scope and increase the popularity of the Association's activities much more than to improve its qualities of scholarship, if it is to result in alliance

---

[1] This letter is in the Andrew D. White Papers in the Cornell University library.

[2] John Franklin Jameson entered the Hopkins as a graduate student and became, in 1882, the first Ph. D. in history. Henry Carter Adams who had in 1878 received the previous doctoral degree granted to a student of Herbert B. Adams was, of course, in economics. Dr. Jameson remained as assistant and associate in history from 1882 to 1889 and returned to the Hopkins as lecturer in 1890-1891.

with the local societies rather than with the university and collegiate teachers. That seems to be the tendency. This year, for the first time in the history of the Association, I think, its executive council is mainly composed of persons who do no teaching of history. Now I consider the hope of good historical writing in the future to rest with the teachers, now that the instruction of graduates has reached such an extension as to make "schools," personal followings, and the learning of the trade possible. The historical societies I consider of little account intellectually, except as trustees of material and as possible furtherers of publication. The Rhode [Island] Society, for instance, stands above the average; I have been ever since I came here an interested and, for a newcomer and a busy teacher, an active, member of it; and I am sure that, except in those two ways, it has very little value. I think it must be so elsewhere. A movement to maintain and strengthen the alliance with the professorial body appears to me, therefore, likely to be of more benefit to the *quality* of the Association's operations than this. But as I am, if critical, a wholly friendly critic, I wish the movement success; it is at all events likely to increase popular interest, and, if the standards of the central body can be kept sufficiently high, it may do something to lift the local organizations out of their pettiness and sterility. You will surely get a detailed report from the Rhode Island Historical Society, though, *me judice,* they have in the whole year done nothing worth reporting to the scholars of the country.

I thank you very much for your Hopkins news, of which I hear far too little. I shall be sorry to have Wilson go out of New England. I wish there were news here that might be of interest to you. Our new president is doing a great deal for us, and proving an admirable choice. I have a graduate student, and am soon to have another. But there isn't as much satisfaction in attempting to direct the studies of men ten years older than I am, as there would be in teaching younger men. Our little historical club progresses well, and has interesting meetings, though it is composed almost entirely of amateurs. Weeden is finishing the proof-reading of his book. Foster is seeing through the press a revised and expanded edition of his bibliography of the Constitution. Our lecture-course this year was an immense success. Walker's slaughter of Bellamy in the February "Atlantic," by the way, was his lecture given here in our course. Our hall has generally been *full* at our lectures. The courses of last winter and of this have been important factors in bringing about the better relations of town and gown which now prevail here. The community, indeed, " has took us up " again. With many thanks for your letter I am

Very sincerely yours,

J. F. Jameson.

Please give Ely my regards and congratulations.

68 — From Woodrow Wilson

Middletown, Conn.,
27 March, 1890.

My dear Dr. Adams,

I have been somewhat surprised and distressed by the character of Iyenaga's examination paper in Administration.[1] It shows what seems to me a very meagre knowledge of the subject indeed. I should say, however, that, reckoning it numerically, he might fairly be credited with answering fifty *per cent.* of the questions. If that entitles him to a certificate from me, you may file the enclosed to his credit; if it does not, why of course the matter must be reconsidered. I suppose that it is only fair to take his present over-worked condition into account and his comparative inability to express himself fully and exactly in English. I have taken these things into account in making out the certificate. I would not have given it on this paper to an American student.

---

[1] Toyokichi Iyenaga received the Ph. D. degree in 1890.

9

I am hard at work here again, and fairly recovered from the grippe. With warmest regard,

Faithfully Yours,

Woodrow Wilson

Dr. H. B. Adams,
Baltimore, Md.

69 — From Daniel Coit Gilman

Paris, May 25. 90

My dear Adams,

I have been very much interested in all the information conveyed by your long letter of May 13. I am sorry that every hour before I leave this place is so appropriated that I can only send you a brief response but I think you will prefer brevity to delay. On all the work of the year I can surely congratulate you, & with your suggestions for next year I concur in the main. The illness of Dr. Ely gives me much pain,—& I shall be anxious until I hear that he has quite recovered. I know from experience what a prolonged weakness may attend such an attack. When you see him please give him my kind regards & good wishes. Tell him that I have just returned from Montpellier where I took luncheon with his friend Professor Gide, who expressed much sympathy when he heard of his illness. He knows & values what Dr. Ely has written. I found him a very sensible & pleasant man, & I inferred that he would rank himself among Christian Socialists,—but I am not quite certain, as his writings have not come under my eye. To consider your suggestions:

I quite concur in the views you express re W. Wilson. (Mr. Boutmy of the School of Polit. Sci. & his friend Mr. Durand both praised his work highly.)

You certainly should engage Jameson if such a sum will bring him ($250). It is little enough.

As to Vincent, you know much better than I his value,—but I see no reason to question his reappointment.

I might say the same of Dr. Smith.

The other allowances (100 + 300) seem reasonable.

I am very desirous of promoting intercourse with Washington, & unless there are strong reasons at the Treasury why the appropriation should not be renewed, I hope it will be again appropriated ($1000.) It seems to me that we miss our opportunity, if we do not make the most of our proximity to the capital. I am in favor of renewing the appointment of Dr. Ely,—but I should prefer to talk over the terms of reappointment before expressing myself definitely in respect to them.

I have no doubt that Scaife's lectures will be valuable. Blackmars pages, I shall study. It will not be difficult to prepare the Hopk. chapter for the Md. report, if you wish me to do so. I congratulate you on " so many & such " candidates for the Ph. Dr. degree. Mr. Wards' art. in Bost. Herald is one of the most gratifying " tributes " ever paid to our work. If you are writing him, please tell him thàt I was much pleased by what he said. You may, if you wish, announce a course of lectures on the Mediterranean considered with respect to its Geography and History,—which I will give in the midwinter.

I hope to see you before many weeks—with kind regards to all your associates, & congratulations to each one of the Candidates for Ph. Dr.

Ever yours Sincerely

D. C. Gilman

70 — To Frederic Bancroft

American Historical Association.
Baltimore, Md., June 2, 1890.

Dr. Frederic Bancroft,
Library, Department of State,
Washington, D. C.

My dear Mr. Bancroft:

I received your letter of May 28 and made various inquiries without success. Finally, on Friday evening, May 30,

I called upon Miss Randolph herself. I had a good errand, for she has in her possession a package of Jefferson letters, which I had lent her after the completion of my Jefferson monograph. My point was to ascertain whether she had any use for these letters; if not, I proposed to return them to their owner. I found that Miss Randolph was ill and had been so for a year or more. Her assistant, Miss Armstrong, assured me that Miss Randolph had not been able to do anything whatever with the Jefferson letters; in fact, she had been abroad for nearly a year and left her school in other hands. I requested Miss Armstrong to ask Miss Randolph to inform me by letter whether she was likely to have any use for the Jeffersoniana which I had lent her. I have been expecting a reply, but none has been sent at this writing. I think you may assume that the Jefferson project is in statu quo. I think she has a good command of the situation and that it would be unwise at present to encourage anyone else to prepare an edition of Jefferson's writings. Indeed, it will be impossible to do so without her cooperation. I think the entire policy of allowing private individuals to monopolize historical materials belonging to the government and to publish them in luxurious editions of 500 copies, for the private benefit of mercenary publishers and paid editors, very unworthy of this republic. The government ought to take the whole matter under special control and to authorize editions of the writings of American Statesmen in such form that an ordinary citizen and student of history can afford to buy them. The present method of publication does not begin to be so generous or public spirited as was the work of Jared Sparks. Whatever criticisms may be made upon his editorial methods, which belong to a former generation, it will not be easy to supplant his popular work by limited editions that appeal only to the pockets of the rich.

Very cordially yours,

H. B. Adams

71 — From George D. Ferguson

Queen's University,
Kingston, Canada.

Herbert B. Adams Esq   Kingston June 13th 1890.

Dear Sir

I presume that I am indebted to you for a copy of your article on " The Study of History in Germany & France." [1] I had already read the article as it appeared duly in the Series of the Johns Hopkins Studies & I was delighted with it—& handed it to Principal Grant of our University to read as I am anxious to obtain his aid in carrying out a scheme of Historical Studies based on original research.

I am more & more convinced that any attainment in Historical Study can only be through familiarity with the original sources of information.

The current histories of the day are interesting & are valuable as showing current views on the period but are of comparatively little value to the student. The article of Prof Fredericq has confirmed this view, *tho* I knew, in the main, the general facts before. The mere lecturing before a class of students is, I always feel, unsatisfactory. I believe we must take them in to the library as the Prof of Chemistry or of Physics into the Laboratory & make them do practical work for themselves. The great difficulty on this side of the Atlantic is the meagreness of our original authorities unless we entirely confine ourselves to the history of our respective countries. The British government has given us the publications issued from the Record Office & we are daily expecting a collection from the French Government & these with the Pertz Monumenta & the Bouquet Collection certainly open the way for the study of European history. I take the liberty of sending you our College Calendar & you will see that for

---

[1] Paul Fredericq, *The Study of History in Germany and France.* This as well as a companion monograph on *The Study of History in Belgium and Holland*, also by the professor of history at the University of Ghent, appeared in the eighth volume of the Hopkins *Studies.*

the higher degrees I insist on some acquaintance with original authorities.

Very many thanks for the article. I may mention that I took a semester at Halle in *Leo's* & *Witte's* time & *tho* I was then a divinity student I was especially fond of history. I have since then been frequently in Germany especially Stuttgart & was a student in the library there.

With best regards

Yours very truly

Geo D Ferguson

I send you a small pamphlet on the Etruscan question in review of a theory of a Prof Campbell

72 — From John Franklin Jameson

18 Mystic Avenue,
Winchester, July 2, 1890.

My dear Doctor:

Some way, I missed knowing, until it was too late, that the time of Amherst Commencement had been changed, and so did not come up, as I meant to do. I should imagine that it was an interesting week, and am much disappointed that I did not get the chance to run up and see what was going on, and talk with the brethren under the patulous trees. How many changes our Alma Mater is likely to undergo, these next few years! I am glad Seelye resigned. From what I had been hearing, I feared he would not consent to do so. An Amherst citizen told me the other day that he didn't believe Montague would be allowed to return. What is the true inwardness of that?

I wanted particularly to have a talk with you before the return of Mr. Gilman, as to the lectures which I proposed giving. I wish to make the proposition definite, yet do not know exactly what will best fit in with your plans. In a dozen lectures one cannot cover a large subject. But just how special it should be made, I cannot perfectly judge. It is possible to take a period of American constitutional and political history, as I did three years ago, and devote the 12 lectures to the period 1789-1793, say. Then a course could be given one year on The Establishment of the New Government, 1788-1793, and, if you liked, another a second year on The Rule of the Federalists, 1793-1801. Or, secondly, I could in the twelve lectures take up the constitutional and political history of the 13 (or 15) states from 1775 to 1800 or so, which I think would offer more that was novel and original, or at least not to be got out of the standard books on American history. This would give me more pleasure than the other. Thirdly, if it would not be too special, I should like very much to devote the 12 to the history of the Southern states simply, 1775-1800; that would give room for a closer treatment, and one more instructive in respect to methods. Or, one could treat the Northern states one year, and the Southern another. Of course, twelve lectures on the Hauptpunkt of the formation and adoption of the Consititution would be possible; but nowadays, with Bancroft and the new Curtis, that doesn't seem as well worth while as in Austin Scott's time.

Are you coming down to Boston soon, or nearer to it, so that I could meet you and talk of these things? I could come up to Amherst if you deem it necessary. I am strongly desirous of making this engagement, for I greatly feel the need of more stimulation than I can get in Providence. Visits to Harvard, you can easily conceive, bring one the stimuli of patronizing remarks rather than any vital quickening. I feel no doubt that the consent of our people can as readily be obtained as in Diman's case, and hope you will not fail in securing that of Mr. Gilman. I am sorry that the arrangements, if made, cannot appear in the Circular, which I have just received; still, that must in some cases be so, this year.—
Believe me,

Sincerely yours,

J. F. Jameson

73 — From Frederick Jackson Turner

Department of History,
University of Wisconsin,
Madison, Wis.
September 27, 1890.

Dear Dr. Adams:

Mr. Thwaites tells me that he has invited you to deliver the address before the State Historical Society this year. I am more than glad that he has done so, for I think that you are pre-eminently the man who has a message for us. This meeting occurs at the time of the biennial session of the legislature which makes it especially important. As you perhaps know, the Historical Library is supported by the state and is managed by the State Historical Society as the trustee of the State In this respect it is almost unique, so far as I know. It is also out of the usual line of historical societies of its class in that it does not devote its time to collecting information as to the first white child and that sort of thing; but rather to accumulating what is already one of the best libraries on Americana in the country—particularly in respect to Western history and local history.

As you know, we have developed a spontaneous and peculiar form of University-Extension in Wisconsin in our Agricultural Institutes and School Institutes, under the guidance of the State University. They are steadily growing into a natural *inter*relation. The district school is being brought into a healthy connection with both; and preparation is being made to open a way for district schools to send students directly to a primary agricultural course in the University. It is hoped that this may act as a feeder to the supply of district school teachers, now sadly deficient in point of educational fitness as well as in capacity for bringing their teaching into connection with the life and work of the community in which they live.

The thing that is needed is a utilization of the resources of of the State Hist. library to *fertilize* and *spiritualize* the system. Wisconsin is not so thoroughly Philistine as some other States, but there is decidedly a need of some such movement as this. I do not wish to make any suggestions as to a subject but I desire to say that you as the representative of the idea of University Extension, and the use of *libraries* in this end, have here a field in which to do a missionary work, and help on a movement of great significance, and direct it into the higher path. I sincerely hope that you will embrace this opportunity to see our West and help on that process of cross-fertilization which you and your institution has [*sic*] been so instrumental in promoting. The West needs Eastern ideas; I think the West, too, has a word for the East.

It is a delicate task to bring home to our legislators the utility of the higher education and the practical value of an institution like the Historical Society. Heretofore the state has supported it nobly and it has escaped attack—partly perhaps, because it has not made itself over prominent; but the time has come I think when it ought to be more of a force in the movement of higher education of the people. Of course it stands in a peculiar relation to the commonwealth. The library cannot be utilized as at Buffalo because Madison is not a great city. Its importance lies as a fertilizer of students and teachers of the state. A word from you on this subject would not be amiss. But at any rate I earnestly ask you to accept the invitation and come to see us. It would do our historical department good—but that is incidental. *The main point is the opportunity to present University extension in its higher aspects to a State ready for the seed by its spontaneous acts in the same direction.*

Very truly yours,

Frederick J. Turner

74 — From William R. Harper

The American Institute of Sacred Literature.

Dictated.   New Haven., Conn., Oct. 13, 1890.

My dear Dr. Adams,
   Your kind favor of Oct. 9th is at hand. It gives me pleasure to send you some material which will give information to your friend, Dr. Hausknecht. I am much obliged to you for the opportunity to lay the matter before him.
   Of course, you will refuse the presidency of the State Univ. of Colorado at $5000 and the presidency of the Univ. of Wyoming; but when you let me present the attractions of the position I want you to take in the University of Chicago (and you have no idea what it is,—perhaps I may whisper it before meeting you, viz., the Deanship of the Graduate Department), I am sure you will consider the matter favorably.

I remain

Yours truly,

W R Harper

Prof. H. B. Adams, Ph. D.,
Baltimore, Md.

75 — From Reuben G. Thwaites

The State Historical Society of Wisconsin,
Madison, Wis., U. S. A.
Reuben G. Thwaites, Secretary.   Nov. 8, 1890.

Dr. Herbert B. Adams,
Johns Hopkins University,
Baltimore, Md.,

   My dear Sir:—Our institution is supported, for the most part, by standing legislative appropriations. The Society is the incorporated trustee of the commonwealth, for which it holds its funds and other possessions. In the matter of printing, rooms, janitorship, heat, lights, repairs, stationery, postage, and the principal salaries, we are on the same footing as any state bureau. But owing to the feature of Society management, of course we are wholly free from political control in the matter of tenure of office.

The library, now the largest reference library west of the Alleghanies, is resorted to by scholars from all over the west, as well as those within our own state. It is used by the students and professors of the State University far more than their own library, which is chiefly scientific and technical. In purveying for our library, we have the wants of the students continually in view, for they form 90 per cent of our readers.

We have a considerable ethnographical and historical museum, and a very good portrait gallery of Wisconsin worthies (175 oils, besides crayons, and portrait busts in marble and plaster). These are the popular features, and are visited by from 35,000 to 40,000 persons yearly.

In active work, we have for forty-one years gathered manuscripts and data of every character, throwing light on the history of Wisconsin and the whole west. Pioneers have been interviewed, and others encouraged to write their reminiscences, and over 20,000 manuscript documents—letters, reports, diaries, account-books, and what not—have been accumulated, many of them of very great value. Turner's Fur Trade monograph, for instance, was almost wholly evolved from these documents. This work, together with antiquarian research, is constantly in progress. I go next week to rummage in some old French garrets in Green Bay, to get fur-trade documents heretofore overlooked. We have published eleven stout volumes of Wisconsin Historical Collections, and have enough good material on hand for thirty more, if we could only get them printed,—we are restricted by law to one volume every three years, which is perhaps frequent enough for careful editing.

So you see we are at work in many directions, and are

constantly enlarging our field of usefulness and research. Our inquiry into the foreign groups of Wisconsin, you may possibly have seen something of; it is still in progress.

Thus much to acquaint you in a general way with our status. I can only express a hope that you can say something, incidently, of the value of such work as the Society is doing, to the people of this State and the west; of the credit which rests upon the state, for its active encouragement of such an enterprise, which in a new country, where endowments cannot be secured, could not have met with any notable success unless aided by official patronage; of the wisdom of the organic act, in securing the management free from all suspicion of partisan control,—trained experts being necessary to properly conduct such an undertaking; of the wisdom of increasing the state patronage, from time to time, that the several departments of the Society may keep pace with the rapid growth of the State,—Wisconsin is now at the front, in this sort of thing, and should keep there; and of the wisdom of some day bringing the State University and the State Historical Society into even closer relationship, at least in the direction of placing both libraries under the same roof, with joint management, thus avoiding duplication and doing the greatest possible amount of good,—a scheme, *sub rosa,* which both the University and the Society are devoutly praying for. Lastly, if you could say that you are surprised to see such a priceless collection as the Society has, in quarters ill-adapted for it, in every way,—quarters of awkward construction, ill-ventilated, dark, in extent only capable of holding the accessions of five years more, and apparently a regular fire-trap; and strongly suggest that there ought to be a new and fire-proof building,—and if possible, the University library also placed under the same roof. The State is wealthy enough to build one, and the need is crying.

You invited suggestions. I give them in a hap-hazard fashion, but the points cited cover the main ideas, some of which I would delight to have elaborated. Our legislature is good enough to us, on the whole, but it requires to be continually spurred up to its duty, and the coming assembly is composed almost entirely of new men wholly unacquainted with our growing needs and the importance of our work. A few words of suggestion and encouragement from an outsider will go much further than anything we can say. Our Western people naturally like to hear praise for their state and its institutions.

We have not fixed upon a date, yet, but will soon. About a fortnight before the time—perhaps ten days would do—I would like to have you forward to me either a synopsis of the paper, or the paper itself for me to synopsize. I want to be sure that the press is accommodated in this respect. They will, as you well know, publish much fuller reports if they can have the matter by mail, and some hours in advance, than they will if it is left to the wire.

Very truly yours,

Reuben G. Thwaites

76 — From William P. Trent

Sewanee, Tenn.,
Nov. 13th, 1890.

My dear Dr. Adams,

I received today a letter from Dr. Wm. E. Boggs, Chancellor of the University of Georgia which sends me to you for advice. I became acquainted with Dr. Boggs through some correspondence we had relative to the essay I wrote for Dr. Jameson's book and since then he has gone to the Univ'y. of Ga. He writes me a long letter to tell me that a professorship of History & Political Science is to be established in the University of Georgia, that institution expecting money under the Morrill Bill. He then dilates on the prospects etc. of the University & asks how the suggestion strikes me that I should send him such testimonials as would serve to let the Trustees know who I am. The tone of the letter would imply that Dr. B. will have the choice of the professor pretty much in his own hands & I also infer that he wants me—although of course he may have written similar letters to others. Such things are done.

Now the point is just this. For many reasons I don't care to leave Sewanee for any place in the South because I am fond of the people here & I am doing good work. On the other hand the salary in Georgia is $2000 ($500 more than I now get) with a prospect of a raise. I am worked very hard here on two very different branches—there I would only have to work in my specialty—with I presume, less hours of work in the class room. Since I have been at Sewanee my studies have been far more desultory than I could have wished & I had about made up my mind to serve out the term for which I was elected (four years) & then not apply for reelection but go back to the Hopkins. Then again I don't like the governing system at Sewanee for the Trustees are very unreliable in their actions. But on the other hand this is a critical period in Sewanee's history & without conceit I can say that if I draw out it will have no good effect—for I am very popular with the students & these latter are not in the best of humour with the management here at present. Besides the rumour has gone abroad owing to the fever here this summer that the place is unhealthy—an absurd rumour but one that has its effect—& I don't like particularly to look like a deserter at a critical moment.

Another point ought to be mentioned, however. There is no future for a place that hasn't a head with a policy—We have no policy that I can discover & our new Vice Chancellor though a fine man is not calculated to give us a policy. The institution simply *drifts*. Each man is a law unto himself & I never know whether we shall not drift on the rocks before the year is out.

I think the Univ. of Ga. is better off in many respects, but in a social way I imagine that S. is superior & I certainly will meet more influential people here. As I have often told you my ambition is to do good historical work & to make whatever mark I can in that way without thinking

too much of money or position. I would rather get a subordinate place in a large university with a *library* & the
chance to make a scholar of myself than to be *full professor*
in a very *unfledged university* (so called! God save the
mark!)

Now you know how the Univ. of Ga. stands better than I
do & you can calculate the chances of my getting a place,
from there or from here, in a large city better than I can,
so I ask you whether I ought to consider Dr. Boggs' proposal very seriously. I shall of course write him for further
information & shall keep the matter open; but I confess that
there are so many pros & cons that I hardly know what to
think.

At any rate though this is a long letter filled with myself,
I am glad to let you know of this proposed chair which ought
to be filled by some Johns Hopkins man. If you think I had
better not meddle with the matter, let me know the name
of some *Hopkinsensian* whom I can work for. I shall always
stand by the H. Only the other day a friend in Nashville
wrote to me to recommend a Univ. of Va. man for an assist.
professorship of Latin. I could name no one but I urged
him to write to the J. H. He writes now that there will
be no vacancy this year, but when I see him I shall convert
him to Hopkinsism. But I wouldn't dare say this to a Virginia man. My reason for preferring the Hopkins may be
selfish but it is natural—you have done more for me.

I doubt if I shall have enough information for a separate
place in the programme. I will try to make my paper as
acceptable as possible but I am overrun with work. I leave
in about a month for Charleston & then the tug of war begins
as far as Simms is concerned.

With best wishes, yours sincerely

W. P. Trent

77 — From Frederick Jackson Turner

Department of History,
University of Wisconsin,
Madison, Wis.

December 8, 1890.

Dear Dr Adams:

The report from Mr. Thoms on the relation of Agricultural Institutes to the district schools I have been unable to get owing to his pressing official duties. It is not essential however. The idea is simply that this bringing the farmers together in connection with University lectures and so on, stimulates the district school so that a better interest is taken in it and the teachers are awakened to better work. The report of Prof. Marxs is also delayed owing to the fact that his work is not yet fully formulated. He goes to various cities and studies the local conditions relative to industrial matters. Then a course of graded lectures is arranged by him. He calls in the aid of expert mechanics in the city and a local club is organized. Professor Marxs may lecture, for example, upon *materials* in mechanics relative to some special industry of the city one week and the next a practical mechanic will give a practical demonstration of the principles developed by Prof. Marx. He will also give instruction to these local bodies in draughting leaving the immediate charge of the work to local experts. Special lectures will be added by local talent and by others. The local manufacturers are brought into the work. This may grow into a system of manual training schools in connection with the public schools. Prof. Marxs hopes to see it develop into a system of Gewerbe Schulen, but Pres. Chamberlin does not lay any stress on this,—indeed he wished that it should not be mentioned in print. A particular aim of the work is to prevent the students of public schools from rushing to the shops at the age of fourteen, or younger, as they do in our manufacturing towns.

This gives the industrial side of University Extension here. A combination of Agricultural Institutes and Mechanics

Institutes. The " Culture side " of the work has not yet been developed to a great extent. The faculty have now under consideration a plan for bringing all departments into relation to the work but it is yet too undeveloped for public notice. *The President regards the industrial side of the work as only a part of it, however.* He has asked me for a report on historical extension and says that he finds a particular demand for this work. He suggests the question of whether the demand can be filled without taking too much of the time of a member of the faculty and whether we might not *appoint* certain workers in the historical field throughout the State as adjuncts to the faculty for this purpose, after the fashion of the Agricultural and Mechanics system. I would be glad to have any printed material that you can lend me for a few days, if you feel at liberty to do missionary work in this direction. I am to report next Monday so that if I make use of any suggestions or material it should be here before then. We are counting on your lecture with much interest. Pres. Chamberlin is to speak on University Extension at the teachers convention which meets here in the holidays.

Very truly yours,

Frederick J. Turner

Can I be of any further service to you in the way of Wisconsin matter? I find there is a " Travel Class " at Columbus where I am lecturing.

78 — To Daniel Coit Gilman

University Club
1005 North Charles Street

Dear President Gilman:

You kindly inquired whether the proposed arrangement would be agreeable to me and I was frank in expressing my feelings with regard to the title. I have no ambition to be known as a Professor of American History. At least five

10

sixths of my three years' course of lectures to graduates and *all* of my undergraduate classes are in the European field. I do not object to the phrase " Institutional History," for that describes very happily the nature of my university-work in class and seminary.

As " Professor of Institutional History " I could have a fair field for comparative studies in Church and State and in the Institutes of Education, without being regarded as an American provincial. If it seems expedient to define and therefore to limit my department of History, I cheerfully assent to the use of the above title.

Very respectfully,

Dec. 22, 1890   H. B. Adams

79 — From George W. Knight

Ohio State University.
Department of
History and Political Science
Columbus, Feby 23 1891

Dr. H. B. Adams:
Baltimore, Md:

My dear Sir:

Your recent favor is at hand. Regarding the kind of a man we *may* want next year, just what we should want him to do, and how much we could give him for it, these are questions not yet easily answered, and cannot be until the 1/20 mill bill is passed or defeated in our State Senate. We have encountered a snag in the opposition of the other two alleged State colleges (Ohio University at Athens, and Miami at Oxford) who both insist that they ought to have a share. We have finally and definitely told them that we won't consent to a " divide " but will let our bill fall through in preference if necessary. We think we have a majority of the Senate in our favor, and are going to " try conclusions "

within the next ten days. If the bill passes, our annual assured income from all sources will be raised to about $150,-
000, which will enable us to adopt a definite educational
policy hereafter. As soon as we know our fate, I will write
you again concerning our probable need of one of your men—
or at least of a man—as assistant in this department.

*   *   *   *

Yours truly

Geo. W. Knight

80 — From Charles Kendall Adams

President's Rooms,
Cornell University,
Ithaca, N. Y.

Feb. 26/91.

My dear Professor:

I congratulate you most sincerely and heartily on your
well earned promotion. Nobody during the last few years
has done so much for historical study in this country as
yourself, and it would have seemed to me a culpable neglect
of a great opportunity if you had been allowed to go to any
other institution, if, by a permanent appointment you could
be held at Baltimore. The little pamphlet showing what
you do is most inspiring, and I cannot for a moment suppose
that you will abandon your post there for any picnic at
Chicago or elsewhere. I hope you will drive in your stakes
so deep and strong that nobody will be able to pull them up.
One who has built up such an opportunity as yours ought
to hesitate a long time before abandoning it for any reason
or inducement whatever. You are doing a great work for
American scholarship in history and I hope you will keep
your place. For a long time I had a hope that we might
transplant you to Cornell; although I never intimated my
desire to you, it was never absent from my mind until the
peculiar combination of circumstances here seemed to make

it impracticable. I trust you will have every success and satisfaction in your work.

Very heartily and truly yours,

C. K. Adams

Professor Herbert B. Adams

81 — To Frederic Bancroft

Johns Hopkins University,
Baltimore, Md., March 5, 1891.

Dr. Frederic Bancroft,
Department of State,
Washington, D. C.

Dear Sir:

At this University there is a little company of graduate students, who are greatly interested in American history and in its scientific promotion. They have heard something of the manuscript historical materials preserved in the Library of the State Department, and would be very glad to see some of these treasures with their own eyes. Would it be possible for you and consistent with your duties to the State Department to meet a delegation from my Historical Seminary upon your library premises on some Saturday after the Easter holidays, say on the 4th of April at about 3.30 P. M. and to show them such selections from your archives as might seem proper for exhibition? Such a privilege would be highly appreciated not only by the Historical Department but also by the Johns Hopkins University.

Enclosed please find the most recent published statement concerning our school of history and politics. You will observe that the Hon. John A. Kasson, at one time U. S. Minister to Austria and afterward Minister to Germany, is to give our department ten lectures on the history of diplomacy in the months of April and May.

Very respectfully yours,

H. B. Adams
Prof. Hist.

82 — From Frank W. Blackmar

Kansas State University
Department of History and Sociology
April 6th, 1891

Professor H. B. Adams,
Johns Hopkins University,
Balt., Md.

Dear Dr. Adams:—

At a recent meeting, the Regents of the university granted me an assistant for the coming year and thereafter.[1] The salary is fixed at $800.00 per annum with a prospect of $1000, within a year or two. The amount of work required is three hours per day in regular work which consists mainly of instruction in history. The new man will take part of my work and would be expected to do it *well*.

I will enclose a list of subjects for the coming year. With a slight exception the students will be seniors and juniors in all classes.

Our library is growing; I have $325, to expend for books and maps for the next year. There is a good opportunity here for an energetic man to make his *work* felt and to *rise* in the *profession*. I know that the salary is low but it is the regular price for assistants who come for the first time. But this is the best town in Kansas for residence, and living is cheap.

Have you the man that I want?—one who is *able* and at the same time *willing* to *practice* in the west, where there is plenty of room, on a small salary? I have written to you first and shall await your reply before applying elsewhere.

Tolman said something to me some time ago, about coming west. I presume that he would not come for the salary.

I want a good man; personally I would prefer not to have an assistant unless he is to be a number one.

---

[1] Frank W. Blackmar received a Ph. D. degree from the Hopkins in 1889.

Our western newspapers are inclined to be rather hard on the venerable president of Harvard. I enclose a species of the sentiment that is going the rounds at present.[1] The west seems to have sense enough to know when it is snubbed. Please let me hear from you as soon as possible.

Yours truly,

F. W. Blackmar

83 — To Daniel Coit Gilman

University Club,
1005 North Charles Street.

President Gilman:

Dear Sir:

On the same day that I was promoted by the trustees of the Johns Hopkins University I was elected by the trustees of the Chicago University professor of history and dean of the graduate department at a salary of $5000, with a year's preliminary vacation on full pay.

I did not know this fact until very recently, for in Chicago I declined all overtures, on account of my promise to accept the formal proposition of your executive committee. Last month the offer came to me from President Harper and I was pressed for an immediate answer. Within forty-eight hours I declined the call. Last week there came to me from the same source an offer of $6000 and a year off on full salary, with other generous conditions. In justice to all parties I feel that you and the trustees ought to know these facts.

---

[1] The editorial from the Atchison *Champion*, if I can decipher the fragment of the name written on the clipping, said in part, " Among other things this cultured and highly inflated snob said: ' The west, in a mass, is incapable, dense, ignorant and wrong.'

This is about the most impudent and execrable manifestation of ill-breeding and of a criminal lack of a just perception of facts of which we have any knowledge. It is the very acme of scholastic conceit and of literary dudeism, and brands its author as a man whose shallowness is only exceeded by his want of good common sense."

Certain apparent limitations to my prospects in Baltimore compel me to take the Chicago opportunity into renewed and serious consideration.

Very respectfully,

April 6, 1891.   H. B. Adams.

84 — From James A. James

Madison, Wis.,
April 8. /91.

Prof. H. B. Adams;

Dear Sir and Friend:—

This afternoon I attended Prof. Turner's Seminary. It is Hopkins S. on a small scale. Turner and Haskins are both doing very effective work. It is not a difficult task to make the students here, who contemplate a higher education, come to the conclusion that J. H. U. is much preferable to Harvard. Some of my friends will enter the Historical Department within the next two years.

As suggested by you, I talked over the subject of a thesis with Prof. Turner. He spoke of one which you had recommended to him and on which there are some original manuscripts in the State Hist. Library. Although somewhat difficult to state exactly, it relates to the " Relations of the Federal Gov't. to the Indian."

Prof. T. thought it might be prepared somewhat after the manner of Dr. Brackett's monograph on the Negro. He said farther that the manuscript material at Washington would be especially useful. Will you be so kind as to let me know what you think of this field?

At present I have considerable time which I shall devote to special research after hearing from you.

Sincerely yours,

539 State St.   J. A. James [1]

---

[1] James A. James received the Ph. D. degree in 1893. His dissertation entitled " English Institutions and the American Indian " was published in volume twelve of the *Studies*.

85 — To Daniel Coit Gilman

University Club,
1005 North Charles Street.
Apr 13, 1891

President Gilman:

Dear Sir:

Last Saturday I received another letter from Dr. Harper, urging me to accept his $6000 proposition. If I decline to go for that figure, I am told that he means to offer me $8000. Mr. J. D. Rockefeller is behind Dr. Harper and agrees to the policy of large salaries.[1]

I shall refuse to go to Chicago at any price, if the Hopkins trustees put my department upon a satisfactory *historico-political* basis and give me a salary of $5000, beginning with the next academic year, and a leave of absence, when I ask it, at some future and more convenient time.

Anything less would obviously be unsatisfactory to one who has served the Johns Hopkins for fifteen years, at great pecuniary sacrifice, and who now has the opportunity of going to Europe with an assured salary of $6000.

Any economic discrimination in my present case would compel me to consider Dr. Harper's proposition.

Very respectfully,

H. B. Adams

---

[1] In his reply dated April 21, Gilman wrote " The Executive Committee at their meeting this afternoon directed me to say to you, that they cannot recommend to the Trustees to comply with the request contained in your letter to me of April 13. They expressed their hope that the present agreeable relations between you & the university may continue, & I have no doubt they would confirm the suggestions that I made in my talk with you on the 5th of April, & then reduced to writing. But it is clear that we have not the funds to compete with Mr. R. or Mr. Stanford."

86 — From Walter Hines Page

The Forum,
253 Fifth Avenue, New York.
Apl. 28, 1891.

Dear Mr. Adams—

I am going to publish book-reviews in the *Forum,* and the task is harder than any other that I have in hand. For this reason I come to you for help.

Generically, the book-review is dull—perhaps must be dull; and I seriously doubt the scientific value of any contemporary criticism. I have got into this somewhat pessimistic mood after a good many years' effort of my own and a good many years' direction of other people's efforts to make reviews interesting. For the point where failure comes in and is wellnigh universal is the point of interest or dullness. Nothing, I hold, is pardonable that is dull.

And all this, of course, I write—not, I pray you, believe me, with any personal application but—only to justify the departure I am going to make in admitting reviews to the *Forum;* and I am going again to try to see if they cannot be made interesting.

My first invitation of a review, I take great pleasure in sending to you, if you will be kind enough to help me; and I ask if you will not prepare an article on Henry Adams's recently published historical volumes. I shall publish it as a *Forum* article, putting it in the body of the magazine. This will give you scope, therefore, to wander over the technical bounds of a review, properly speaking, and allow you to write about histories of the early administrations *ad libitum;* and I should say that an essay on this wider view of the subject with Adams as a text would be more instructive and more interesting than a mere review. We can leave to the purely academic journals the task of criticising minor and technical things and throw our consideration of the subject on a higher, at least more comprehensive, plane.

I shall very highly value your cooperation if you can give it; I would not have you regard my rambling remarks as suggestions about the treatment of the subject—not at all; I beg to ask that you will buy a set of the books, if you need them for this use, at my expense; I shall ask you to be as brief as you can to give yourself comfortable room; I shall ask you to accept our check for $50; and I beg—(if you will consent) to have your manuscript by May 10.

> Very Sincerely Yours,
>
> Walter H. Page [1]

Prof. H. B. Adams,
Baltimore

87 — From George W. Knight

> Ohio State University.
> Department of History and Political Science.
> Columbus, April 29 1891.

Dr. H. B. Adams:
Johns Hopkins University
Baltimore, Md.

My dear Dr. Adams:

Can you name to me a first class man, whom we could be likely to get, for an instructor in the department of history and political science? I should want a man who had made history his major specialty, and who was especially well grounded in mediaeval and modern European history. The work to be carried by the man next year would be a general course (for sophomores) in mediaeval and modern European history (2 hours a week for the year), mainly text book work, *perhaps* another partial course in European history for juniors and seniors, and in the preparatory department, which we hope to cut off and close in two or three years, work in U. S. or general history, and in Civics. The total would range from nine to twelve hours a week, in part repetitions on account of double sections in some classes. As our organization gives

---

[1] Walter Hines Page had been a graduate student and a fellow in Greek at the Hopkins during the years 1876-1878. A later letter shows that Adams refused this request to review a nine volume history in ten days.

to heads of departments only, seats in the Faculty he would
not be charged with Faculty duty or responsibility. The
salary will range between $800 and $1200, depending on the
man, presumably $900 or $1000.

I may say that in all probability though it is *by no means a
certainty* and should not be taken as an implied part of the
contract for next year, my department will be divided in
two or three years and the chair of European history (perhaps all history) will be open to be filled. In such event the
instructor now to be appointed if he proved the right man
would have a reasonably good future before him. This last
paragraph is written not for the benefit of prospective candidates but in order to show *you* what we are aiming at, and
what sort of man we would like to start in with now. The
right man can do much by his work, toward bringing it about.

Have you such a man now available? If so please tell me
what you can say for him. An early answer will be especially
appreciated as our attention has already been called to one
or two others.

Yours truly

Geo. W. Knight

88 — To William R. Harper

Johns Hopkins University,
Baltimore, Md., May 1, 1891.

Professor W. R. Harper,
Yale University,
New Haven, Conn.

My dear Professor:

I have given the whole matter renewed and thorough consideration. I never have been so near a decision in favor of
Chicago as I have been this week since our interview Sunday
morning. The two cities and the two universities have stood
face to face in my mind for the past five days. Your letter
of April 28, with the enclosure from Professor James, presses
me to a final decision. While it is evident that I should gain
very much in material and administrative ways by a removal

to Chicago, it is now perfectly clear to my mind that my professional and scientific interests lie here in the Johns Hopkins University. I observe that Professor James has two great objects in his life work: (1) a great department of history and politics, which shall be at once a place of instruction and a centre of scientific publication equal to any in this country or in Europe; (2) a school of practical affairs, having history and politics for its liberal basis and affording useful training in administration and social science. These two objects I have already virtually realized in Baltimore. I cannot, therefore, believe it is my duty to go afield for the purpose of discovering or reproducing what now exists under my very hand. I see the following substantial reasons for remaining in Baltimore and, under the circumstances, you are entitled to know exactly what they are:

1. I have the best department of history and politics in this country.[1] It is at once the largest and the strongest. It has a wide-spread colonial system and a very loyal body of graduate students.

2. From this department have gone out nearly twenty published volumes under my editorship. These University Studies are my scientific capital. I cannot afford to throw it away or to lose my present control of the best established series of University publications in my chosen field.

3. I am reluctant and indeed unwilling to spend the next ten years of my life in the work of preliminary organization and preparation for doing what I can do already. My track is laid. My machine is built. Steam is up and, although we are still on the up grade, there is a certain momentum in a moving train like the Johns Hopkins University.

4. I prefer the East to the West, the Atlantic seaboard to the shore of Lake Michigan, an international outlook even to the broad view over the Mississippi valley and the great

---

[1] In saying this Adams was reporting a fact not boasting. At the previous commencement Ph. D. degrees had been conferred on Frederick Jackson Turner, Charles H. Haskins, John Martin Vincent, James A. Woodburn. The class of the year before had included Charles M. Andrews and Albion W. Small. Among those receiving the degree a month after this letter was written were W. W. Willoughby and Edward A. Ross.

Northwest. My friends and associations are all along this coast and Washington is only 45 minutes away. I like this mild Maryland climate better than Chicago grippe.

5. I think I shall be happier here in Baltimore doing my own work than I could possibly be in Chicago doing some other work, even for a higher salary.[1]

---

[1] The considerations that led Adams to reject the offer from Chicago which Harper pressed so insistently are listed in a note among his papers. It casts such a significant light on Adams and on his estimate of the contemporary advantages of the two places that it is worth reproducing in full.

Balto. *vs.* Chicago

	Baltimore		Chicago
1.	Department	1.	None as yet
2.	*Men*	2.	Coeducation
3.	Studies	3.	None
4.	Colonies	4.	None
5.	Europe	5.	Doubtful
6.	Washington	6.	Remote
7.	Peabody	7.	Newberry
8.	Friends	8.	None
9.	Climate	9.	Raw & dirty
10.	Hist. Assoc.	10.	Lost
11.	Smithsonian	11.	Lost
12.	Bureau [of Education]	12.	Too far
13.	East	13.	West
14.	Quiet	14.	Rush
15.	Continuity	15.	Broken
16.	Ideal	16.	Lost
17.	Non Sectarian	17.	Baptist
18.	Secular life	18.	Theology
19.	$4000	19.	$5000+
20.	*My* work	20.	Administra for Harper
21.	Vacation	21.	None
22.	Liberty	22.	12 hour law
23.	Liberal sys.	23.	2 courses
24.	Experience	24.	Experiment
25.	Gilman	25.	Harper
26.	Society	26.	New people
27.	Conservatism	27.	Boom
28.	Univ. club	28.	Dining club
29.	Literature	29.	Lacking
30.	Duty	30.	Advantage
31.	Seaboard	31.	Interior
32.	Communica easy	32.	Travel
33.	Cheap living	33.	Expensive
34.	Arundel	34.	Boarding
35.	Assured position	35.	All new
36.	Settled	36.	Moving
37.	Mother & H.	37.	Distance
38.	Nat. Univ.	38.	Local
39.	Identification	39.	Lost
40.	Future hopeful	40.	Doubtful

These are the reasons, my dear Professor Harper, why I must positively and finally decline your generous and altogether magnanimous offer. You have treated me very frankly and very handsomely. I wish it were in my power to show my heartfelt appreciation of your great kindness and wonderful patience. Be assured that I am sincerely grateful for your manifest confidence in me. I have equal confidence in you and am sure that you will work out your great academic problem with acknowledged success. There are two men to whom you can turn now for efficient co-operation in the organization and up-building of the University of Chicago: President Albion W. Small, or Professor Edmund J. James. I doubt whether you can get the latter. His position in Philadelphia is as strong as mine in Baltimore, perhaps stronger in a financial and public way. I have the highest estimation of the moral and educational qualities of Dr. Small. In a Baptist university he would be a tower of strength.

Very cordially and sincerely yours,

[Herbert B. Adams]

89 — From Frederick Jackson Turner

University of Wisconsin,
Madison, Wisconsin,
May 7, 1891.

Professor H. B. Adams,
Johns Hopkins University,

Dear Dr. Adams:

I believe that there is some rule that requires the thesis to be published before a year from the granting of the doctor's degree unless the fifty dollar deposit is to be forfeited. Is not this construed to permit publication in the Studies at a later date, as in the case of my thesis? I would like to add a couple or three maps of a simple character to show changes of Indian location, and to show the effect of the fur-trade upon the boundary proposals of Great Britain in 1795, and 1812. Have you any means of knowing about what extra expense would be involved in this? I notice some changes in the order in which the theses are to be published; about what time shall I have to send in my matter?

I am sorry to learn from Mr. Moseley that you are not coming West this summer. We are counting upon the pleasure of having President Gilman here at Commencement. If you have not received extra copies of your address here please let me know. Mr. Thwaites has gone to Europe but I think I can arrange matters with Mr. Durrie for you. President Chamberlin has recently come to some arrangements with the regents whereby he is enabled to do more "cultural" university extension work in the future. There was a lively fight made in the legislature to put some Democrat in place of Mr. Morrison the conductor of the Farmer's Institutes, and also to make the organization independent of the University and the conductor an appointed officer of the governor's. This would have plunged the whole institution into politics, and we managed to kill the bill, but it was a close shave. We also made a lively effort to secure the refunded direct tax money for a Memorial Hall but the Democrats would not do it this year, though making us many promises for next session. They increased the University income very materially.

Please give my regards to Dr. Ely.

Yours very truly

Frederick J. Turner

90 — From Frederick Jackson Turner

University of Wisconsin,
Madison, Wisconsin,
May 17, 1891.

Dear Dr. Adams:

I have it in mind to prepare a syllabus of my work in American History. My particular effort this year has been to get the students to working on the original authorities. Taking for my mottoe that all history is comment on a text, I have aimed to indicate to the class such texts as would best serve as the material for discussion. My first thought has been to get up an outline something like Professor Hart's, except that the references would be chiefly or entirely to the original authorities, rather than to secondary authorities. It strikes me that a better plan however would be to *print a collection of texts.* In libraries there are seldom sufficient duplicates to permit the class if it be large to use the documentary material as the sole basis of work. Why could not something like *Stubbs' Select Charters* be gotten out to illustrate, or rather to furnish the basis, of a course in American Constitutional and Economic history? Preston's Documents are too meagre. My idea would be to print a good sized volume or perhaps two, containing significant speeches, Presidential messages, selections from debates, treaties, Supreme court decisions, laws (Alien and Sedition, e. g.), Reports, like Hamilton Walkers, Gallatin's, etc., etc.

I have not fully thought the matter out, though I have been for some time collecting references to original authorities in this line. I am not prepared to get the book up purely as a personal venture, though if it was judiciously compiled I think it would be used in a large number of colleges. Would it be possible to get the book issued as an extra volume of the Studies and secure co-operation in the compilation from some of your graduate students, and particularly from Hopkins graduates who could use the book in their classes? For instance if Professors Jameson, Wilson, Blackmar, Andrews, Small, and others could be interested, the work would be made easier, *better* and more certain of paying for itself. I would gladly become one of such a co-operative company, under your editorship. Please let me know what you think of the scheme.

Yours truly,

Frederick J. Turner

91 — From Charles H. Haskins

University of Wisconsin,
Madison, Wisconsin,
May 23, 1891.

My dear Dr. Adams:

I have your letter of the 21st. I had not heard that Barnes was going to Stamford, although I had wondered whether he would not be called there. I have just written to Woodburn inquiring about the place at Indiana. I don't feel at all sure that I should want to go there, and should prefer a similar place here, but at the same time I haven't so good a place here and feel that a professorship at Indiana is at least worth looking up.

I hope that President Chamberlin will get Sherwood, as I think he can if he offers him a respectable salary. I think he is excellently fitted for the work here, and Turner and I should enjoy having him with us. Either Turner or I would have written to you earlier in regard to him, had we been in a position where we could have done so with propriety. The department however is entirely distinct from ours, and we could tender no advice until asked, especially as we knew that Professor Parkinson had personal plans with which we had no right to interfere.

I was much gratified to hear that one of the best undergraduate students desired my return to Baltimore. I look back with a great deal of pleasure on my class work there. I have no reason to complain of my students here or of the work they do; at the same time I notice their lack of preparation, especially for classical history. It is hard to do much work in classical history with students most of whom know no Latin. Greek is of course out of the question with nearly all of them. Ignorance of Latin is also a drawback in the work in mediaeval and parts of English history. In view of their preparation I think the upper classmen do excellent work; the contrast with my Baltimore students shows strongly in the case of the Freshmen. The work-spirit, too,

11

is not so strong as in Baltimore. The western student is also thoroughly practical, and, vitalize ancient history as thoroughly as you may, it is to him still ancient.

The department is certainly to be congratulated on the acquisition of the Scharf and Birney collections. It has for a long time seemed to me that the opportunity of Johns Hopkins lay in the line of southern history, and I am glad that matters are opening so well in that direction. I regret very much not being able to hear Dr. Jameson's lectures; I have become particularly interested in that field after my work in Yazoo. I haven't yet given up hope of future work in American history.

My dissertation is nearly in final form. I am waiting to see the latest book on the Spanish intrigues. Col. Jones has kindly consented to look over my manuscript. Dr. Jameson made the same promise in the winter. Do you know whether he is in position to do so soon? Does he return to Providence immediately after the close of his Baltimore lectures?

I had a note from Vincent a few days ago in regard to some thesis material which I have out of the library. I can return it next week, if that is not so late as to inconvenience him.

Very sincerely,

Charles H. Haskins.[1]

92 — From Charles H. Haskins

Madison, Wisconsin,
Sept. 29, 1891.

My dear Dr. Adams:

I have been back here for a month and in the harness for three weeks. Matters have begun auspiciously. The department of history has all the students it can handle. We have fewer required students than last year, and the number of

---

[1] Haskins received an A. B. degree from the Hopkins in 1887 and the Ph. D. degree three years later when still in his twentieth year. The dissertation of the young scholar who was to become the most distinguished of contemporary American medievalists was on " The Yazoo Land Companies."

electives is much greater. Turner has forty in Nineteenth
Century; I have twenty-five in classical institutions. Turner
gives American constitutional history, American colonial
history, nineteenth century, and seminary—twelve hours; I
have general English history, English constitutional history,
history of institutions, Greek history, and seminary—fourteen
hours; and the fellow has six hours' work in dynastic and
territorial history with the Freshmen.

University extension promises well here. The professors
have announced nine courses, and from the number of ap-
plications coming in it looks as if all would be taken. I will
send you one of the circulars when they appear.

President Rogers of Northwestern is, I hear, trying to form
an association of the colleges around Chicago to pool their
university extension interests in some way. Is Harper in it?
I have a suspicion it is some sort of a scheme to head him off.

A propos of the University of Chicago, it is rumored in
the newspapers that Judson of the University of Minnesota
has been offered the chair of history. Is it true? It rather
surprised us. Who will follow him at Minneapolis? It ought
to be a good opening for some one. After Nebraska, who can
tell what is coming?

Can you tell me what is the character of the National
Cyclopaedia of American Biography? Your name is given
as a contributor on one of the announcements that fell into
my hands, but I was not sure that it was genuine. They
want me to do a little local Pennsylvania work; there is
almost no money in it, and I don't want to undertake it unless
the Cyclopaedia amounts to something. Something, in the
Nation I think, aroused my suspicions. And Gilmore's
Cyclopaedia, what is that like? Gilmore wrote to Turner
and me for biographies, but we are rather shy of it.

I finished the page proof of my A. H. A. paper some time
in August. Will it not be out soon? I didn't reach Jameson
until too late. I ordered 150 sent directly to Mr. Murray.[1]

---

[1] His dissertation was published in volume five of the Papers of
the American Historical Association. Mr. Murray of the Hopkins
Press had charge of the distribution of printed theses.

Pennsylvania education still hangs fire. The returns come in but slowly from some of the colleges. Some of the earlier work is already ancient history, but I hope to keep it going.[1] My university work is lighter than last fall, and I shall have some time for my own work, if I don't get loaded up with university extension and candidates for the master's degree—they are coming in fast.

I heard from Sherwood recently. Was sorry to learn that he is still unsettled for the year—wish we could do something for him, but see no way. I see he has improved the vacation by going the way of all flesh and taking his second degree.

It would have been pleasant for us to have you at Chicago, but I think you did right in declining.

If nothing prevents, I shall be at Washington in the holidays to read Sanford's paper. There is a chance of Turner and Sanford's being there. Thwaites will probably not attend; he is on his way back from six months in England.

With best wishes for the year and regards to Dr. Ely, I am

Very sincerely yours,

Charles H. Haskins

93 — *From Bernard C. Steiner*

Williamstown Mass.
Sept 30, 1891

Dear Prof. Adams;

I have been here nine days, have become a little used to being called Professor and Doctor, have attended a faculty meeting, have written divers and sundry lectures, have delivered some of them, and am settled, on arriving at which period I promised to write you.

I like it here very well, the students are a fine class of men and the faculty have been very cordial and friendly to

---

[1] Adams was editor for the United States Bureau of Education of a series of studies of higher education in each of the States. That for Pennsylvania by Haskins and W. I. Hull was published by the Bureau in 1902.

me. I have two large rooms one for study the other for bedroom, occupying the whole third floor of a house, which frees me from noise and disturbance. I board at a place where are five others of the young, unmarried members of the faculty and find it very pleasant. This fall I have two classes, after Christmas another a four optional in American History (or really an eight hour one) I instruct now only Juniors and Seniors after Christmas I am to have Sophomores in English history. Three times a week I lecture to the Juniors, 80 of them on American Colonial History. They have behaved remarkably well so far and seem quite interested. I am going to give them bi-weekly examinations. An optional class of about twenty five in English Constitutional History, which runs through the year, turning into European History in the latter part, I meet thrice a week for two hour sessions. For text-books I use Thwaites' "Colonies," which is full of inexcusable mistakes but has good bibliographies, and imitating you, I am trying to get the men to do some outside reading; and our old and bulky friend Taswell-Langmead. In my English Constitutional History I find my notes a perfect gold-mine and I hope Prof. Emmott will not be offended, though I do plagiarize at times.

The library is *fine* for my purposes. History, though with some strange omissions, is remarkably complete and they manifest a willingness to get the books I want.

We have a freshman class of 115 men, by far the largest ever known here. I like the place very much now that the temperature is bearable. Talk of mountain air, I would as soon be in the city as in such humidity as we had until Tuesday. I think I have told you the most important things.

Last summer I nearly finished the History of Guilford, which I had been working on for four years, though I don't think I ever told you of it. I have material for what is left up here and hope to complete it this winter.

I wrote a life of Gov. Wm. Leete last Summer; you may remember you said last Spring that if it turned out worth anything you would give me a chance to read it before the

American Historical Association. It does amount to something: I am convinced that he has never had justice done him, especially in regard to the part he took in the proceedings which ended in the absorption of New Haven Colony by Connecticut. I am established in the belief, through reading of colonial records and the correspondence with Winthrop that that union of the two colonies would have been almost impossible but for his firmness and moderation and yet even the histories of Connecticut scarcely more than allude to him. Cotton Mather judged him better than anyone else in this regard.

I hope you will have as large a seminary and as prosperous a winter this year as last. Remember me to everybody and believe me

Yours sincerely

Bernard C. Steiner [1]

94 — From John H. T. McPherson

Athens [Ga.]
Oct 4, 1891.

My dear Dr. Adams:

I have been just three weeks in my new field, and have things now working very nicely. They had assigned me quarters in a very unsatisfactory place in a remote corner of the campus, over the Gymnasium; but after a good deal of persuasion and insistence, with some tact and wire-pulling, I succeeded in capturing the rooms belonging to the vacant chair of Geology. These are just what I want. They are situated just over the Library, much like the History rooms at J. H. U. and have great possibilities. I have the whole floor, 100 x 55 feet. After this success I made a bold strike for money to fit them up, and have had the floors covered

---

[1] Steiner received the Ph. D. degree in 1891. His history of Guilford, Connecticut was published in the Proceedings of the Celebration of the 250th Anniversary of the Settlement of the Town, Sept. 10, 1889, and his sketch of Governor Leete appeared in the Annual Report of the American Historical Association for 1891.

with cocoa matting, and am now putting up shelves like
those in the Bluntschli, dividing half the room into alcoves,
which I'll fix up with tables and chairs. When this is done
I'll make a raid on the General library and get all the books
I can. I have $500 to order books for my Dep't, and have
hopes of $1000 more at the next meeting of the trustees.

Can you tell me the best agent from whom to order books
and maps? Or is it best to write to the publisher in each
case?

Behind this combined Historical Library and Lecture-
room is a large room 55 ft square, which is now a geological
museum. Here my ambition projects a fine museum of
Southern and General History. I've already arranged to have
the stones packed away elsewhere, *leaving the cases behind.*
These cases cost $500, and just suit my purposes. My Museum
has started with an old cannon ball, and fragment of cannon
from Fort Marion, St. Augustine, Florida. There are lots of
valuable things around Athens & Augusta and Atlanta that
will flow in when it gets once well started.

I succeeded with some difficulty in getting 11 hours a week
for the present, which I divide in this way.

Seniors: 3 hrs. Polit. Econ. Walker with Mill & Ely &
Marshall for reference.

Juniors: U. S. Johnston's U. S. Const. 3 hrs. Johnston's
Amer. Politics. Lectures.

Soph.: England— S. R. Gardiner 2 hrs. France—Duruy.
Fresh: Greece—Oman. Rome—Mommsen.

The faculty of the Literary Dep't consists of 14 men, 8 of
whom are progressive young men under 30 years of age: 3
are from J. H. U.—Campbell, Prof of Biology, & Herty,
Instructor in Chemistry. Instructors get $1200.00; I shall
call on you for one as soon as I feel able.

The only difficulty I've met so far is a peculiar one. The
editor of a local paper, *the Banner,* picked up Johnston's
U. S.—the Britannica reprint, you know, which I thought
above reproach—and discovered what he is pleased to consider unsound doctrine. I heard of it accidentally, and headed

him of[f] just in time to prevent the appearance of a flaming
sensational article " showing me up." It has gotten round
to some extent in conversation, and tho' I think most people
know me to be a good Southerner there is still some danger
of stirring up a regular hornet's nest. That editor wants
to know "whats the matter with Alexander Stephens?"
What would you advise me to do? Use Stephens nominally
as a parallel?

I've sent Murray the corrected galley proof of Liberia.

I trust you have had a pleasant vacation, and that everything is well with you at old Johns Hopkins. I should be
glad to have your guidance in the purchase of my $1500 worth
of books and maps.

Very sincerely yours,

J. H. T. McPherson.[1]

95 — From Frederick Jackson Turner

21 W. Gilman St
Madison Wis.,
Oct. 19, 1891

Dear Dr. Adams:—

I have already returned galley proof to Friedenwald with
(I hope) all important changes. Will be glad to send page
proof to you.

I do not know the financial side of the Studies very well.
Where a paper makes a double number what do the 150
copies for Hopkins cost the author? Will there be other expenses to me besides this? How large an edition is published?
It is not impossible that there may be a little sale for the
Study in Wisconsin. I shall want some extra copies, how
many will depend on my other expenses in connection with
it. Of course the fifty dollars now on deposit will be applic-
able to the purchase of the 150 copies for . . . [?].

---

[1] Ph. D. 1890. His dissertation, "History of Liberia," was published in the ninth volume of the *Studies*.

You are very kind to make the suggestion in regard to a Study on the Northwest. Sometime we may have something for you, though it is President Chamberlin's intention to use a fund at our disposal from the State, to publish a series of University Researches before long, to which, I suppose, our contributions will naturally go. We are working in our seminary at the period 1830-40 with particular reference to the reciprocal influences between East and West at that time. Our fellow is doing a thorough piece of work on the German immigration into Wisconsin at the same time. She finds interesting currents connecting us with German life and particularly politics & religion—Some schemes for making Wisconsin a German colony are particularly interesting.

I shall return your Extension syllabus in a few day[s]. They are just what I wanted, as explaining the English method. Of course we shall adapt our work to our environment, as we have always tried to. I do not think that our lectures will be given at Chicago, though it is likely that some of them will. But the policy of the institution will certainly be co-operation with all of the other Universities while not resigning any Wisconsin ground which she is asked to *till*—The rivalry with Chicago University will be a good thing for us all.

James worked very faithfully, and I believe, very intelligently at the Indians this summer. His excellent work at our University makes me confident that he will succeed well with you. Certainly I hope so. I expect that several of his friends, particularly Sanford, will be doing postgraduate work at Hopkins before long. James is enthusiastic over his work.

Mrs Turner wishes to be kindly remembered.

Very truly yours

Frederick J. Turner

Professor H B Adams
Johns Hopkins University

96 — From John H. T. McPherson

University of Georgia.
Athens, Georgia, Nov. 11 1891

Dr. H. B. Adams,
Johns Hopkins Univ.

My dear Dr. Adams:

I have your letter of the 9th, and should be glad to have your office send copies of my monograph to the *Frederick* (Md) *Times,* the *Detroit Free Press,* and to Mr. *Pleasant A. Stovall,* editor of the Augusta Chronicle; also to Mr. Wm. Coppinger, Colonization Building, Washington, Pres. J. B. Angell, Profs R. Hudson & A. C. McLaughlin, of Ann Arbor, and to Haskins and Woodburn; I think among these I could get some sympathetic reviews.

I've had a mildly exciting time since I last wrote you. In spite of all my efforts, and after staving it off for three weeks, the " Banner " at last came out with a flaming, sensational, two-column attack on Johnston's History, and kept it up daily for over two weeks.

I took no public notice of it, and the rest of the faculty, though indignant, maintained silence. The students took it up, however, and answered it in another paper, publishing also Resolutions upholding the course in U. S. Hist. and condemning the Banner. The Augusta Chronicle is a personal friend of mine, and came strongly to my defense, but most of the small local papers in Georgia applauded the Banner. The Constitution is influenced by the faculty, and kept quiet.

Gradually as the facts quietly developed people became disgusted with the tone and effrontery of the Banner, and now I am decidedly on top, and the Banner is quieted. Most of the Stockholders are indignant, and both editors, it is said, will be dismissed at the next meeting of the board. The loyal support of the students was very gratifying to me, as were also the numerous expressions of good-will and sympathy I received on all sides during the attack. I've had a tremendous amount of free advertising, though!

You will be interested in a scheme of University extension to which the faculty is now practically committed. Our first center will be in Atlanta, where the Young Men's Library Association are to provide the Hall and enroll the students. I am one of the Standing Committee on Univ. Extension, which has succeeded in eliciting the promise of a course from at least eight members of the faculty. The courses will contain six lectures apiece, and will be delivered once a week, on Friday nights. They are to be solid and instructive, with nothing of the superficial or popular. It is an experiment in which I am deeply interested and for which I am partly responsible. My own course is to come after Christmas. The lecturers will have expenses paid, but receive no remuneration. I know how deeply you have gone into this subject and should be glad to have your opinion of our scheme, and any concrete suggestions.

I have not published anything beside this monograph. I was ground down with 15 hrs a week class work last year, but hope I may strike some line of creative work this winter.

Sincerely yours,

J. H. T. McPherson

97 — From Barrett Wendell

358 Marlborough St

Boston, 13 November, 1891.

My dear Sir:

I shall trust you to pardon my delay in answering your kind letter. It was so complete a surprise that I have not quite known how to reply.

Nothing would give me more pleasure than to prepare a paper for the meeting at Washington. But I do not feel sure that I can offer you anything that you would care for. Indeed, I am at this moment so busy with college work that I certainly cannot prepare anything not already pretty well formulated in my mind. And the only idea I now find there

is this: in my studies for "Cotton Mather," I found much
trouble in understanding him & his fellows, until I forced
myself to feel as they did. They were essentially idealists—
thinking unceasingly of things unseen, of what nowadays
people call unknowable; but thinking of them always in
concrete terms. In concrete terms they were forever talking
of them, too, forever making dogmatic assertions about what
any man may believe but no man may know. Naturally from
this incessant habit came an inextricable confusion of belief
& knowledge which resulted in an inevitable breaking down
of any such sense of strict veracity as would nowadays be
held the first requisite of honesty. Yet they weren't dishonest a bit.

In talking with Mr. Parkman & Mr. Winsor about Cotton
Mather, I have found both of them indisposed to see how
inevitable the rather misty uncertainty of Mather's sense of
fact was. It seems to me, then, that perhaps an attempt to
analyze the curiously material idealism of the Boston Puritans might interest students of colonial history, when sympathetic imagination is in a state of partly Teutonic dormancy.
But I don't feel at all sure. So I write frankly. If you would
like a twenty-minute paper on this subject—"Some Characteristics of the Boston Puritans"—I will gladly prepare
it.[1] If not, I shan't be in the least put out to have you say so.
I am a "literary fellow," you see, rather than a professional
student & not perhaps quite the sort of person that professional students have to take very seriously.

I shall be very happy to be proposed for membership of the
Association, however; & happier still to be enrolled. And I
am very grateful for your cordial words about my Lowell
lectures.

Faithfully Yrs.

Barrett Wendell

To H. B. Adams Esq.

---

[1] His paper on "Some Neglected Characteristics of the New England Puritans" was published in the Annual Report of the American Historical Association for 1891.

98 — From Brooks Adams

Quincy.

Nov 21st 1891.

My dear Sir.

I have just received a letter from Mr Bowen asking me to read a paper at the meeting of the Am. Hist. Soc. next month. As I have had no idea of any such invitation I am of course unprepared, nor have I any distinctly historical subject on hand now which is fit to be treated in such way. But I have been rather intending this winter sometime or other to read a paper on universal suffrage as one of the phenomena caused by the passage of a society from the condition of status to contract. I may as well say at once that it is part of a theory which I mean to develop into a book, but which is I think capable of being separated. If such an essay falls within the scope of your meetings, I should be very happy to put what I have to say in shape. But if you are limited to distinct investigations of special periods, I suppose you would hardly want it.

Please let me know as soon as you conveniently can if you care to have such a paper, and also the day on which I shall probably be called upon.

Very truly yours,

Brooks Adams.

Prof. Herbert B. Adams
Baltimore.

99 — From Frederick Jackson Turner

University of Wisconsin
Madison, Wisconsin, Dec, 9, 1891.

Professor H. B. Adams,
Johns Hopkins University,

Dear Prof. Adams:

I have just received the 25 copies of my Study. Although I am very much dissatisfied with the way I have put my ideas now that I see them in final form, I think I must have a few extra copies in addition to use among friends. Can you tell me what the charge for ten or twenty more copies would be and whether the printing has involved me in any other expenses than the supplying of the copies to Hopkins correspondents, provided for by my deposit?

You desired to have me remind you that you promised to put Mr. Sanford's paper on the Am. Hist. Assoc. program. Kindly let me know if this is all satisfactorily arranged.

Our extension work is astonishingly popular. I am entirely unable to satisfy all the demands that are made upon me. We will in all likelihood have some special extensioners next year as a part of our faculty. I suppose you know of our Northwestern Association.

Very truly yours

Frederick J. Turner

Does the JHU Publication Agency collect criticisms on the Studies. If so would it be possible for me to see those affecting my own?

100 — From Frederick Jackson Turner

Madison, Wisconsin,
January 18, 1892

Professor H. B. Adams,
Johns Hopkins University,

My dear Dr. Adams:

Thank you for your kind words regarding my syllabus. I am fairly well satisfied with the success of my Extension work, for I shall have given seven courses of six lectures each in as many places, before the close of the season. In one little community of six hundred inhabitants—farmers, etc.— I have an audience of over two hundred people. But the work is too wearing with my class work in the University, and I shall not do any of it another year if I can possibly escape. I must have some time for *intension*. You may be interested in knowing that the gerrymander case has been brought before the court.

We are indeed proud of the success that James has achieved and I am glad to know of Winston's good work. Our Wisconsin men are an earnest lot of workers at any rate, and I believe that a steady stream of postgraduates will go out from us. Harvard has made some efforts to attract our men in the way of making it easy financially to go there, but you will certainly be the goal of many of our graduates nevertheless.

I enclose a letter which I was writing to you in regard to Sanford's paper.

Very truly yours,

Frederick J. Turner

P. S. Apropos of Extension, there should be some institution to turn out young men who would carry on this work, at least preparatory to taking collegiate positions. All of your good men will be too well provided for next year to engage in this occupation, I presume—

I received your letter in regard to expenses of my thesis, thank you, and have written Mr. Murray.

101 — From Justin Winsor

Harvard College Library,
Cambridge, Mass., Jan. 21, 1892

Dear Adams,—

I chanced quite by accident today to light upon what you say of the *Nar. & Crit. Hist.* in your Seminary Notes (8th series of your tracts). I had not seen it before.

The reader would infer from what you say of the period since 1789 (p. 532), that the book came down to the present date, whereas it only comes down for the U. S. to the close of the Mexican War. Even with that curtailment the space given to the later history of the U. S. may be too scant, but you must remember that the proportions of the entire work were determined by the amount of material of critical importance, not by the duration of the periods. What you call educational, social & economic phases were only incidentally mentioned, & would have swelled this later period, had they been systematically treated. I left them out purposely as intending at some future day to add 2 or 3 more volumes of special essays to the work, covering such topics from the beginning. The book was big enough without them for a first go-off. I did this special essay business in my *Boston*.

My plan included a treatment of slavery, piracy and witchcraft, as inheritances from the mother country, and early in progress this section was assigned to Abner C. Goodell; but I got only promises after promises from him—illness really interfered—and finally I saved space for it as an appendix to my last volume; but there was no prospect of using it there without postponing the completion of the work indefinitely, and so I was reluctantly compelled to leave it out altogether. I would have made the references to these subjects much fuller throughout the work had I not expected to have this essay. I may yet get it in one of the additional vols. of the work, if I ever determine to prepare them.

Have you seen what I suppose to be Professor A M Wheeler's review of my *Columbus* in the *Providence Journal*, nearly 4 columns long. It is really the only notice of the book out of hundreds I have looked over in which the writer brought some knowledge to the matter, outside of what he got from the book itself. It is not so unreservedly commendatory as that in the *Nation*: but more knowing. His main point is that in my microscopical treatment of Columbus, I have blurred the general conception of his character. This is not unlikely. My object was to strip off the later accretions to the historic figure, springing from ignorance and sentiment, and I devoted myself to that. This accounts for my method of examining all my predecessors ways of looking at him. To do so was a part of my plan. I aimed to get down to hard pan, and there was a lot of over-soiling which the wriggling worms had created, which I wished to sweep away.

Yours

Justin Winsor

102 — *To Frederic Bancroft*

American Historical Association.
Baltimore, Md., February 5, 1892

Dr. Frederic Bancroft,
Department of State,
Washington, D. C.

My dear Bancroft:

I have your letter of February 3 regarding the appropriation for the historical manuscripts. I am willing to do anything in my power to aid you, for I believe you are engaged in a good and helpful public work. You can count upon me for anything that I can do in an individual way or as a representative of the Johns Hopkins University. The Executive Council of the American Historical Association, as you know, is opposed to the exertion of any corporate influence by the entire Association, but you can certainly enlist the aid of any individual member of the Council or of the society.

I am interested in what you say about Dr. Toner's reception on the 22nd of February and on many accounts I should like to come; but that day is our Founder's Day on which we always have public exercises and academic reunions. Possibly I can arrange to be absent but I am afraid President Gilman would not like it.

I am now going over carefully Ford's edition of the Writings of Washington and I am amazed at the extent of his plagiarism of Jared Sparks' footnotes. I should like very much to see the original letter-books of the Ante-Revolutionary period. I suppose all Washington's papers are now in your keeping and I should greatly appreciate the opportunity of an examination one of these days. I want to have you and Dr. Toner see what I have written about " Ford's edition of Sparks' Washington." Any suggestion that you can make to me upon this matter would be especially valuable at the present time. Moore, of Columbia College, gave me a list of all the discrepancies between Sparks' edition of the

12

Diplomatic Correspondence and Wharton's new edition. While numerous they are not very important and certainly do not justify the hyper-criticism which has been bestowed on Jared Sparks.

Very cordially yours,

H. B. Adams

103 — From John Martin Vincent

Paris. Feb. 15, 1892.

My dear Dr. Adams,

Your letter reached me a week or so ago and I was much pleased to note the general prosperity prevailing at the University this year. I have been glad to find also from the circulars and annual reports that the proportion of graduate students is so rapidly growing. I hope that it will continue at the same rate.

I find it easy to fit into things at Paris. The Bibliotheque Nationale is an agreeable place to work and one gets very nearly all the books he asks for. Besides a regular session at the Library, I go nearly every day to some lecture or other at the Sorbonne or the College de France choosing those of historical or literary character. We are located right in the Latin Quarter only a block or two away from these institutions and are able to observe well the student life. It is a great satisfaction after the turmoil I have been through during the last five years to sit down to study and literary work without interruption.

Your very kind interest in my future career is gratefully accepted. Your advice as well as your mediation will be of great value to me, and it is especially pleasing to have both freely offered.

Your suggestion that I should stay over here another year falls in with my wishes, for I should be able to accomplish a good deal, yet I hesitate somewhat on account of business matters which demand attention at home. I have enough work mapped out to keep me on this side indefinitely; some of it, however, is already well advanced.

The keel is laid and the frame up for a book on the science of historical research. This is intended to be a practical work for the use of those who expect to take up history as a profession. It will discuss the nature of historical material, the kinds and relative value of sources, the criticism of documents, nature of historical evidence, methods of writing history, etc. etc. all in practical rather than in a theoretical way. I know of nothing in English that covers the ground in the way I intend and I think the book will be useful. I was led to think so from the experiments made in the course of lectures I gave in the Seminary. I have already assembled pretty much all of the matter in the way of definitions, etc.; the remaining effort will be to get illustrative examples which will appeal particularly to an English & American public.

It is now definitely understood that the literary partnership with Mrs. Prof. Hug, will go into effect. The plan now being to undertake a scientific history of Switzerland from the ground up. All the present histories in English are of a popular character, and it was my proposition to write a standard work in a couple of volumes which will answer the requirements of the student public without necessarily excluding the popular reader. I think this will be carried out and the schemes for a history of Zürich and for monographs on various topics will be kept in sight as well.

My aim is toward a future academic career. I am not well enough off in this world's goods to devote myself to literary work alone even if I thought that my most useful mission. My travel and study over here has been undertaken as an investment for the benefit of a future educational activity, and that object always kept in view because I am not rich enough to travel for the fun of it.

It has been rather my hope that something or some place would turn up for my benefit the coming autumn. Yet I am not inclined to grasp at the first straw that floats along just for the sake of getting located. I can afford to wait a while

yet for the proper avenue to open, yet I should feel easier
about staying over here another year if there was something
more or less definite in view at the end of that time.

I am of the opinion which your advice implies, that it
would be better to be over here writing a book than to be
occupied in some subordinate capacity as a teacher at home.
I should come quicker into notice. Yet I am tempted to
conjure with the future a little, impertinent as it is. However, I shall not definitely fix the date of my return for a
while yet. I expect to go to London about the first of April,
and have promised myself a busy time at the British Museum.
Just how long it will take me to get that book ready is hard
to say. I have been working quite steadily at it since November but even with the time I have at command things move
slowly. I have thought best also, while on the ground, to
devote a good deal of time to French History, and enjoy it
hugely, having the sources and the scene of action before me
at the same time. I shall do the same in England.

However long I remain, I hope to get back under the same
size of hat that I wore when I left. I find nothing thus far
that equals the *possibilities* of our American educational life.
There are many advantages here, but methods are often petri-
fied and fossilized beyond belief. I did not have the worship
for Germany that I had when I went there as a student ten
years ago, and in France things seem to be up to the hubs
in ruts. The personal attention I get is of course very agreeable but is not the continual fête the *Correspondant* would
have you believe. I am obliged, by the way, for that cutting
for it was my first knowledge of the notice in the *Literary
Anzeiger*.

I suppose the affair of the Chicago Library—the search for
a librarian—has blown over. I am not opposed to such a
career as that, and feel that my studies lead up to such a
position. I have moreover been taking notes of things in the
Library line over here, but I should prefer to be a professor
of history and political science sometime as there is more
freedom.

But as a fellow does not always know what is good for him,

and as you have had your eye on me for a number of years, I shall value your counsel very highly, in determining these matters.

Please give my kind regards to Dr. Ely and to the rest of the fraternity.

Yours very truly,

J. M. Vincent.

P. S. Dr. Borgeaud received your " Thos. Jefferson " the other day. He will doubtless acknowledge it himself,—was very much interested in the Geneva proposal—said it was news to the present generation there.

Would you mind sending me a letter of introduction to Mr. Freeman? I can get such a thing by other means but would rather have your letter, if you are willing. I shall not bother him much but would like to see him a few minutes, on the subject of method in history.

Yours very truly

J. M. V.[1]

104 — From Michael D. Harter

House of Representatives U. S.,
Washington, D. C.,
February 16th, 1892.

President D. C. Gilman,
Johns Hopkins University,
Baltimore, Maryland.

My dear Sir:—

Please give me below every historical illustration you can recall of the cheaper money, iron, copper, silver, paper, shells,

---

[1] John Martin Vincent, Ph. D. 1890, was an instructor in the department from 1889 to 1892, associate from 1892 to 1895, associate professor from 1895 to 1905 and professor of European history from 1905 until his retirement in 1925. His dissertation on *State and Federal Government in Switzerland* was published as Extra Volume IX of the *Studies*.

etc., driving the dearer out. Begin with the Grecian iron money, or earlier, and if possible, omit no historical proof of this kind in any country or in any age, winding up with the Argentine Republic, Mexico, and all others in that condition to-day. We are yet to have a great struggle here.

Yours truly,

Michael D. Harter [1]

Kindly give name of history opposite each in which I will find full account.

105 — From John Martin Vincent

Paris, March 12. 1892.

My dear Dr. Adams,

Your letter of Mar 1. had a remarkably quick passage reaching me, with all its stops in England, within ten days.

The business matters mentioned therein have been duly considered and I answer in general terms that I accept the position offered; understanding the duties to include the general oversight of the department library, with a regular assistant, undergraduate instruction of one of P. H. E. courses and the History Major, & a course of lectures to graduates.[2]

For this latter I will offer the subject " Science of History " with practical exercises in methods of research, one hour a week throughout the year.

In regard to the P. H. E. course I should like time to consider a little further as to choice between the Greek & Roman Hist. and the Outlines. I had the former before and am inclined to think it ought to be kept in line with the medieval and modern history, since this class is a nursery of the Dept, while the other is for those who want only as

---

[1] Adams evidently sent some information to this Maryland Congressman because on March 9 he wrote Adams thanking him and two graduate students.

[2] The P. H. E. courses were undergraduate courses in the department of Politics, History and Economics.

little history as possible. At first sight my preference is to train up these beginners myself.

There is too much water between us just now to discuss the financial question. I was inclined to think however that an Associate touched $1,200. In the modern language dept, that was the amount Fred. Warren received—about others I do not know. In either case it cannot be said that one is induced to come for lucre. If you can see your way clear to the adoption of the higher figure, I think the department will get value received. Whatever salary I have had since the beginning, I have not spared myself to do what I could for the University, and purpose to do the same in the future.

It is very gratifying to know that my relations with the Dept. have left on the whole a pleasant impression. I reciprocate this fully, and have repeatedly said to others, that I could not ask for better men to work with, nor more considerate treatment than I found at the Hopkins. I am, moreover, in full sympathy with the work going on there and shall do my little part to make it the best school of History in America.

This subject has been submitted to Madame V. and meets with her full approval. It will not do for me to publish her flattering opinion of Prof. Adams.

I think I shall stay abroad till the latter part of August, and will put in my appearance at the University Oct. 1 or a little before. The time left is altogether too short for what I wish to do but I shall try to make the most of it. Mrs. V. is also extremely busy with her art work, attending one of the best academies here and copying in the galleries. We meet only at breakfast and dinner. Since my last letter I have been industriously getting acquainted with the important men in History & Economics here. Dr. Gould's letter of introduction opened up the Economists and one from Prof Arndt of Leipzig set the ball rolling among the historians. Mr. Monod of the Revue Historique gave me the freedom of the Historical Club. Mr. Delaire editor of the Reforme Sociale had me at dejeuner with a select party of specialists & professors, and invites me to the monthly dinner of the Societé d'Economie Sociale. The other day I presented the hommage of the Hist. Dept. of J. H. U. to Mr. Taine and had a very pleasant conversation on the subject of methods of historical study. So it is going on; the introductions have grown like the grain of mustard seed. All of this not because they have known anything about me, but because of my recent connection with the J. H. U. They have a very good opinion of " Chon Opkins " and the Studies are surprisingly well known.

The Jahresbericht is promised for May 1. & I hope to have it ready by that time.[1]

I thank you very kindly for your good words and good efforts in my behalf, and hope to merit your confidence in the future.

Very sincerely yours

J. M. Vincent.

106 — From John Martin Vincent

Paris, le 18 Mr. 1892.

My dear Dr. Adams,

I wrote you a " letter of acceptance " last week which, if it safely arrived, has already explained my intentions for next year. I am very glad to know about the matter at this early date because I can organize my work so as to profit very greatly the class-room duties next season. Time goes very fast, however, and I find there is none too much left.

I write this time to ask if you would like to have me do anything about getting up a report on American Hist. Literature for the *Revue Historique*. Please do not take this for impertinence, but as a wish to help you out of your multiplicity of affairs. As I have been dabbling in that sort-of-thing for some time I could perhaps assist you more than anyone else on the premises. The last report comes down into

---

[1] The section on Nordamerika in the *Jahresberichte der Geschichts-wissenschaft* was prepared yearly by Adams and Vincent during this period.

1889 only and the material has accumulated very rapidly since then.

If you would like to have me do anything about it while I am working up the other report I shall be very willing to do so.

I have been examining into methods of historical instruction at the Sorbonne and the Ecole Pratique des Hautes Etudes recently. In some of the advanced classes, thóse studying for higher degrees, there is some very good work, naturally the best in French history. The report of Prof. Fredericq, published in the Studies remains true in general outline, but as his observations were taken in 1881-2 names and courses have changed considerably, a fine new building gives the history work at the Sorbonne pleasant quarters and things generally have probably improved.

Mr. Monod is doing some very close work at the Hautes Etudes and his students are apparently doing the same. I went in also to an exercise of the Abbé Duchesne, in early christian history. He is the great catholic authority on that subject here and is taking his men to the bottom of the matter. The meeting was very informal but a student presented a research in early christian epigraphy which showed wide research.

I shall keep on taking notes of things till I find out pretty well how they do it. I do not get much that is new but it is an inspiration to see the machine work when it works well. The seminary room where Mr. Monod and others are giving their courses is modest in appearance compared with ours but it has the proper environment. It is simply one of the anterooms of the University Library in the old old Sorbonne and reminds one of the den Dr. Browne used to have for an office below you.

If there is anything else I can do for you over here I should be glad to do it. I wish I had a lot of money to spend for books and maps for the Seminary library, but I do not expect to see it.

I shall be greatly interested to learn who is to be Dr Ely's successor when the time comes for publication. My vote would be for H. C. Adams.

Mrs Vincent always joins me in kind regards, and I remain

Yours very sincerely,

J. M. Vincent.

Mr. Murray tells me that my book has suffered by Friedenwald's fire.

Too bad the rest of the edition was not all burned up heavily insured,—I should have had some financial returns from it.

107 — From James Bryce

April 7/92

I should be much obliged if you could tell me whether it is true that the College of William & Mary has lately been, or is shortly going to be, restored. I seem to have heard some rumour of this. Is it true that R. T. Ely is leaving you? Where is he going?

You will understand what a terrible blow the loss of Freeman has been to us. He had been unusually well this winter; and left for Spain in excellent spirits. We have just heard of the appointment of his successor which is not only in itself a scandal but little less than an insult to Freeman's memory. In Oxford the strong feeling had been for the selection of S. R. Gardiner.

54 Portland Place, London.[1]   J. Bryce

108 — From James Bryce

July 28/92

Dear Mr. Adams

Many thanks for the William & Mary Catalogue. I am very glad it has been re-vivified.

It is not easy to persuade the Treasury, which controls these matters, to present sets of our official publications to

---

[1] This was written on a postcard.

foreign libraries—or even to home ones. I have tried already in vain on behalf of Italian Libraries of high rank. However no University in the world has a better claim than Johns Hopkins: & I have sent on [to] the Treasury the letter of the Librarian which Mr. Emmott handed to me, & have earnestly pressed that the gift be made. I have explained things fully to Mr. Emmott, whose acquaintance I have been glad to make.[1]

Is it possible to get some of the J. H. U. Studies of the first & second series, to complete a set? I fear that a few are missing from my set.

You will be annoyed to see a malignant & captious attack upon Freeman in the Quarterly for this month. Vermuthlich by one Round who was always nagging at him.

I have just heard from your President & am hoping to see him. I wish you would get somebody to write a Contemporary Study on Pinkerton's Men & another on Lynch Law— not only in the West, but in the contemptible form of Ind. White-cappism. Also, I wish you would stir up Congress to publish a continuation of Poole's constitutions—W. L. Wilson promised me to move about it.

Yours very sincerely

J. Bryce.

109 — From James Bryce

54 Portland Place
London W
Oct. 10/92

Dear Mr. Adams

I am sorry to say that the answer which the Treasury have at last sent me—now the vacation is over—to my appeal, made at the instance of Professor Emmott, on behalf of Johns Hopkins Library for our government publications is in the negative. I am not surprised, for they " donate " to very few

---

[1] George H. Emmott was Lecturer from 1885 to 1892 and Professor of Roman Law and Comparative Jurisprudence from 1892 to 1896, when he returned to England as Professor in Victoria University, Liverpool. Each year he gave courses in the history department.

British Libraries: and if the precedent were set even in so
eminently strong a case as Johns Hopkins, they would find
it impossible not to follow it in a great many other cases. I
wish heartily they were more liberal: but they are economical
to niggardliness—stinting even the British Museum of its
due allowances. As I am not sure whether Prof. Emmott
has now returned to J. H. U., I send this to you. If he is
there, will you inform him, & say I could not answer him
sooner?

I am revising my American Commonwealth with a view to
a new edition. If you have noted, or if any of your students
have noted, any errors or material omissions in the chapter
on Universities, or any where else in the book, I shall be
much obliged if you will let me know. It is no easy matter
to keep abreast of the frequent changes in your constitutional
arrangements as well as your politics. I don't know whether
Johns Hopkins has undergone any material changes, beyond
its constant development.

Always truly yours

J. Bryce

Freeman's biography has been committed to a Mr. Stephens
who wrote the life of Dean Hook. I dont know what sort of
person he is. But our friend deserves a really intelligent &
appreciative biographer

110 — From Theodore Marburg

Kenwick House,
12 Bradmore Road,
Oxford.
Jan. 7th. 1893.

Herbert B. Adams, Esq.
c/o University Club,
Baltimore.

Dear Sir,

I enclose a cablegram which will explain itself. It would
hardly be just to the artist to refuse this request, and I ac-

cordingly cabled you from Dublin, where we were spending
the Christmas holidays, requesting that you let the World's
Fair Art Committee have the two Turner pictures.

The Bolton Jones I should like to leave at the Club, if
quite agreeable to you. Life in Oxford is very fascinating,
as you predicted. There are so many interesting people here,
and the place itself is so attractive. A man whom I have
become particularly fond of is D. G. Ritchie of Jesus; you
probably know his little books "Principles of State Interference," and "Darwinism in Politics." He is at present at
work on a treatise on Equality.

Ritchie lectured last term on political theory, taking up
Hooker, Hobbes, Locke and Rousseau—going over much the
same ground as Professor Dunning of Columbia. Ritchie does
not, however, confine himself to an exposition of the authors
mentioned, but whilst recognising the part that the theory
of natural right has played in the development of modern
politics and institutions, at the same time shows wherein it
fails. Whilst a legal right is that which is recognised by the
State and which the Law Courts will enforce, and a moral
right that which public sentiment will uphold, there is no
tribunal to which a question of natural right can be carried.

Natural rights he defines as rights, which in the opinion of
the individual claiming them, ought to be recognised by law
or by public opinion, or by both. This implies that an individual conceives of a better state of society than any which
exists, and his natural right is one which would be recognised
in such a society. Everyone agrees that we ought to do what
is just but to determine the justice of an act we must con-
struct a State; justice in one society is not justice in another.
The natural rights theory is, therefore, of no help to us, and
it is better and more practical to appeal directly to social
expediency.

Ritchie expressed surprise that a writer in a recent number
of the North American Review should still base his arguments at this late day on the natural rights theory. We have
been accustomed to look upon England as a conservative

country; I find that they go to greater length with respect to socialistic theories and legislation, than we have dreamed of doing in America. Not only has their Land Legislation invalidated contracts—a thing which our constitution prohibits —but the prominent radicals place absolutely no limit to State interference except social expediency.

They say that as all property is dependent upon the existence of the State, the State would have a right to abolish private property of every kind, if it considered it socially expedient to do so. It is the great good sense of the English that has saved them heretofore from subversive measures but as there is absolutely no limit to the power of the House of Commons, the constitution being at all times in their hands, and as the extension of the franchise is putting power into the hands of a different class from that which has wielded it heretofore, it seems to me the immediate future is not without some danger.

I do not know that these things interest you particularly; if not I trust you will pardon this lengthy letter.

My permanent address is 12 Bradmore Road, Oxford. If I can be of any service to you whilst in Oxford, do not hesitate to command me.

The list of books you gave me to read during the Summer I read with much interest. They are quite free to admit here that America is doing more in political science at present than England, but by gathering up all the threads at Oxford, I find enough to keep me interested here for a year at least. They are most friendly towards Americans and appear glad to have men come here to follow a study for its own sake, instead of working for a degree. By the advice of several of the tutors I have not matriculated as an undergraduate is more or less restricted in his intercourse with the tutors and professors.

Yours very truly,

Theodore Marburg

111 — From John W. Perrin

The University of Chicago.

February 24. 1893.

Dear Prof. Adams,

Your letter came to hand several weeks ago. I regret that illness and a pressure of work have prevented my answering at an earlier date.

On the receipt of your letter I sent you the first number of Current Topics containing the best report I have seen of Prof von Holst's address. Later I have sent you a copy of the Arena, containing his address also. These two periodicals have no official connection with the University though both are in a sense fostered by it. I send you with this letter the February number of Current Topics. It contains two papers which I believe will be of interest to the Seminary. One of the articles is on " Ernest Renan " by Dr. E. G. Hirsch; the other is entitled " Municipal Government in its Relation to Party Politics," by Judge I. K. Boyesen. The latter paper was first read before the Political Science Club of the University. Judge Boyesen is one of the leaders in a movement here towards a reform in municipal government. He is a Scandinavian by birth and a brother of Hjalmar H. Boyesen of New York.

⁂   ⁂   ⁂   ⁂

I have had two [or] three talks with Prof. von Holst about the Hopkins since I last wrote you. He understands and appreciates the Hopkins spirit. He has asked quite a number of questions about the Historical Department. In his seminar we are now at work on " Thomas Jefferson's Economical doctrines and their influence on American Politics." Besides this Seminar, he has what he calls a " Preparatory Seminar," for students who are just beginning their course or have had but one or two semesters. He is also giving a course on " The French Revolution." He is universally liked, and seems to be in great demand as a lecturer. He has been to Indianapolis twice since November,—and to other cities about or near Chicago; besides these, he has given quite a number of addresses in Chicago. He is an untiring worker, and seems to be improving in health.

About the only news so far as the University is concerned is the attempt to raise $500,000, now being made. It will be raised by May 1, the time set. Four new buildings will also have been completed by that time. The buildings are all of stone, and are a credit to the city. The Newberry library building will be completed by May 1, so too will the Art Institute building. The Public Library building for which the city appropriated $1,000,000 last year will not be ready for use before next fall.

I think the " World's Fair " buildings will be a great surprise to most people who will be here next summer. I have tried to get some good " Kodak " views of them to send to the Seminary; but so far I have been unable to get anything worth having mounted. I hope to be able to get some soon however.

I am glad that the seminary is increasing in numbers. I have recommended two young men in Chicago who have asked me where they should go next year, to go to the Hopkins. Neither of them have done any graduate work as yet.

Cordially, Your friend,

John W. Perrin.[1]

112 — From James A. Woodburn

Department of   Indiana University,
American History.   Lafayette,—(on the Extension wing)
                     March 4, 1893

My dear Dr. Adams:

The " excellent " monograph of which you sent me a favorable notice, is receiving some left-handed thrusts.[2] I enclose

---

[1] He had been a graduate student at the Hopkins during the years 1890-1892.

[2] James A. Woodburn, Ph.D. 1890, published in the tenth volume of the *Studies* a monograph entitled *Causes of the American Revolu-*

a long review from the Richmond *Despatch* of Jan. 29. This review is just in some of its criticism—no one sees more than I how many things deserve to be said which I omitted from my essay—but in other respects it is unjust and ungenerous. The editor has reviewed my monograph as if it were a *history* of the American Revolution instead of an *essay* on the causes. He has disregarded all perspective and proportion. The article shows something of the earmarks of the *Henry* family, or at least of the patriotic Virginian who is always jealous of any precedence accorded to the men of Massachusetts in the Revolution. I was aware of the controversy over the " claims " of Patrick Henry and perhaps I disposed too summarily of that subject since I mentioned it at all; it did not seem to me to be pertinent to my task to go into " evidence " on that theme. You may be interested in the article, which I should like to have returned after you have read it.

Yes, Ross is taking quick rank among university economists. He is a bright brainy man, of sure promise, but he needs ballast. He will get it on the coast, about the time he sets his students to working up the expose of the Pacific R. R. dealings *a la Stanford*. Will, then, the " spirit of reform " continue with him its perfect work?

I wish the Historical Congress at Chicago might have a conference on " *Problems in Representative Government*," or on some such historico-political theme. A symposium of brief papers on " The Gerrymander," or " The American Speaker," " The Quorum and the Cloture " etc. would be interesting to many people. I feel sure the Congress can be made an interesting and valuable success. For what time is it set? I suggest the first two weeks in September.

There is a strong probability that Indiana University will again soon be without an executive head. President Coulter has received a call to the presidency of Lake Forest University, near Chicago, and there are personal reasons which

---

tion. His dissertation, *History of Higher Education in Indiana*, had been published as U. S. Bureau of Education, Circulars of Information, No. 1, 1891.

13

indicate that he will accept. He will leave an aching void with us. Do you have in mind a man to suggest?

Yours truly,

J. A. Woodburn

113 — From James W. Black

Oberlin College
Department of Political Economy
Oberlin, Ohio, March 13, 1893

My dear Dr. Adams:—

As soon as the announcements of your work for next year appear, I wish you would send me a few. I have already received inquiries from some of my advanced students about the courses at the Hopkins, and could readily distribute such announcements where they might do some good.

The Department of Political Economy is booming, and is larger than ever before. There are 118 students in my classes this term as against 48 in the fall term. The advanced classes in " Finance " and " Money " are small, but in " Economic Problems " and " Amer. Institu. History," there are 50 each. In the latter course, we are using Thwaites', Fiske, and Hart's Formation of the Union, though the work is largely conducted by class lectures upon a schedule of topics previously prepared. In " Economic Problems," we have been studying the history of labor, trades-unionism, remedies and reforms, and in connection with the course recently had an excursion to Cleveland to look into the progress of mechanical invention and its effect upon hand-labor (a la Hopkins methods). The results, including topics treated in this course, titles of class essays with bibliographies, we are now preparing for publication in pamphlet form. During the past two weeks, and owing to the illness of Prof. Monroe, I have had his class of 92 in Pol. Econ'y, and will have it through the term. Though this entails extra work, I am enjoying it, for it brings me into contact with one-half the students in the College proper.

Our greatest trouble here is lack of funds, and we are in something of the same plight as the Hopkins a few years ago. There has been a deficit for the past year of $14,000, and there is an estimated deficit in the budget for the next school year of $20,000, but Oberlin cannot afford to take a step backward, so the work goes on with the hope that ways and means may be forthcoming soon from sources now unforeseen. The administration is friendly to me in granting privileges for the conduct of the work of the department, and the President and a committee of the Faculty have already asked me to remain next year at a small increase of salary. As it is, however, salaries in Oberlin are uniformly too low.

In the spring term I have courses in Pol. Economy (beginning) 5 hrs. wk.; Socialism—3 hrs; and Amer. Polit. & Constitu. Hist.—2 hrs. I shall take pleasure in sending you our forthcoming catalogue, when it appears, which will contain a full description of the work of this year, with alternating courses for next year, many of them being new.

The prospects for University Extension in Ohio do not seem bright, for the Ohio Association with all its organizers and courses has not stirred up much enthusiasm this year.

I was sorry and surprised to read of the death of Lauer recently, for only a few months ago, I saw him in Cleveland in good health and spirits.

Very Respectfully Yours,

J. Wm. Black.[1]

(I send you several papers under another cover.)

---

[1] James William Black received a Ph. D. degree in 1891 in history.

114 — From A. Howard Clark

American Historical Association
Smithsonian Institution
Washington, D. C., March 15, 1893

Dear Dr. Adams—

Dr. Goode, Librarian Allen of State Dep't & myself have talked over the proposed sending of the Declaration of Independence, Constitution of U. S., and other original documents to Chicago and think that just now and without any delay is the time to protest against the ridiculous risk to which those priceless records would be endangered. The best course to pursue is for you and other influential historians to write to The Honorable Secretary of State and in earnest language ask him to carefully consider the matter and urge him in the interest of the preservation of American Archives to substitute facsimiles for such documents as are of special interest to the public and to carefully guard the originals from loss. Call to his attention the lamentable fact that the Declaration of Independence is already almost illegible, a condition caused largely by an unfortunate handling some fifty years ago while producing a facsimile. Only the most careful method of protection in hermetic sealed case and shield from sunlight will preserve what ink remains on this most valuable of American parchments.

To speak plain it is pure vandalism to risk transportation by rail, and to exhibit these records in a non-fireproof building, a building in most respects identical in structure with the Exhibition building at Genoa not long since destroyed by fire with all its precious contents.

If it will not cause you too much trouble please write yourself and ask Prof. Hart, Prof. Gross, and perhaps Dr. Winsor of Harvard, Prof. MacMaster and as many others as you think proper to promptly address the Secretary of State in regard to this matter.

Earlier action would not have been advisable for the reason

that while Congress was in session a joint resolution might have been passed specially ordering such sendings to Chicago, though I hardly think Congress would be so rash. The only authority now is the Secretary of State and the President and they must listen to protests from American historians.

I will have a resolution passed today by the Sons of the American Revolution covering this matter.

Let me know if I can assist you.

Very truly yrs

A. Howard Clark

Dr. Goode as head of the Museum has taken the ground that nothing should be sent to Chicago that cannot be replaced— for this reason the valuable Washington and other relics will not go.

AHC

Dr. H. B. Adams
Baltimore
Md

115 — From Herbert Friedenwald

Washington D. C., 945 K St., N. W,
March 21, 1893.

Dear Dr. Adams:

I came across, to-day, a very interesting & important early controversy (1776) between Maryland & the Continental Congress, in which the " back lands " were the disturbing elements. From what I have found, I gather that certain letters by President Hancock must have been written, between September 15, & November 15, 1776, to the Maryland Convention at Annapolis, & I write to ask, if it be not too much trouble to you, to let me know how I can be put on the track of them. If the revolutionary papers have been published,

I will probably be able to find what I want here. If not, would you let me know to whom, in Annapolis, I should write in order to procure copies of the desired letters?

With kind regards, I am

Very truly yours

Herbert Friedenwald.[1]

116 — From Justin Winsor

Cambridge, Mass.,
Gore Hall, 22 Mar. 1893

Dear Adams,—

I am told that there is to be a safe constructed in the Government Bldg. at Chicago to hold the Decl. of Indep. ms, which they propose sending there. The Government also promises some such protection to an irreplaceable relic of Washington, which the Corporation—not to my liking—have ordered to be sent from this library. I have no better opinion of the Government sending there the documents to which you refer; but I do not feel like writing to the Secretary of State. I have consistently from the start declined to have any personal connection with the big Fair, for reasons which I am entitled to hold; but I am met with intimations that my declinations are from unworthy motives. Every thing I have done in respect to the Fair, heretofore has been necessitated by the conditions of the case, and I shall only lay myself open to the charge of going out of my way " to oppose the fair," as it is called, if I volunteer advice to the Secretary of State,—and this is why I can not help a protest which I say to you, privately, I wish to have successful.

Poole wrote to me the other day giving the names of those invited to read papers at the historical Congress and designating those

---

[1] Herbert Friedenwald had received an A. B. from the Johns Hopkins in 1890.

1. who had declined
2. who held back
3. who took no notice
4. who accepted,—the last a pitiful show. He added a
list of additional invitations to make up for the failures of
the previous list, and asked my opinion. I replied that the
statements under nos 1, 2, and 3, did not, in my judgment,—
to say nothing of the quality of no. 4, which was not on the
whole of average excellence—warrant the asking of any
reputable writer to take part in the Congress to the extent of
reading a paper. The conditions are not favorable I fear
for a creditable show for American historical scholarship, and
I am sorry to intermit my interest in the meetings of the
association for even a single year. I am sorry the prospect
is not better, both for your sake,—and to you the asso'n owes
much—and for Dr Angell's sake, who is deserving of better
things. If there is a rally at a late hour and an improvement
in the outlook I shall be glad.

I have been hoping to see your Sparks before this. Where
is it? I shall very likely go to press this summer with a new
book, of some such title as this: Explorations of the St.
Lawrence: a study of the relations of history and geography
in the interior of North America.

I have just been developing the forgery of a pretended
1507 edition of the Vespucius Voyages, " into Latin from the
Spanish," which came to me via Chicago (!) from Berlin
and Italy, with a price of 5000 marks. I shall expose it in
next weeks " Nation."

This letter, as you perceive, is personal and not for others
eyes.

Very truly

Justin Winsor

Dr H. B. Adams.

117 — From Lynn R. Meekins

18 East Townsend street,
April 10, 1893.

Dear Dr. Adams:

In our brief conversation yesterday at the University Club you said that you thought of making a complete study of the negro in the various Southern states. I earnestly hope that you will do so and largely for the reason that this is an important dividing line between generations and valuable material will soon be slipping away. I write you this note in order to offer a suggestion or two which may or may not be useful to you.

In the study of the negro there is much interesting and amusing material for a capital monograph upon benevolent and mutual and insurance enterprises which have been organized by negroes among negroes. I think that if you will put one of your bright young men upon this you will be astonished at the extent and financial aggregate of these societies. You will also enjoy the humor of their high-sounding titles.

There is great need of a careful and comprehensive account of the Chesapeake Bay. The greatest indentation on the Atlantic Coast and one of the most extensive and beautiful bays in the world is practically without a historian, unless my information is very much mistaken. The Bay is undergoing constant changes and places that have historical importance are being obliterated, especially the eastern islands which are growing smaller every year.—The Susquehanna river also needs such attention as you can give to it. It would be a noble subject for another of the bright young men whom you seem to be so successful in stimulating to good work of permanent value. I am, Very truly yours,

Lynn R. Meekins

118 — From Henry Adams

1603 H Street.
Washington, D. C.
May, 1893—

Dear Sir

At the meeting of December 1890, the Historical Association did me the honor to make me one of its Vice Presidents. As I was then in the South Seas, and had no knowledge of the election, I could do nothing about it. In 1892, at the next meeting of the Association, I was still abroad. In a few days I start for another absence which will prevent my attending the meeting at Chicago in July. Naturally I feel somewhat anxious lest the Association should think me deficient in courtesy; and I write to ask that, in case comment or inquiry should be made, you would take any private occasion that may offer to express my sense of the compliment offered by the Association, and my regret that long and almost continuous absence from the country should have prevented my attending the meetings of the Association, especially the particularly interesting one at Chicago.

Having no official excuse or warrant for addressing the Association, and indeed no official knowledge of my election except from the printed Annual Report, I am obliged to ask you to consider the matter as private, especially as this is the last chance I shall have of communicating with you before the July meeting.

I am very truly yrs

Henry Adams

Herbert B. Adams Esq

119 — From Newton D. Baker

Professor H. B. Adams,
Johns Hopkins University.   [1893?]

Dear Sir:—

In accordance with your suggestion I beg leave to submit the following account of my work in the University. I may be justified in mentioning the fact that when I entered the University I was very ill prepared and had perhaps more " conditions " than have ever been allowed to any other student. These conditions were not finally worked off until the latter part of my graduating year, so that I was, during my whole course, doing double work.

I stood thirteenth in my class, taking my degree in the Historical-Political group of studies. Under your instruction I took the courses in Church History, and International Law. In the latter class I prepared two papers: " The International Relations of the Jews " and the " Annexation of Canada," both papers being read in class and there meeting your approval.

During the Summer vacations I have collected annually the Vital and Mortuary statistics of the State of West Virginia, as they appear in the Report of the Secretary of the State Board of Health, and have done other work on that Report. I have been employed by the tax conference of the State of Pennsylvania, for a short time, during which I determined the ratio of the real value to the assessed value of real estate in York county.

As a graduate student I have taken the work of the Department in History, Jurisprudence and Administration, and, having selected the subject of " Bills of Rights in State Constitutions " for original investigation, I have worked at the subject in my spare time.

I enclose you my plan for the original work that I have undertaken and also a partial list of books read on the subject, or as preparation for the work. So far I have written little except the sub-section on " The Declaration of Independence as a Bill of Rights " which section is now seeking a publisher in the North. From the character of the Subject, it being wholly analytical, I doubt its acceptance in the Yale Review, to which I have offered it.

My efflorescent " University Extension Lecture on History " is hardly worth recalling. The enclosed letter is from Judge Faulkner to the President of the Board of Regents. As I have been known to Mr. Faulkner all my life I feel particularly gratified that he feels able to say such kind things about me. I take the liberty of enclosing the copy as the opinion of a neighbor.

Asking your indulgence of this encroachment on your time, I remain

Most respectfully yours

Newton D. Baker, Jr.[1]

---

[1] Newton D. Baker, after receiving an A. B. in 1892, remained as a graduate student in the history department during the following year. The plan of his dissertation which he enclosed is as follows·

Bills of Rights in State Constitutions.

I. Constitutions
General Propositions and Remarks.
State Constitutions.
(a) History and Contents.
(b) Modes of Adoption and Amendment.
II. Bills of Rights
Magna Charta, Petition of Right, Bill of Rights and the Act of Settlement.
The Declaration of Independence as a Bill of Right.
The Articles of Confederation as a Bill of Right.
The Constitution of 1788, (particularly the first ten amendments).
III. Bills of Rights in State Constitutions
Enumeration of the Various Constitutions of the States, pointing out the Bills of Rights
History of the Provisions found in the Bills of Rights, pointing out the coincidences and differences between the several States, when discoverable.
Self-Operative Provisions vs those Requiring Legislation to Make them effective.

List of Books.

Bryce, American Commonwealth. 2 Vols.
Poore, Charters and Constitutions (Parts only).
Tasewell-Langmead, Constitutional History of England.
Cohn, An Introduction to the Study of the Constitution.
Hitchcock, American State Constitutions.
Wright, American Constitutions.
Stubbs, Constitutional History (2 Vols. and parts of the others).
Gneist, Constitutional History. Parts.
Taylor, Constitutional History.
Federalist. Parts.

120 — From Shirley C. Hughson

Sumter, South Carolina,
July 9th. 1893.

Professor Herbert B. Adams:

Dear Professor Adams;—

In my recent rambles around Charleston I met with numerous indications of proof of your theory concerning the influence of early Hebrew history on the lives and customs of the lately emancipated negroes. I enclose you something of interest I picked up. There is a certain abandon of grammar about it that imparts to it a distinctly archaic flavor.

I have been hard at work on the negro, and think I am going to overturn some of the long established notions about the revival of the slave trade by this state in 1803. I have found a great deal of what I believe to be wholly new material. I gave several weeks to research in the confused and uncatalogued libraries of Charleston with fair success, and am going to Columbia next week to work on the colonial and state records. I think I shall find a mine of material there which has been hitherto unexploited. I trust that my study of the subject will be a successful one.

I am delighted to see that Bassett is going to take hold of that Seminary of Southern History. I think we can produce some great results.

With assurances of regard, I remain,

Yours obediently,

Shirley C. Hughson.[1]

---

[1] Shirley C. Hughson was a graduate student during the year 1892-1893.

121 — From Justin Winsor

Sep. 24, 93.
74 Sparks Street,
Cambridge.

Dear Adams,—

I have just finished the first volume of your Sparks. I
skimmed the early parts; but have looked carefully at those
pages chronicling the growth and results of the historical
aims of Sparks. I wished I had had the Journal of 1826,
and the other journals of which you give the skimming in
the appendix and could have profited by them when I was
working on my paper on the ms. sources of the Rev. in the
appendix of my last vol. of the *America*. I am sorry you did
not annotate this part of the volume; I personally could have
spared some of the matter of the earlier chapters, for a clear
exposition through notes of what this ms. material stands for
today in prints and archives; what Sparks missed and what
he saw which is now not to be found. There was a good
chance to show what this part of our Revolutionary sources
has developed from since Sparks' day. As it stands the
journal does not have all its interest, and is of not much importance to the investigator, since so much of what he found
has been printed, by the original states and individuals and
the student has now so much better means of understanding
the history and condition of such papers.

On p. 47 you make a curious slip in leading the reader to
understand that the average age of graduation at Harvard
was 23 in Sparks' day as it is now. Even when so young a
man as I am was in College it was two years less than now,
and in Sparks' day it was certainly a year still less, if not
more. Of Sparks' classmates Francis was 20 at graduation;
Harris, 20, Palfrey, 19, Parsons, 18, Eustis 19. These are
all the names which are in Drake's *Biog. Dict* and I have
no doubt that further search in other directions would yield
much the same result for the rest of his class mates.

I have been looking over lately the records of a dining

club in Cambridge, now about fifty years old, of which Sparks
became a member in 1848 and remained one till his death,
giving a paper each year, when it met at his house.[1] I am
secretary of the Club and the members have asked [me] to
prepare a privately printed a/c of its career, emending all
the papers &c. I have done a little work on it during the
summer in the country; but there is much yet to be done in
collating the records of it in the personal diaries of some of
its members. I have had those of E. S. Dixwell, Joseph Lov-
ering and Everett, and perhaps your 2d volume when I get
at it may reveal something in Sparks' journals. Do you remember anything? If there is anything I must look it up in
the Sparks' papers which you had, and which are now in the
College Library.

I was struck with the word "heredity" in the first paragraph of volume one. I fear that word will start surmises
and perhaps utterances in some of the critics. I think it was
a mistake not to make clear the relation of "Mr. Joseph
Sparks;" but your principals were entitled to their own
notions.

Very truly

Justin Winsor

122 — From Clarence W. Bowen

American Historical Association.

New York, Oct. 10, 1893.

My dear Adams:—

I finished the other day the two volumes of your "Life of
Jared Sparks" and I do not know when I have enjoyed reading books as much as I have these. I was interested in the
allusion you made to my great uncle Thomas Aspinwall of
Boston and was also pleased to see some reference to my own
recent book. Willington is not many miles from Woodstock,
perhaps eighteen or twenty, and some time I mean to drive

---

[1] Winsor enclosed a card listing the twelve men who were members
of the Cambridge Thursday Evening Club in 1892-1893.

over there. If you should ever come to Woodstock to visit me we might go together unless, indeed, you have already visited the place.

Robert C. Winthrop of Boston has been in New York during the past week attending the Peabody trustees meeting. He is very feeble but I had a most interesting call upon him with my wife on Sunday. I spoke to him regarding your book and told him what you had said regarding the Lord Mahon Controversy and he replied that he was glad to hear that you had done justice to Sparks as editor of the Life and Writings of Washington. Mr. Winthrop said he thought a great injustice had been done to Sparks as an historian. He referred to what you said in your book; namely, that the Controversy had been amicably settled by Lord Mahon at the time that Mahon proposed Sparks to the Society of Antiquarians in London. Mr. Winthrop added what I did not know; namely, that Sparks afterwards moved the resolution to make Lord Mahon an honorary member of the Massachusetts Historical Society. Mr. Winthrop said that he should get a copy of your Life of Sparks and looked forward to reading the book.

I recently wrote as good a letter as I knew how to Henry Cabot Lodge about continuing his membership in the American Historical Association but he has resigned as you will see in another letter I wrote you.

Replying to your letter of the 4th inst. I think the report of the Treasurer ought to be printed and I do not think the fact that we are worth some money would operate adversely to our interests.

Hon. John A. King took Mr. Jay's place on the Finance Committee.

Very truly yours,
Clarence W. Bowen

123 — From Edward P. Cheyney

University of Pennsylvania
Department of History
Phila. Nov. 12th 1893

Dear Dr. Adams,

I send you by the same mail a copy of a mediaeval document in which you may possibly be interested. I prepared it for use with my graduate students in Eng. Ec. Hist. as a starting point & thread for their work in the manorial system.

I want to ask some advice from you about a matter we are just starting on. We are about to begin printing a series of translations or other reprints of documents illustrative of European History, somewhat on the lines of the American Histy Leaflets. We want them for our own students here but think that they may be of sufficient usefulness to other teachers to pay their expense & make it possible to sell them at say 15¢ each, each of the six or eight numbers a year being from 15 to 25 pp. We have thought that other teachers were possibly feeling, like us the need for something in the way of available original sources to put in the hands of even undergraduate students; and even where they do not it might be missionary work to try & encourage a rather higher kind of teaching. Will you tell me what you think of the plan? Moreover any suggestions at all you would make we would be very glad to get, as you must know from the large number of your former students now teaching in colleges what would be likely to make such a series of use to them. We thought of beginning with either a translation of a typical *cahier* of 1788, or The Rights of Man, Declaration of Pilnitz, & one or two other documents of 1791 & 2, or in Eng. History, Magna Carta, with Henry I's Charter, & the Coronation oath &c. We have thought that you would at least take an interest in this plan.

Yours truly

E. P. Cheyney

124 — To Macmillan & Co.

Johns Hopkins University,
Baltimore, Md., November 17, 1893.

Messrs. Macmillan & Co.,
66 Fifth Avenue,
New York City.

Dear Sirs:

I beg to acknowledge your favor of November 10 with regard to a text-book on " The American Citizen: His Rights and Duties." The little volume by Mr. Wyatt on " The English Citizen " has come to hand and last evening I examined the work with some care. It seems to me that there is a good opportunity for a similar book in this country. Indeed, I have long thought that an American Citizen Series, corresponding to the English Series, would be welcomed by students and by the general public.

As you perhaps know I have edited an annual series of " Studies in History and Politics " for the Johns Hopkins University since 1882. Enclosed you will find a complete list. Mr. Edward A. Freeman, at my request, prepared the introduction and Mr. James Bryce contributed a monograph to the series of 1887, before the publication of his " American Commonwealths." In spite of the fact that much of our material has been rather heavy, we have made the Studies self-sustaining.

It seems to me that a more popular series could be devised which, with better agencies than ours for publication and circulation, would prove a business success. Such general subjects as the following could be treated in a readable and instructive manner:

(1) Local and City Government in the United States
(2) State Government and State Institutions
(3) Federal Government and National Institutions
(4) Church and Charitable Institutions
(5) Education in America

14

(6) Land Laws of the United States
(7) Railroads and Interstate Commerce
(8) Commercial Relations of the United States
(9) Foreign Relations
(10) Army, Navy, and National Defence
(11) Taxation and Economic Problems
(12) Labor and Social Problems

There are many good materials already existing which might be utilized in the preparation of such volumes as those proposed. Frequent references to Mr. Bryce's "American Commonwealths" would promote the academic and further use of his able and comprehensive work. Suggested parallels from English experience and occasional mention of the English Citizen Series would perhaps increase the use of those excellent volumes in American schools and colleges.

With regard to your immediate proposition I feel favorably disposed; but I am not able at the present time to undertake the work. I am under contract with the Bureau of Education for an extensive report upon "Higher Popular Education in England and America." This report will include all the agencies outside of public schools for the education of the people. My work is well advanced and I hope to complete it during the present academic year. Next summer vacation I might begin the preparation of a text-book on "The American Citizen." Many of the materials which I am now gathering would be of service in the proposed work. If I should undertake the task I think I should prefer a fixed sum for the production of the volume. In case you should conclude to make it the introduction to an "American Citizen Series," I wish you would kindly state what honorarium you would allow to me as editor and what to each author that I might engage. I should seek able men and good writers. If such a series were projected I should like to write the volumes on "Education in America" and on "The Church and Charitable Institutions."

I have been editing for the Bureau of Education a long series of monographs called "Contributions to American

Educational History." Enclosed please find a partial list. The first two are out of print, but I send you reserved copies under separate cover, with one or two other specimens of these educational studies. There will appear under my editorship similar reports for every State in the American Union. This work has all been contracted for and much of it has been delivered to the Bureau of Education. An edition of 20,000 copies of each report is published and freely circulated by the Government. Some account of this educational series you will find in my paper called " The State and Higher Education," p. 705, of the Smithsonian Report for 1889. A reprint is sent you with the other papers.

Such a book as you propose, followed by an " American Citizen Series," would undoubtedly prove of great educational and public service in this country and ought to meet with a wide sale in American schools, libraries, and colleges. I should be glad to hear further from you regarding the whole matter.

Very respectfully yours,

[Herbert B. Adams] [1]

125 — From William R. Harper

THE UNIVERSITY OF CHICAGO
Founded by JOHN D. ROCKEFELLER
WILLIAM R. HARPER, President
Chicago Jan. 30, 1894.

Prof. Herbert B. Adams,
Baltimore, Md.

My dear Friend:—

We are proposing at Chautauqua this summer to make History and Political Economy the leading subjects. We are desirous of having present during the summer the leading historians. We now expect among others Prof. von Holst, Pres. C. K. Adams, and Prof. George Adams. We think an

---

[1] See letters Nos. 128 and 129.

historical combination without H. B. Adams would be lacking. I write to propose to you to come to Chautauqua for three weeks beginning July 5th, or three weeks beginning July 20th, the service to include a daily course of lectures with two or three general lectures, and the compensation to be $400. for the three weeks. Will you not say " yes " and delight our hearts? [1]

> I remain
>
> Yours very truly,
>
> William R. Harper

126 — From Frederick Jackson Turner

> University of Wisconsin
> Madison, Feb. 5, 1894

Professor H. B. Adams,
Johns Hopkins University,

My dear Professor Adams:

I send you herewith my paper for the Historical Association.[2] I leave to your discretion the question of whether the " sub-heads " shall be retained. I presume I shall see proof on the paper.

You are quite right, I think, in your policy in regard to recommendations. I presume that your opinion may be asked in the near future by the authorities, unless James's friends find that it is best not to present his name. He enters the fight late, after it had practically been settled in favor of another Wisconsin man; but I hope he may get it.

> With regards,
>
> Yours very truly
>
> Frederick J. Turner

---

[1] Adams had lectured at Chautauqua for a number of years. Anyone writing the history of that movement could find helpful material in his correspondence.

[2] This was his famous paper on " The Significance of the Frontier in American History " which was published in the Annual Report of the American Historical Association for 1893.

127 — From James W. Black

Oberlin College
Department of Political Economy.
Oberlin, Ohio, Feb. 19, 1894

Professor H. B. Adams,
Johns Hopkins University,
Baltimore, Md.

My dear Dr. Adams:—

I trust that everything is going pleasantly at the J. H. U. I cannot say the same for Oberlin, for the hard times have struck us a severe blow. The College has been in a weak financial condition for some years past. The annual deficit is large. For this academic year, it will reach something over $26,000, including some losses from bad investments. The deficit as estimated in the budget for next year will be $21,600. In addition to this, the College has about $100,000.—in foreclosed mortgages upon western farms. Little can be realized from this source at present, due to the stress of the times. The condition is a serious one, and is partly brought about by the fact that the College began three or four years ago a policy of expansion with the expectation that money would be forthcoming to sustain the work. Such has not been the case, however, and the institution has been running behind financially ever since. The problem of retrenchment now stares the Faculty and Trustees in the face in a way that it has never done before.

The Faculty at a recent meeting voted to prepare a budget in which the expenditure and income columns should balance, and appointed a committee to arrange the details. Among other things, it was proposed that College tuition fees be raised from $40.- to $50.-, that salaries over $1000.- be cut 10%, and that several teachers be cut off. Some of these propositions have already carried, including the giving up of the chair of Political Economy which I hold. As the latter is one of the newly expanded parts of the curriculum, it was thought that it could be spared sooner than some others.

This was done in the face of strong opposition, for many feel that the Faculty will make a serious mistake in abandoning this work which is popular, and is elected by such large numbers of students; but the financial situation compels it. It is discouraging to see upset the plans and work upon which Prof. Commons and I have spent so much labor, but there is nothing to do but to take it philosophically.

If all of the radical measures now proposed be ultimately carried, the deficit will only be reduced to $7000. You can readily see that the problem is a grave one to contemplate. How far the Faculty and Trustees may go, will probably be settled within the next few weeks.

Provision is to be made for some of my work in the following way. The elementary courses are to be divided among three other members of the present faculty, including Prof. Thomas, who is now out on a two years leave studying Sociology at the Univ. of Chicago; the rest of the courses are to be abandoned for the time. I think it is expected though, that when Prof. Thomas and Prof. Hall, who is with you, return, much of this work will be resumed; so that even after Prof. Monroe Senior-Prof. of Pol. Science retires, it will not be necessary to restore the chair of Pol. Econ'y, or certainly not for a long time.

Despite this turn of affairs, however, I am enjoying my work very much, and have the cordial support of our Faculty. I was somewhat handicapped last term by a mild spell of typhoid fever which came at the opening of the year and continued five weeks. In addition to my regular work, I assumed Prof. Hall's course in English History, which runs through the year, in order to save the College this extra item in the budget. Several of my courses this year are new, and have all the charm and interest of newly-planned work. I take my class in Practical Sociology to Cleveland in a few weeks for two visits to the Charitable Institutions of that city. We had Dr. Dike, of Divorce Reform fame, with us last week for four lectures to my classes and the students of the Seminary.

We all have a common bereavement in the death of Merriam

at Ithaca last fall. I thought your recent memorial as recounted in the Studies an exceedingly good and worthy tribute to such a bright, faithful student and thorough gentleman.

I see James has gone to Cornell College, Iowa. That recalls the fact that I received an invitation there last year, thanks to your kind recommendation of my name, but could not accept, as I had already entered upon my duties here.

I congratulate you upon the appearance of your "Jared Sparks," and hope this excellent work may have a heavy sale.

A lecture which I gave here before the College at the opening of the year on "Savagery and Survivals" will appear before long in the Popular Science Monthly, and I take pleasure in confessing that much of the inspiration that led to it came from you.

What my plans for next year may be, it is too early for me to say. I am anxious to go to Europe, and feel the need of it, though I am hardly financially ready. If a desirable opening in History and Economics fails to present itself, I may decide upon this course.

I understand that Prof. Hall is much pleased with the J. H. U., and I daresay you find him an excellent and interested student.

Very Respectfully Yours,

J. Wm. Black

128 — From Woodrow Wilson

Princeton, New Jersey,
13 March, 1894.

My dear Dr. Adams,

I trust that my delay in writing has not caused you any inconvenience. To speak without reserve, it has gone hard with me to decline the volume you proposed to me. That particular volume,[1] and the whole scheme, have great attraction for me; and the temptation to undertake the job was very

---

[1] Adams wrote in the margin "Federal Government." See letters Nos. 124 and 129.

great, in spite of the inadequacy of the pay. I wanted the
subject, not the money. But here at home, in the immediate
presence of the other work I have begun, I have realized the
" must " of the case. I must decline,—with genuine regret,
and with renewed apologies for being so long about it.

With the warmest regard.

Most sincerely Yours,

Woodrow Wilson

129 — To Macmillan & Co.

Johns Hopkins University,
Baltimore, Md., March 26, 1894.

Macmillan & Co.,
66 Fifth Avenue,
New York City.

Dear Sirs:

I have not forgotten the project of the American Citizen
Series. Opportunities for conferences with good advisers have
been afforded and I have been considerably encouraged by
what has been said. I have opened correspondence with various desirable writers. Although several of them, e. g. Seth
Low, Woodrow Wilson, and J. F. Jameson, have not proved
available in consequence of other literary engagements, some
have replied in terms more or less favorable. I enclose letters
from the above named gentlemen and one from Professor
Seligman, whom I asked to undertake " Taxation "; also one
from Dr. Albert Shaw, a former student, whom I asked to
write on " City Government." Shaw is in delicate health and
I am not sure that he can be relied upon. Dr. James Schouler,
author of the History of the U. S. and various law books, has
been lecturing here and has promised to undertake the volume
on " State Government " if the plan is carried out.

The following subjects and authors represent the plan, as it
is now shaping itself:

(1) Local Government, by E. W. Bemis, of the University of Chicago, and the Editor.
(2) State Government, by James Schouler, of Boston.
(3) City Government, by Albert Shaw, of New York City.
(4) Federal Government, by A. B. Hart, of Harvard University.
(5) Taxation, by E. R. A. Seligman, of Columbia College.
(6) Social Problems of Labor, by E. R. L. Gould, of Johns Hopkins Univ.
(7) Government Expenditures, by W. F. & W. W. Willoughby, of Wash. D. C.
(8) Good Citizenship, by H. B. Adams.

I feel reasonably sure of Bemis, Schouler, Seligman, Gould, the Willoughby Brothers, one of whom is connected with the Department of Labor. Prof. A. B. Hart is still in Europe and I have not yet written him.

I have just received the enclosed letter from the Willoughbys, with their plan for a volume on " Government Expenditures," and it looks promising. The Willoughbys are both graduates of the Johns Hopkins University and wrote for our " Studies," a monograph on " Government and Administration of the U. S.," which is now used as a text book in the Washington public schools. " Government Expenditures " would be a very good companion volume to Seligman's " Taxation."

You see that I am making progress in the development of our project, although I am cautious about contracting for more than I am able to execute.[1]

Very sincerely yours,

[Herbert B. Adams]

---

[1] This series never appeared, but in 1903 Longmans, Green published an American Citizen Series edited by Albert Bushnell Hart.

130 — From William F. Willoughby

Department of Labor,
Washington.
April 3, 1894.

Dear Professor Adams:—

A few evenings ago I had quite a long conversation concerning historical and economic matters with a Mr. E. I. Renick, Chief of the Consular Bureau of the State Department. I became so interested in a subject to which he had given a great deal of study and attention, that I thought that you as director of the Seminary and Editor of the Studies might also be interested.

For a number of years Mr. Renick tells me he has given a great deal of time to going through Southern Records family histories etc. In the course of this he came across a good deal of material concerning Richard Gadsden of South Carolina the father or grandfather of Gadsden of Gadsden's Purchase. The qualities of the man impressed him, and he began to look up everything he could find concerning him. His association with a great grandson of Gadsden as roommate for some time increased his interest and gave him advantages for study.

The causes of the American Revolution have been largely written by men of the Northern and border states. The records of the South being less accessible, the part played by the extreme Southern states has been neglected. Now Gadsden, according to Mr. Renick, stands for the South, and for South Carolina in particular, as the type and central figure of unconditional opposition to Great Britain in her demands upon the colonies. Of him, Bancroft said America most largely owes her independence to Otis of Massachusetts, Henry of Virginia and Gadsden of South Carolina. Mr. Renick, to whom Gadsden has become what William the Silent was to Motley, told me the following anecdotes as illustrating the character of his hero. In one of the early conventions, when the timid ones were dwelling on the unprotected character of the sea coast towns, predicting that England could destroy them in a few days, Gadsden arose and said, " Our houses are

built of brick and wood. If they are destroyed there is mud
and timber in abundance with which to rebuild them, but if
our immortal liberties are taken from us what can we do to
replace them?" Again when the proposition to pay for the
tea consumed at the Boston tea party was under consideration,
Gadsden wrote "Don't pay for a damned ounce." When the
subject as to whether total non-importation and non-exporta-
tion should be applied, was being discussed, the South Carolina delegates made a strong demand that rice should form an
exception as the whole life of their state was dependent upon
its exportation. Gadsden, though he had just built the finest
wharf in the City of Charleston, a wharf which still stands
and is known as Gadsden's wharf, alone among the delegates
demanded that no exception should be made in favor of rice
or any other commodity.

Mr. Renick at one time wrote to Putnam asking if a biography of Gadsden to show South Carolina's part in the
causes of the Revolution would be accepted as a number of
the "Makers of the Commonwealth Series." Putnam, however, did not consider Gadsden's name as sufficiently known to
warrant its inclusion in the series.

At the risk of boring you somewhat, I have written all this
as I thought that by chance you might want to use Mr. Renick
for purposes of the Seminary or Studies. I do not know
whether Mr. Renick would come over or not but I think that
he would.

Mr. Renick is a young man of about thirty-five or forty and
a thorough scholar. He was at one time, I think, a partner of
Prof. Woodrow Wilson before he recommenced his professorial work. I remain,

Yours very sincerely

W. F. Willoughby [1]

---

[1] William Franklin Willoughby, the twin brother of W. W. Willoughby, had received an A. B. degree in 1888. An article on Gadsden
by Renick was published in the *Publications of the Southern Historical Association* (1898), II, 242-255.

131 — From W. I. Chamberlain

Ohio State University
Board of Trustees
Hudson, O., May 21 1894

Prof. Herbert B. Adams,

Dear Sir, I write you at the suggestion of Prest. Merrill E. Gates of Amherst College, though your name has been suggested to us by others. Are you free to consider a call to the Presidency of the above (Ohio State) university with any reasonable probability of accepting if elected? If so, our committee will probably call on you soon & talk the matter over & see whether our work is suited to you & you to it as nearly as we can judge by such conference.[1]

Our regular annual income, above all fees for tuition & incidentals, is about $150,000—$85,000 to $90,000 from state tax of 1/20 of a mill; & from national grants about $55,000. Our domain is 330 acres on the main business street of Columbus with electric cars out to us on one other street & seven miles beyond us on the main street. Under a wise system of leases this land will in time bring us a vast income, much as Columbia's real estate now does. We have over 50 Professors & 800 students. Our work is mostly undergraduate & law work now. We are more like Cornell & the Wisconsin University than like Johns Hopkins, having the Morrill "Land Grant" features of agricultural & other industrial education, though on a liberal basis & with large state aid as in Wis. for all liberal studies. We are singularly free from political influences & have a compact Board of Trustees of seven, one being appointed (often reäppointed) each year by the Governor—for seven years. The Governor always consults the Prest. & the hold-over members in regard to all vacancies. The members of the present Board are nearly all college & professional men who will give the President intelligent &

---

[1] For the rest of these interesting negotiations see letters Nos. 132, 133, 134, 135, 136, 138, 139, 140.

loyal support. Our possibilities are great. We need a leader
& a builder.

Kindly write me at the *Neil House, Columbus, O.* so that
I may get it by the evening of May 25th.

> Respectfully
>
> W. I. Chamberlain
>
> Ch'n. Com. on Prest.

132 — To W. I. Chamberlain

> Johns Hopkins University,
> Baltimore, Md., May 23, 1894.

William I. Chamberlain, Esq.,
Neil House,
Columbus, Ohio.

My dear Sir:

I beg to acknowledge your favor of May 21 regarding a
possible call to the presidency of the Ohio State University.
While I am free to consider any proposition which your committee may see fit to make, I can give no positive assurance of
an inclination to accept. My Department of History and
Political Science in this University has absorbed my energies
during the past eighteen years and the thought of leaving
special for administrative work is very serious. Some of my
friends are persuaded that I ought to undertake larger responsibilities, but I have not yet seen an academic field more
inviting than my own department, with my present relations
to the Bureau of Education and other interests in Washington.
I do not feel like encouraging your committee to take the
trouble of coming to Baltimore, but I should be glad to know
what salary you propose to pay your next president and what
are the most pressing needs of the Ohio State University.

I am this morning compelled to leave Baltimore to attend
an Amherst College trustee meeting at Springfield tomorrow.

I shall there see President Gates who will perhaps give me
advice and information regarding the field of academic labor
in Columbus.

I shall return to Baltimore May 26.

Very respectfully yours,

[Herbert B. Adams]

133 — From W. I. Chamberlain

Ohio State University
Board of Trustees
Hudson, O. May 28 1894

Prof Herbert B Adams,

Dear Sir, Our Board at its meeting May 26th instructed me
to confer further with you. I have asked Prest. Scott to write
you & Secy Cope to send you our annual report & an
illustrated " Chicago Graphic " with some facts & photo-
engravings.

The Ohio State University is not yet 21 years old. It was
first built on the Morrill national land grant, but now has
also from Ohio 1/20 of a mill on the state tax duplicate,
yielding $85,000 or more per year. Our fixed income annually
from the state & nation is about $150,000 *besides* all fees from
students, leases etc, & *besides* special state appropriations for
buildings & equipments. Our domain is *330 acres* of land
with a very long frontage on High St, the principal business
street of Columbus, a city of over 100,000 inhabitants. The
business blocks already have nearly reached our grounds tho'
not continuously. This large domain will in time be the basis
of a large income from 25 year leases, somewhat after the
manner of Columbia, N. Y. We have already some 60 Professors & Instructors & some 800 students. At present our
work is chiefly undergraduate work (except the law school),
& chiefly along the lines of pure & applied science, history,
literature, & economics.

I know most of the state universities, & I certainly know no

other that can compare with this in bright prospects of future
greatness, aside from Cornell, Wisconsin, Michigan, Minn.
& Pa.

Kindly let me know soon whether you are likely to regard
a call with at least even chances of acceptance should it be
extended to you. Then we can confer with you & give further
facts.

Respectfully

Please address me at Hudson, O.   W. I. Chamberlain

Ch'n Com. on Prest.

P. S. As to salary, we have not thought it wise in view of the
present finances of the state & of the university to offer more
than $6000 & President's house. We have within three years
spent $200000 on new buildings & equipments of a permanent
character. W. I. C.

134 — From William H. Scott

Ohio State University.
Columbus, O., 30 May, 1894.

Dr. Herbert B. Adams,
Johns Hopkins University,
Baltimore, Md.

My dear Sir,—

The committee appointed by the board of trustees of this
institution to nominate a suitable person for the presidency,
informs me that the position has been offered to you, and asks
me to write to you on the subject. I am glad to comply with
the request, for I am sure that your acceptance would bring to
the post the qualities which it especially needs.

The present income of the university is about $160,000 a
year. The legislature is kindly disposed, and will no doubt
provide for future growth. Public opinion has become more
cordial year by year, and the high schools of the state are
adapting their courses of study to the requirements of the
university.

There is an interest-bearing debt of $110,000 which is to be paid in annual installments of $10,000, and the treasury of the state is somewhat embarrassed; but the recent session of the legislature resulted in several enactments which will probably replenish the state treasury, and then the university will be almost certain to receive additional appropriations.

I have great confidence in the future of the institution, and for a man who is equipped for such work and whose tastes lie in that direction I do not know of a more promising field. It affords an opportunity to do a great and permanent work— to build up a great university, the fountain of educational light and power at the heart of a great central state.

It would afford me much personal satisfaction, if you should decide to come here, and the pleasure of laying down the responsibilities of my office would be greatly enhanced by the fact that they were to be assumed by one in whose abilities and fitness I have so much confidence.

Very truly yours,

W H Scott

135 — From William H. Scott

Confidential.

Ohio State University.
Columbus, O., 30 May, 1894

Dr. Herbert B. Adams,

My dear Sir,—

I feel bound to inform you on one other point. Your success and satisfaction in your work here, if you come, will depend much on the understanding that may be established between you and the board of trustees before you accept their offer. They are excellent men and have the interests of the university much at heart; but they do not appreciate the position of the president or view rightly his relation to them and to the university. Much of the authority that should be exercised by the president is retained by the board. The trustees seem to regard him simply as an adviser, while the exercise of power belongs mainly to them.   This fact may be partly due to the character of the present incumbent of the office, and I might think it altogether so, if the same thing had not existed in a still greater degree during the administrations of both of my predecessors.   Indeed it was in some respects even worse then than now; for I was forewarned in part and provided for the "privilege" of attending all the meetings of the board. The previous practice had been to grant the president an audience for the presentation of such matters as he might wish to bring to the attention of the board, after which he was expected to withdraw.

The welfare of the university requires that the president should be supreme and I should have insisted on it long ago if I had not expected from year to year to retire.   You are in a position to dictate terms, for there has been a brief period of enlightenment of late and I think that the board begins to see the importance of the matter.   Besides, to you, a new man whom they are anxious to secure, they will readily make liberal concessions.   You need not, therefore, let what I have said deter you in the least from coming, for I have no doubt that you can make just such terms as you may choose.

With a renewed expression of my desire to have you as a leader and fellow-worker, I am

Faithfully yours,

W H Scott

136 — To W. I. Chamberlain

Johns Hopkins University,
Baltimore, Md., June 4, 1894.

W. I. Chamberlain, Esq.,
Hudson, Ohio.

My dear Sir:

Your letter of May 28 came duly to hand and I have since received copies of the annual report of the board of trustees

15

and of the catalogue of the Ohio State University. Although we are in the midst of examinations I have given some thought to your proposition and have made some inquiries concerning the academic situation in Columbus. I am impressed with the prospects of the institution and have studied its history as recorded by my friend, Dr. George W. Knight, in a government report which I edited for the Bureau of Education.

There are some matters, however, which seem to me rather doubtful from an administrative point of view:

(1) The present unstable tenure of your president and all the faculty. I understand that they are all subject to annual reappointment by the board of trustees.

(2) The president seems to me to lack sufficient power and influence with reference to the appointment and tenure of professors, and the shaping of the general policy of the University.

(3) Is the president necessarily the chaplain of the University or can religious functions, which are important, be discharged by a ministerial member of the faculty?

(4) Is there any such office as a Dean or Secretary for the conduct of routine college business?

(5) The question of the president's salary seems to me somewhat uncertain, even if fixed by the board of trustees at any one time. What is to prevent the legislature from reducing it at pleasure?

I should be very reluctant to change my present stable position for an insecure tenure of office, with a salary subject to modification by a changing majority in the board or by the action of the legislature. While I appreciate the honor of being considered as a possible successor to the presidency of your State University, I do not feel like encouraging you to elect me to the office. If, however, you are inclined to give me your views upon the above points, I shall be glad to receive them.

Very respectfully yours,

[Herbert B. Adams]

137 — From Daniel Coit Gilman

Office of the President. Johns Hopkins University,
Baltimore, Md.

Dear Dr. Adams

The Trústees, yesterday, adopted the enclosed minutes, for my guidance, as well as yours in respect the work of next year;—and not for publication.

Yours very truly

D C Gilman

Professor Adams June 5. 94

Minute adopted by the Trustees of the Johns Hopkins University,

June 4, 1894

D. C. G.

The Trustees of the Johns Hopkins University regard the discussion of current political, economic, financial and social questions before the students of this University as of such importance that the lessons should be given only by the ablest and wisest persons whose services the University can command. They request the Executive Committee to consider this subject and to make a special report thereupon. The Trustees are of the opinion that no instruction should be given in these subjects unless it can be given by persons of experience, who are well acquainted with the history and principles of political and social progress. Until this report is presented the Trustees recommend great caution in the selection and engagement of lecturers and other teachers.

138 — From W. I. Chamberlain

Ohio State University
Board of Trustees
Hudson, O. June 5 1894

Prof. H. B. Adams,

My dear Sir, Yours of June 4 is before me.— (1) The plan of annual elections was adopted in an early day, as I learn, to prevent legal trouble in case of an offensive & " cantankerous " professor. *In fact* the tenure is as stable as in any college or university in the land—too stable, sometimes, for the good of the University.

(2) The appointments are usually made on the recommendation of the president & the tenure of the professors would depend largely upon his advice. If he advised that a professor be asked to resign & supported his advice with good reasons, in my opinion there is not the least doubt that the trustees would unanimously act on such advice.

(3) I think trustees, faculty & the community at large would prefer that the president should be a man of Christian belief & spirit, who would be willing to conduct chapel exercises himself at least a part of the time. Still Dr. Orton the first president never conducted chapel exercises himself, tho' a man of reverent spirit. The chapel exercises are not compulsory upon the students, partly from the fact that our chapel will not seat the entire student body. There is but one minister in the faculty, I think.

(4) Secretary Cope is " bursar " & does much of the routine work done by the president in smaller colleges. The president also has a clerk.

(5) I do not think the legislature ever will or ever can reduce the president's salary except during an interregnum. The legislature this year removed the old salary limit & thereby placed the fixing of the salary & the contract with the new president in the hands of the trustees, where it belongs. For any future legislature to reduce the salary of an incumbent would seem to me to break a contract which the

legislature had itself authorized to be made. It would be
unprecedented in Ohio.

As to "a changing majority in the board" of trustees:
there are seven trustees, one being appointed by the Governor each year to serve for seven years, subject to reappointment even twice. Your position in Ohio would, I think, be
as stable as that of any college or university president.—I
can scarcely conceive a more inviting field to a strong man
conscious of executive ability.—One point in (2) I omitted:
The "shaping of the general policy of the university" would
rest largely with the president, subject however to *its* organic
law. That makes it first a school of pure & applied science;
second a true university in the widest sense, so fast & so far
as its constantly widening resources will permit.

I hope you will see your way clear to write me at the
Neil House, Columbus, O., by Monday next, that my letter
has met your doubts & that you will consider a call if extended,
with probability of accepting it.

Respectfully

W. I. Chamberlain

139 — To W. I. Chamberlain

Johns Hopkins University,

Baltimore, Md., June 9, 1894.

My dear Sir:

I beg to acknowledge your favor of the 5th instant and
to express my satisfaction with your practical views on most
if not all of the points raised in my recent letter of inquiry.
Calm reflection has convinced me, however, that it would be
unwise to let my name go before your board of trustees for
possible election to the presidency of the Ohio State University.

Attractive and honorable though the call might be to a
man in my position, I cannot persuade myself to abandon my
present field of historical labor, with a large following of
graduate students in a department which I have created and

now direct. This Baltimore work, with my various editorial connections, seems peculiarly my own and I am reluctant to undertake another man's public and administrative responsibilities for which I have had no previous training.

My salary here is considerably less than that which you propose and I have no expectation of any increase in these hard times, but somehow I prefer the things I have in Baltimore and Washington to those I know not of in Ohio. I have given careful and honest thought to your generous overtures and have taken no counsel with authorities here; but I cannot bring myself to the conviction that I ought to change my academic base from the Johns Hopkins University to Columbus.

I believe that your State University is superior to all denominational institutions in Ohio and I have confidence in the ultimate triumph of State education and of the sound principles which your institution represents; but the simple truth is, I am too fond of my own department to leave it now and to take up an entirely new work, although it is manifestly larger, more distinguished, and better paid.

Regretting the loss of time which negotiations with me and my serious deliberation may have caused you, I remain

Very respectfully,

[Herbert B. Adams]

William Chamberlain, Esq.,
Chairman of Committee on President,
Columbus, Ohio.

140 — From Walter Quincy Scott

Moscow Penn
June 13th 1894

Dr. H. B. Adams
Johns Hopkins University
Baltimore, Md.

My dear Sir:

Your letter has just reached me at this place where my family is located for this summer—

1. My own belief is that the chief controlling reason for my removal from the presidency of the O. S. U. was the purpose of the majority of the Board to put the University under the control of the Campbellite denomination.

This was the opinion of many judicious men in Columbus at the time.

When Bishop (a Campbellite) was Gov. the democrats reorganized the State institutions, including the University. His private secretary was made Secretary of the Board of Trustees of the University, a majority of whom were Campbellites.

2 But the "trouble" actually appeared in this way; At the close of the Class Day Exercises (to which the graduating class had summoned me to receive a gift of a handsome bible for the Chapel, in recognition of the "magnanimous and wise" manner in which as President I had peacefully settled the question of introducing prayers into the University) I was met at my home by a district messenger boy with a notice that the "Board of Trustees declined to reelect me for the coming year and had elected W. H. Scott president pro tem. and prof. of pol. economy," and a request was added that I should not disclose this action of the Board until after the close of the Commencement exercises on the following day.

No explanation whatever accompanied this extraordinary notice. I was not aware of any personal difference with any colleague or with any students, nor of any disagreement with any members of the Board which could in any way account for such startling action.

3. The technical ground of the action was a By-Law of the Board, that the members of the faculty should be elected annually. When I accepted the presidency I was assured this rule was merely a convenient rule for dropping inferior teachers and employees, and was not intended for application to the presidency and professorships.

4. The action of the Board caused a deal of excitement in the Univ. and in Columbus. So far as I knew it was unanimously denounced by students, by alumni, and by leading

citizens of Columbus, and by newspapers. The press kept up a racket for a couple of weeks. Meetings of students and alumni, and conferences of citizens caused Gov. Foster to summon the Board of Trustees to give reasons for their action. They came to Columbus and answered in effect that their By-Law gave them the right not to re-elect a president, that I had withheld an important document from the Board, had neglected to carry out a resolution of the Board and in general lacked executive ability, and had uttered unsound doctrines in political economy!

No intimation of such charges had come to me at any time from any source, and the Board refused to give me any hearing on any point.

The "important document" turned out to be a paper which was not addressed to the Board, but to myself—a request by Prof. Short that I would whenever I might deem it best, lay his resignation before the Board. He was dying of consumption, and the object of this paper was to quiet the Professor's mind while I and other colleagues were doing his work to the end of the year so that he could draw his salary. And this arrangement I made with the personal and full approval of the president of the Board (T. Ewing Miller) and other members!

The resolution I had neglected to carry out was in relation to prayers in Chapel—which resolution I myself drew up and urged the Board to pass, and upon their passing it, I announced it the same day, and the following morning began to conduct prayers, and alone continued to conduct them for many months until the day of my removal,—with the goodwill of every colleague and of the students, though most of my colleagues, if not all, would have preferred not to have prayers established.

I need say nothing as to economic heresy nor as to executive ability—since there was no specification nor hearing in the whole matter.

5. Other facts doubtless had an important bearing on the "trouble,"

1. President T. Ewing Miller and Secy Allen wanted me to recommend as Assistant Prof. of Latin, a son in law of Allen's (who had been dropped for incompetency from the High School.) I told Miller I was entirely unacquainted with the young man, had never met him, and further that I could not recommend any person as an assistant to a head of a department unless the head of the department was entirely satisfied. This made Miller very angry. He wanted to know what a president was for if he couldn't sign a recommendation when desired to do so by members of the Board.

2. President Miller's son, T. Ewing Miller Jr., was dropped from the University because he failed in two-thirds of his examinations [chiefly under Prof. of Physics, Mendenhall). His parents were both angry. The case was reviewed and the teachers reaffirmed their decisions. Miller wanted me to cause the reinstatement of his son. I told him I could not do so in case of his son any more than in any other case. Mrs. Miller was very bitter against Mendenhall and myself.

3. The Board disposed of many thousands of acres of land belonging to the Univ. and located in the State of Ohio. No tax was paid on this land, nor was it necessary to sell any of it for current expenses. But the star chamber sold it all for next to nothing. I was not a member ex officio of the Board, never met with the Board except when requested to come, but I was opposed to selling the lands of the University.

Now I must leave you to guess what the "trouble" was, as best you can.

Of course it was rooted in "politics." Those seven men were democrats and sectarians rather than trustees of a University. It required and will yet require years of time for the University to grow, like that of Michigan, at least far enough beyond partisan control to permit educational organizations to thrive.

As to the possibilities, I think they are very great. Nothing but deplorable mismanagement has hitherto prevented the University from attaining a position like that of Cornell. A trifling tax in Ohio will give it a large income, and there is no institution in the state that can surpass it, and even now none except Adelbert that can approach it. Ohio has many religious sects, but their colleges are poor compared with O. S. U. If the Univ. takes an agnostic stand in religion it will never be permitted to prosper as it should. If it falls under some sect it will deserve the trouble that will surely come. If it stands squarely as a State University, like the State itself in positive goodwill toward religion, separate from church, it ought to become a great centre of learning. There are hundreds of young men who would be attracted to their own State University, who now go to eastern institutions. The sectarian colleges cannot control these young men.

If they are seeking you for the Presidency, it is clear proof of my hopes. It needs just such a man, that University does, but I cannot envy you the entire experience such a character as yours would have in attempting to develop the University along the lines of free teaching and free learning. There were and are excellent and able men in the faculty. I do not know the present composition of the Board. But I am certain you would make an ideal president for the State University of Ohio, even if you couldn't get the Board to always work on University lines.

But I am very reluctant to think of your getting called away from Johns Hopkins for any reason.

I have written frankly as you deserve.

Very sincerely

Walter Quincy Scott

141 — From James A. Woodburn

Indiana University.
Bloomington, Indiana.
June 16, 1894.

My dear Dr. Adams:

I told Callahan about the fellowship. He was not greatly disappointed, though he would have been elated to have been

successful. I had warned him against too great expectations.
I have encouraged him to go to the Hopkins any how, and
he thinks he will do so. Unless he changes his mind he will
be with you in October. He is a good student, of fair ability,
and of earnest purpose; but he has lacked the advantages of
good early classical training,—the discipline such as I imagine
the German gymnasia give a man. Under your direction I
believe he will prove to be a good University man.[1]

I suppose by this time you are taking a rest, and I am
encouraged to hope that you will have time to write me a letter
about a matter which is of considerable interest to me. I am
planning to go abroad for a year, after spending another full
year in teaching. It may be that I shall be delayed and cannot go until two years from now, but if possible I wish to go
a year from this summer. I have never been abroad, and I
have thought I would not go until I could spend at least a
year. After travelling on the Continent during the summer,
I expect to settle in England, at Oxford or Cambridge, for
the University year. My chief purpose in seeking this year
away is to secure the advantage which comes from observation
and travel and from acquaintance with other life than that
to which I have always been used. But at the same time I
hope to make a study with advantage of English Politics and
English Political History. I should be most interested in
studying English Political Institutions and Institutional History. I probably would not take a regular course of study, but
would like to attend the University lectures, learn as much
as I could of English university life, see as much as possible
of the Extension movement, study current political life in
England, and come in contact with as many helpful and
interesting persons as possible. I would have all these various
avocations, while my vocation would be to study English
History, and it may be that I would be led to give the greater
part of my time to my *avocations*. Do you not think this
would be an interesting program? It is new *life* that I need,
even more than new learning.

---

[1] James M. Callahan was appointed fellow in history for the academic year 1896 and received the Ph. D. degree in 1897.

Now, why am I telling you all this? Because your advice would be very profitable to me. And if you have time to write me your suggestions I would appreciate the kindness very much. I have thought of the possibility of my being able to make myself useful to some Extension centres in England, if there should be any classes interested in American Politics, or in the Political History of the United States. I think I could prove myself a lucid expositor on these lines. I mention this not chiefly from concern for fees, or income from such work, but on account of the opportunity it would give me for advantageous acquaintance. I would like, if possible, to meet such men as Professor Bryce and Mr. Morley. I have been teaching Mr. Bryce's American Commonwealth, and I count myself, in politics, something of a disciple of Mr. Morley. Do you know the English socialist, Mr. Clark, who is a frequent contributor to the *Outlook?* Or, Sidney Webb? or any other who might be the means of introducing me to the English Labor leaders? Could you put me in the way of letters which would help me in the University? You will know better than I what is needed and what is best. Mr. Emmott would perhaps be willing to give me some letters of introduction. I mention this so early because, if I go, I shall wish to plan quite a while ahead. My wife, as might be expected, would go with me, and as an Ann Arbor and Wellesley girl might be expected to do, she is entering into the anticipations with a great deal of pleasure.

There is another thing about which I should like to ask. Do you publish in the Historical Studies anything not brought out by your own men? A student of mine who took his A. B. degree here two years ago, and who subsequently studied a year in the University of Wisconsin, has been working on Anglo-American Relations during our Civil War, especially with reference to the Trent Affair. His essay is to treat of the Trent Affair in a monograph of about 150 pages. He read to my Seminary the first chapter of his study about two weeks ago, and I think he is going to make a very good thing of it. He got interested in this theme and made a term report upon it while he was a senior with me, and I encouraged him to go on with the study with a view to publishing his results sometime. I very much regret that we have no publication agency here, for I should be very glad to see this monograph put out with our *imprimatur*. Would you be willing to accept it as one of the University Studies, if it comes up to the mark? I believe a good presentation of " The Trent Affair " would find acceptance among historical studies. Mr. T. L. Harris, who is doing this work, is Principal of one of the High Schools in this State. He is a thorough worker, and you would be pleased with his clear style of presentation. Would it be worth while for him to send his manuscript to you?

*   *   *   *

As ever, with kindest regards,

James A. Woodburn

142 — From Frederic Bancroft

Washington, D. C., June 16, 1894.
c/o Metropolitan Club.

Prof. H. B. Adams,
Johns Hopkins University, Baltimore, Md.

My dear Adams:

It occurred to me the other day that the Historical Association ought to show some appreciation of the man who has written the best work on American history since Henry Adams', excepting John Fiske. I am thoroughly convinced that next to the men of positive genius, such as Motley, Parkman, and Fiske, no one has made a better contribution in our science than my good friend Rhodes. The third volume covering 1860 and 1861 will be out this year. I am not his advance agent, or speaking from any impulse except that of a sense of justice and impartial friendship. It is because I feel so sure that our ideas about the best interest of the Association agree, that I take the liberty to give myself the pleasure of this one-sided talk with you. I suppose the aim of the Association is to honor those who most honor our profession. Rhodes is as modest as he is generous; and he attended all but one, I think, of the meetings that were held in Washington. It would probably surprise him as much as it would please me, (and you too after you know him), to receive any office of honor from the Association.

I have been keeping my nose on the grind-stone all the year except when lecturing in New York, and have made good progress with Seward, aside from having gathered lots of material for a more elaborate work. In a few weeks I am going to Auburn to spend some time examining the balance of Seward's manuscripts. If I shall still be there when the Association meets I may run over to Saratoga for a little jollity with the grey-beards, or an innocent walk along the midway with yourself.

I hope when they count the ballots at Amherst you will find yourself a trustee. Sometime ago I had so interesting an interview with Galusha A. Grow about political events of thirty and forty years ago that he quite won my affections by his vivid and picturesque recollections, and if I had not already sent in my vote for one of the namesakes of our first ancestor I might have been won over by Grow's eloquence.

So much for lack of an opportunity to have a friendly chat with you. This does not call for an answer,—unless you happen to have a stenographer and an abundance of time.

Very cordially yours,

Frederic Bancroft

143 — From John S. Bassett

Trinity College, Durham, N. C.
July 31, 1895.

Dear Dr. Adams,

I have just returned from Raleigh, N. C., where I have been working for a month getting materials for " The Negro in N. C." & for my Constitutional Hist. I got all I wanted for the latter. The negro matter is not so rich. I think however I shall have no trouble with him except as to his religion. It is going to be rather hard to tell how much he has, where he got it, how fast he got it, & just what kind it is. Do you mean for me to write on Slavery or on the Negro? The history of the Negro since the termination of Slavery will alone make a good number of the Studies. Before 1865 the two subjects are virtually the same.

I had a very pleasant letter recently from Ballagh. He was not placed at that time. Trust he can make a better report by this time. I trust that all the boys are located well. I cannot send you any boys next fall. I have several in soak but they are at work now trying to make the money necessary to take them.

The prospects for our college are some brighter. The President is a good preacher and has awakened great enthusiasm wherever he has gone. Efforts at endowment are a making. A wealthy man in the town has offered $50000 on condition that the church will raise $75000 more. This would endow five chairs. In the meantime salaries are $1200. Another wealthy man has given $5000 to beautify the campus. I hope this may be the beginning of a new era.

Yours very truly,

John S. Bassett [1]

144 — From John A. Fairlie

1035 E. Bay St.
Jacksonville, Fla.
Aug. 10th 1895.

Prof. H. B. Adams
Baltimore, Md.

Dear Sir:—

I have been considering the advisability of continuing my study of History and Politics by a year at Johns Hopkins University, and with that in view have been examining your

---

[1] Ph. D. 1894.

Register and statement of courses of instruction as given in the University Circular for July 1895. I find however several points that are not clear to me, and so write you about them.

First I should like to explain what I have done in the line of History etc., and why I want to take a year at your institution.

I have been for the last four years at Harvard, during which time I have completed five years work; but as I did not apply for my A. B. until this year I cannot get the Harvard M. A. until next June. I may say that the Administrative Board of the Graduate School has recognized my extra work, & agreed to grant me the M. A. degree on the work done the past year over the work required for the A. B. degree.

For the last two years I have specialized almost wholly, in History, Govt. & Law, and Economics; having taken in all 8 and a half courses, six of them being graduate courses. The list of my courses is as follows:—

Mediaeval & Modern European History 375 A D—1750
         Prof. Channing.
Modern European History 1750-1894. (½ course). . . . .
         Prof. Macvane.
English Const. History to 1400 A. D. . . . . . .Asst. Prof. Gross.
Const. & Political History of England. 1760-1893. (½ course)
         Prof. Macvane.
American Colonial History 1492-1783. . . . . . Prof. Channing.
Constitutional Government (½ course). . . . . Prof. Macvane.
Government & Political Methods in U. S. . . . . Asst. Prof. Hart.
Research course on Local Govt. in Prussia and Great Britain.
         Prof. Macvane.
Discussion of Mill's Political Economy, Lectures on Economic Development, Distribution, Social Questions & Financial Legislation. . . . . Professors Ashley, Cummings, Taussig.
International Law. . . . . .Mr. Conant

My rank in all of these courses, as in all my work at Harvard, has been very high. Prof. Hart says in a letter to me that my work " gives evidence of intelligence industry and power to grasp principles. Your written work proves that you have learned the approved methods of historical study." The grades given me by him & by my other instructors show that they consider my work equal to any done in their courses. Having done so well at Harvard it would naturally be easiest for me to continue my studies at that institution. But while realizing this, and also the advantages of Harvard, I, at the same time, believe in the benefits to be derived from studying at different Universities under different Instructors. So having spent four years at Harvard, I think a year or two at another university would be better for me than the same time spent at Harvard.

At Johns Hopkins I should have the advantage of studying United States History and Government within traveling distance of the great laboratory at Washington. The special inducement however which makes me want to come to Johns Hopkins *this* winter is the course of lectures on Local Government to be given by Prof. Wilson of Princeton. You will see from my list of courses that I have been making some study of this subject, and I am anxious to continue along this line. But at Harvard there is no special course in Local Government so that most of my work has to be done with little guidance. With Prof. Wilson's lectures I feel that I could do better work in Seminary courses.

If these long explanations have not wearied you I should like to have you answer one or two questions. I have not been able to learn from the register how many courses are considered a fair amount of work for a graduate student. I have selected as the courses I would like to take, your courses in American Institutional History and History of Civilization, Dr. Steiner's course in American Const. & Polit. History, Professor Woodrow Wilson's lectures on Local Government, and the Seminary of History and Politics. Would this be a full year's work, or would it be too much? I should also like to have your opinion as to the suitability of this course, considering what subjects I have already had at Harvard.

I shall also have to trouble you a little in regard to finances. I know both stenography and typewriting (I own a type-

16

writer), and throughout my course at Harvard have had opportunities to use my ability in this line to make some money,
earning about $150.00 a year. Can you tell me if there is any
opportunity for me to earn some money in this way in Baltimore? I hope it is possible for me to do something of this
kind, as without it I should find it rather difficult to get
through the year.

I trust I have not trespassed too much on your time with
this long letter. I hope you may find it convenient to answer
before long.

Very truly yours

John A. Fairlie

145 — From John S. Bassett

Durham, N. C.

Jan. 16. 1896.

Dear Dr. Adams,

I was just getting ready to write to you when I received
your very encouraging letter. I am gratified to have your
appreciation of my work. What I have done has been much
less than I ought to have done I fear. Yet I have tried to
remember that it has been put on me to do God's work in the
field of history. Perhaps I should not have done so much in
a less restricted field. Some large part of the results ought
to be credited to the kind sympathy and encouragement you
have given me.

I am just sending you a copy of our " Historical Papers "
which is the first heir of my historical society, and it is about
that that I was going to write to you. You will see that the
publication makes a pamphlet of 85 pages and, I think, is
not a bad affair for a college in the South. It is true that
there are a number of careless expressions in some of the
pieces. That is due to the fact that the articles appeared
first in *The Archive*—and the editor of that magazine did
not proof read strictly. I am going to proof read for the next
series myself & I hope to have better results. You may be

surprised to know that the whole affair cost less than $25.
I made arrangements with *The Archive,* the college magazine,
by which I furnished them with historical articles on condition that I might have reprints from the articles. I then
made arrangements with the printer to make 200 reprints at
25 cts a page. These have been saved throughout the year.
Now I bind them up as you see. When I came here I was
determined to have a publication. After much consideration
I hit on this plan. The college, since it has seen the work,
has offered to assume the obligation of the affair to the
amount of $25—for the future; so my " Papers " are to be
permanent. So far as I know, this is one of but three historical publications (not including patriotic publications) in
the South. It is the only one in N. C. I should like your
opinion of it, for publication. If it is not favorable, I will
agree not to publish it.

The college is going on favorably. There are some marks of
improvement. We are now working on the library problem.
I think we shall have some progress. I think we shall have
some good legislation on public schools this time. Trinity
and Wake Forest are doing the work for them.

I am not disappointed about the historical prize. If the
association can do so I should like to get it to publish my
paper.

I do not mind my present situation as such. It is narrow
& uninspiring to live in this State just now. If my salary were
larger I could go North every summer and remedy this de-
ficiency. I am hoping for the best—and I am willing to wait.

Very cordially yours,

John S. Bassett.

146 — From George B. Adams

The American Historical Review.
North Derby, Vt.
Sept., 20, 1897.

Dear Professor Adams:—

The editors of the Am. Hist. Review at their next meeting—Oct. 15 and 16—expect to spend most of their time considering the question of the future of the Review after the expiration of the guarantee fund, and hope to reach some definite conclusion as to the suggestion to make to the guarantors at Christmas. As I have thought the matter over myself, it has seemed to me that to make the Review in some way the organ of the Am. Hist. Ascn. is the only possible arrangement under which it can be carried on in its present form. But it seems to me certain that a bonus from the Ascn. of $500.00, in addition to our present subscription list, would not enable the Review to go on without a very considerable reduction of present expenses—which could be obtained only from the editor's salary, and this would make a very serious change. I should be very glad if you would write me what you think of the following suggestions, not officially of course but as a matter of private opinion and advice.

1. Would it be possible to raise the annual dues of the Am. Hist. Ascn. to $5.00, send the Review gratis to every member, and turn over to its expense fund one half the dues, or $2.50 per member? How many of the present members are not now on our subscription list I do not know—we shall have a definite statement of this at our meeting—but the amount received in this way would probably be considerably more than $500.00. Do you think many of the present members of the Ascn. would drop out if the dues were raised to $5.00? Or do you think that receiving the Review in this way would increase the attractiveness of membership and result in a longer list? Do you suppose that by a concerted effort through our friends in various parts of the country we could raise the membership to 1000 or 1200? The case of the American Academy, of

Philadelphia, may be in point, which has a fee of $5.00 and, with much less to offer, has a considerably larger list than ours.

2. Suppose we should receive from the publisher a definite offer to the following effect, do you think it would be wise to accept it? a. The publisher assumes editorial expenses. b. The editors continue to control entirely the contents of the Review. c. 20 pages now devoted to reviews shall be used to increase the number of articles. d. Each number shall contain two articles by writers likely to attract popular attention, like Goldwin Smith, Capt. Mahan, etc., these to be paid for by the publisher and to be satisfactory in character to the editors. Do you think a scheme like this could be made to work in practice without friction, the publisher looking to popular sales to meet expenses and the editors trying to maintain the scientific character of the Review? If it did work, do you think it would be likely to lower the standard of the Review? I do not know that such an offer will be made, but it has been suggested as possible.

3. Do you think our subscription list would be much reduced if the price of the Review were made $4.00 per year, instead of $3.00, as at present?

I have written to Dr. Bowen to the same effect.

I return to New Haven this week, and shall be greatly obliged if you will write me there within a few days and give me any suggestion on these points, or on any other, that may occur to you.

Very sincerely yours,

Geo. B. Adams.

147 — From John S. Bassett

Trinity College, Durham, N. C.
Sept — 26, 1897.

Dear Dr. Adams,

This is about the time for you to get back to Baltimore from your vacation and I will write you about Weaver—

whom you will probably see before the end of the week. He, Weaver, has asked me about his minors—I told him what I took and advised him to be guided by your advice for his particular case. I am a little anxious about him. He has the doing of good work in him and if his interest is kept aroused he will make a good student. I do not believe much in coddling men—who ought to be able to look out for themselves, but still I think that the more you put it on to Weaver the better it will be for him. If you will allow me to suggest I would say make him buckle down to history—Keep him busy on papers etc—and don't let him go wool-gathering through the departments of Assyriology—Sanskrit—Philosophy & a dozen other things that may strike his fancy. He needs work & a plenty of it to keep his fancy in a good condition.

Our college year has opened well. I am doing more satisfactory work, to myself, than I have done since I have been here. Last night I had an excellent meeting of our historical society. The students are interested and I hope for good results. I am trying to put a new spirit into the historical work of the South—so far as my influence extends. Last night I made talk on our historical ideal. I spoke of the freedom of thought in the history department of this college and of the obligation laid on us for a revival of ideas. I appealed to the boys to let it be so that our society would be at least one place in all the South in which a man could present his opinions of our history and get a respectful hearing. At this point they cheered. I think we are making progress.

I have not had any proof from Clark of my article on Anti-Slavery Leaders of N. C. which is in the hands of the Am. Hist. Association. Has the proof been read? If convenient, I should be glad to see mine.

Some of my N. C. friends tell me they met you at Chataqua. They speak highly of you and your lectures. I wish you could find time to come to N. C. and stop & see me. Ballagh passed through this summer on his wedding trip, but I missed him. I should like very much to be in Baltimore now. I find myself continually reverting to my old experiences there. I

always think of you and the men in history when the time
comes for opening another year.   I wish you much success
this year.

Yours very sincerely,

John S. Bassett.

148 — From James Schouler

60 Congress St., Boston, Mass.,
Sept. 28th., 1897.

Prof. Herbert B. Adams,
Baltimore, Md.

Dear Mr. Adams :—

The time now approaches when it would be well for me to
determine what course to take with regard to the next meeting
of the American Historical Association at Cleveland.   I made
you, I believe, the "keeper of my conscience," or in other
words I left you to decide what I had better do.   It seems to
me most natural that I should put in an appearance, and read
the opening address; after which I might resign the chair to
some one else to occupy for the rest of the session.   Please
advise me deliberately but frankly in this whole delicate
matter.

At all events the preparation of the annual address devolves
upon me, whoever may read it at the meeting.   How much
time ought I to occupy with such a paper?   And what do you
think of Federal constitutional changes or a new Federal convention as the main theme?   My "Constitutional Studies,
State & Federal" is about to be published (containing the
substance of Johns Hopkins lectures), and its preparation
has suggested various points of contrast and comparison, as
between our Federal and State systems, which I would like
to elaborate in such an address.   Let me have your suggestions
in the matter.

I earnestly hope that the gathering may be a lively and interesting one, like that last year in New York.   A sort of

symposium or joint discussion is a good feature, I think, as at our last gathering. So, too, we should take care not to make up too long programmes (or double programmes) of miscellaneous papers. Will there be any attractive reports or prize awards, do you think? Obituary records for the past year need also some proper presentation.

Hoping your vacation has been full of pleasure, I am, as always,

Yours very truly,

James Schouler [1]

149 — From Frank W. Blackmar

History and Sociology,
University of Kansas.
December 20th, 1897.

My dear Professor Adams:

I enclose statement for A. H. A. as per request. My vacation begins today and I have begun work in earnest in my study which I shall pursue with unabating vigor until my den is partially cleared of accumulated work. I am sorry that I shall not be able to go to Cleveland. It is merely a matter of expense. Our salaries are cut and living expenses higher which leaves no margin for extras. I hope it will not always be thus.

I would like very much to see you and other good men of the educational world. I am making a desperate effort to keep up my studies and my enthusiasm in this land of beef, corn, and hogs where during the past two years respectability has been a target for the plebeian and the desire for things elevating has apparently declined.

---

[1] In 1891 James Schouler was for the first time appointed to give a series of lectures in the Hopkins. The association lasted many years and he became a warm friend of Adams. The statements at the beginning of his letter were caused by his deafness. His presidential address entitled "A New Federal Convention" was written in even a shorter period than this letter indicates because a later one, dated Oct. 18, shows he had not yet started composition.

Yet there is hope that the State will eventually build up its higher institutions and not sacrifice itself to the cry of the proletarian demagogue who exults in the leveling down process. I speak not of the loss of a few paltry dollars on salary but of affairs in general.

I trust that you will have a good time at Cleveland.

Sincerely yours,

Frank W. Blackmar

150 — From William P. Trent

205 E. Main St.,
Richmond, Va.
Jan. 8th, '98.

My dear Dr. Adams,

Your letter was very welcome as I wanted to have both sides of the Adelbert matter set before me. I am vainly trying to see my duty & my final decision will be made next week when I hear from V. C. Wiggins & from Adelbert as to some minor points.

I realize the truth of what you say, but as I see it at this moment I have to consider my family first & on the whole the move to Cleveland would be advantageous to them. Sewanee doesn't suit a city bred woman & it has its drawbacks for an ambitious man. I could give up my ambitions to my duty, however, if need were—but I confess that when it comes to resolving to walk & sleep on briars all your life I shrink a bit. I mean by this prickly figure of speech the fact that at Sewanee what harasses me is not so much lack of books & of city life as it is the fact that a considerable portion of the people around me consider me a traitor & don't like me & only keep quiet because they are afraid of me, that I am every year denounced by a minority of the board of trustees as a dangerous religious & political heretic & that I am continually made the object of prayers & other pietistic propaganda for my spiritual regeneration. As a man gets older this sort of thing becomes more insulting & ridiculous.

There is no possible chance of my ever affiliating with Sewanee religiously & hence I have risen just as high as I possibly can there. There is no other Southern institution that would touch me—& I must look for advancement either to the North or the West. Am I to repress personal ambition or not? I have abilities both as a lecturer & an executive that are much hampered in Sewanee. I can write it is true but I can do that elsewhere.

It comes down then in my mind to a question of missionary *versus* man of the world & I should not hesitate to say missionary if I really believed my presence to be necessary. But it isn't. The South will only be regenerated by *time*. My present backers in it are largely men who *dare not speak out*— they write me *letters* & they vote for me etc. but they let me do the fighting in the open. I'm tired of it. Furthermore— they all skulk back a bit—say I go too far etc. It merely means that they are afraid of their own conclusions—of the sound of their own voices. Shallow thinking on political matters, provincialism of taste & sentiments—ignorance & vanity are the dominant characteristics of our people & they have got to be made to see these things before a real reformation takes place *speedily*. A reformation will take place unconsciously through the lapse of *time*—but I'm not concerned with that. I see clearly after 10 years life among them that the Southern people will not be set right for more than one generation—that I cannot head a party for active propaganda which might hasten on the process of regeneration & therefore I much doubt whether five or ten years more of me in the South means much to either party.

But I thank you most warmly for your letter & if I'm boring please tell me so. Mrs. Trent desires to be remembered.

Ever yours

W. P. Trent

P. S. Of course don't say anything of the way I have *unbosomed* myself.

151 — From J. B. Paton

Nottingham,
England.
February 8th. 1898.

My dear Professor Adams,

*   *   *   *

A cousin of mine who lives in Michigan was visiting this country last autumn. He was astonished when I told him that 9,999 people out of every 10,000 upheld and applauded the action of the States in the war of Independence, and reprobated the conduct of the English government as being opposed to the true doctrine of English liberty. I told him that we regarded the States as having upheld that doctrine and as having entrenched it absolutely in the history and development of the Anglo Saxon race. I reminded him also how, both before the war and during the war, the greatest minds of our country protested against it and denounced it, and that there were no nobler passages in Anglo Saxon oratory than those in which Chatham, Burke, and Fox denounced this war. My cousin wrote to me after his return to Michigan saying that he had conversed with a great number of persons during his visit to this country, and had found what I had said to be entirely true. He found not a single Englishman or Englishwoman who did not rejoice in the rebellion of the States and the victory by which they achieved their independence. He then said to me, How is it then that in our School Histories in America such a different impression is given as to the attitude of the English people toward the States? and how is it that the history of the rebellion is given in such a way as to nourish antagonism and even hatred to the English people, as though they had been in the last century and even now were responsible for and supporters of the wicked policy of George the Third?

I write this to you now because I feel that you can render great service by using your influence to have the History School books in the United States written so as to convey the real truth in regard to both the English statesmen of last century and the whole of the English people of this century. In this way you would do much to draw and weld these two great divisions of the Anglo Saxon race into a glorious harmony.

With kindest regards

I remain

Yours faithfully,

J. B. Paton.

152 — From Sidney Webb

Ebbitt House
Washington D. C.
8 April 1898

Dear Sir

The enclosed card was given to me by Mrs. J. R. Macdonald of London, but I think I should have ventured to present myself to you even without a formal introduction, on the ground of my interest in your economic work. Mrs. Webb and I propose to come to Baltimore on Monday, 17th April, and to leave that city early on Wednesday the 19th April. If we could have the pleasure of a talk with you in that time, we should esteem it a privilege.

We have been much connected with the attempt to establish—in the London School of Economics and Political Science—a specialized place of postgraduate work in those subjects; and though the resources of the institution are most modest, it has at any rate made a promising start. I should much like to hear from you about the progress of the Political Science side of Johns Hopkins. (Mrs. Gilman has kindly asked us to an evening reception on the 18th, when we shall perhaps have the pleasure of meeting you).

We propose to stay at the Mount Vernon Hotel.

Yours very truly

Professor H. B. Adams   Sidney Webb [1]

---

[1] In October 1897 Mr. and Mrs. J. Ramsay Macdonald had visited Adams presenting a note from Jane Addams. This letter indicates

153 — From Edward Eggleston

210 A St. S. E. Washington D. C.

14 April 1898

My dear Prof Adams:

I have yours of yesterday and I will come as you suggest on Saturday. But I can not leave here by B & O, my nearest station until 9.30—I do not know the time of arrival at Baltimore, probably as late as 10.30 which would interfere with your first proposal. I am at your service if you wish me to talk but I hope you will not arrange a talk out of compliment to me. If you'd just as soon I'd rather not talk platitudes to your young men. It is the evil of being a ready speaker that one has so much of that stuff on his conscience. I dont care for historical study for the sake of American citizenship. Living right at the door of Congress in this tiresome time I don't seem to care much for American citizenship; it is a brand that covers a discouraging lot of clap-trap; —the study of history with reference to it has made half a nation of irrational jingoes. Patient investigation among original authorities is very sobering. If I am desired to say something let me get away from the howl of the congressman & the newsboy and talk on some subject that relates to the higher side of our pursuit; the study of history for the sake of culture and mental enlargement. Suppose I say something about the influence of geography on early American life or I don't care what besides, so I may talk as a student to students, and not on that most common-place 'thing—trodden under foot of men and asses—the American citizen. You will not take this too seriously—it only means that I am constitutionally not interested in politics living or dead. I am much obliged for your invitation to luncheon. I had planned to have you eat with me at the Mt. Vernon. I must contrive to see as many of the Ms. about Blair & his college

the progress advanced scholarly work had made in American universities since Adams returned to America in 1876. At that time no European scholar would have thought of turning to America for light on postgraduate work in any subject.

Royal as you care to show me. If Dr. Tyler had only vouch-safed to state the source whence he derived them I would have had them copied for my own use without troubling you.

Sincerely yours
Edwd. Eggleston.

154 — From D. C. Heath

D. C. Heath & Co.
Publishers of Text-Books for Schools and Colleges

110 Boylston Street
22 Sept., 1898. Boston

Professor Herbert B. Adams,
Baltimore, Md.

Dear Sir:—

Dr. Donald in his address at the Amherst Alumni dinner this year invited the graduates to name to the trustees any persons they thought eligible for the position of president of Amherst, and I therefore write to say that it seems to me if Amherst could persuade Professor Woodrow Wilson of Princeton to take the position of president of our college we should be getting an excellent man.

I happen to know that Professor Wilson believes strongly in Amherst, and thinks it has done better work in the particular lines in which he is most interested than most colleges. I sincerely hope you will take pains to look up Professor Wilson's eligibility for the place while you have the matter under consideration.[1] You doubtless already know that his address delivered at the Princeton Centennial was considered the ablest paper of its kind that has ever appeared in this country. It was printed in the *Forum* of December, 1896. He is the author of *Congressional Government* and *The State*, two books that have given him a reputation at home and abroad with which you are of course familiar.

Yours respectfully,
D. C. Heath

---

[1] Adams was a trustee of Amherst.

155 — From D. C. Heath

D. C. Heath & Co.
Publishers of Text-Books for Schools and Colleges
110 Boylston Street
Oct. 11, 1898.   Boston

Professor H. B. Adams,
Johns-Hopkins University,
Baltimore, Md.

Dear Professor Adams:—

Yours of the 8th received. I hasten to acknowledge it and to say that it seems to me that the trustees will make a great mistake if they place great stress on getting an Amherst man, and still greater mistake if they place great stress on getting a clergyman. I do not object to an Amherst man,—I am one myself, and there are a lot of good Amherst fellows,—but I want to see some better Amherst men than any we have yet produced and I think it is possible to make them but only by pursuing a broader, more businesslike policy than has been the case up to date.

Only yesterday I was discussing the question with some Amherst graduates as to why the Dartmouth graduates in our vicinity seemed to have so much more college spirit and, on the whole, to have succeeded better and we concluded that the " clergy " side of Amherst had been emphasized too much. Now I think this statement will be understood without ampli-fication and yet I should like to see a good magazine article, by somebody who would be taken as an authority in the matter, on the question as to whether a college can in these days be best served by a President who is a clergyman, or perhaps I should say by a clergyman who is President, and a college attain the highest ideals in scholarship, as well as in morals, by starting out with the idea that religion and the ministry are to be the great themes and occupations to be kept always in sight. I believe in religion, but not in religions. I think, however, that the less that is said about religion that does

not come in a very natural and proper way by evolution the
better. I also believe in clergymen, but I believe in them
more strongly than they do in themselves. They should be
a great power in this close of the 19th century but they are
not and the people are discovering it so fully, and the average
college boy even more fully, I think it is a mistake to lay
great stress on this matter.

I know you will pardon me for speaking plainly. You
would rather have my exact opinion if my opinion is worth
anything, and I force it on you simply because Dr. Donald
invited help of this sort from the alumni in his speech at the
alumni dinner, as you know having been present. I know
that Dr. Wilson is not in very good health but that seems to
me the only thing that can be urged against him for such a
position and yet he may not have the proper executive ability
and may lack a great many other things. I mention him only
because he seemed to me one of the men well worth considering.

Very truly yours,

D. C. Heath.

156 — From John S. Bassett

Durham, N. C.
Nov. 15, 1898.

My dear Dr. Adams,

You have been running on a month & a half since your
vacation & I have not written to you yet. I had expected to
do better but very many things have been on me this fall. I
have been busily engaged by my college work & besides that
I have much to do to keep up with the political affairs of the
state & with the warm controversy now on with regard to
Trinity. As to the latter, it arises out of the fact that we get
some money from members of the Tobacco trust. The report
was put into circulation some time ago that we owned stock
in the trust: well, the holy element of the church howled. The
report was not true strictly speaking, but we did for a time

get dividends from $100,000 in that company. There is an element in favor of withdrawing from the support of the college on account of this affair. I wish they would go. They are soreheads in general & will always be a source of annoyance to us. There has been a strong attempt against the President of the college; but he has come out all right so far. The Church Conference meets this week & it will decide the matter of withdrawal. It looks like an overwhelming victory for the college, so far as I can see. There are a lot of fools in N. C. and it takes some time to lick them into shape. We are doing it gradually. Trinity is about the only place in the state that is trying to do it. I used to be aweary of the place; but as long as the fool-killing is to go on I want to be here to see the fun. I regret to say that Weaver's father is one of the leaders in the attack on the unholy habit of taking the money that Providence sends. He is ordinarily a very good man but is in bad company here.

As to the election, I might write you a whole book.[1] We are crowing down here like children because we have settled the negro question. We don't see that we have not settled it by half. At best we have only postponed it. We have used a great deal of intimidation and a great deal of fraud, I fear; although it is hard to get information about the latter. I do not have the honor to agree with most of my fellow Anglo Saxons on the negro question. There are three things at least which we may do with the negro in politics (1) We may swallow him, nauseating as the dose is; & we may thus submit to the small evils that may come from giving him a vote & an occasional office —(2) We may adopt an educational qualification honestly administered—(3) we may resort to fraud & force to keep him out of office. Of these methods the last is the worst, the second the best. It is the last that we have adopted. The campaign has been one of passion. It has raised political ideals which 20 yrs. of wise rule will not lay. It has created a state of insecurity for property in the east

---

[1] Adams evidently thought this portion of the letter particularly interesting because he marked it and sent it to President Gilman. See also letter No. 161.

17

that is most unfortunate for business. It has ended in a riot at Wilmington—justifiable at no point—a riot directly due to the "white man's campaign." After the election was carried—and the county which had a large negro majority went democratic by a large majority—the negroes were quiet. They were really cowed. The whites realized that they controlled the Legislature. They organized a mob. The leader was a lawyer, an ex-Congressman, a campaign speaker. They went down to destroy the printing office of a negro on account of an offence committed 4 months ago—an offence which is after all a mere statement of opinion. The press was destroyed —& the office set on fire. This was the initial action of the riot. The negroes made no resistance. In a negro quarter in the suburbs some armed white men met some negroes standing on the street. There was no claim that the negroes were doing wrong. They were order[ed] to disperse. They refused. They were fired into. It was claimed they fired first. I don't think many white people who understand things in the state believe the charge. After this the riot was well on. About a dozen negroes were killed—almost as many more were seriously wounded—It is now said 21 will die. The republican city government to quiet matters resigned & put in Democrats. They showed a yielding spirit. The first act of the new govt. was to elect the leader of the mob Mayor of the town. He who had just led a mob issues a proclamation commanding that "all further violence" shall stop. If he had any sense of humor he must have split his undergarments laughing at his own joke. This whole thing was not necessary because in 2 months the democratic Legislature will meet & can & will change affairs in Wilmington. You must not be led astray by what you see about negro rule in N. C. If you were to come to N. C. & talk with the leading citizens— white democrats—you would hear a good deal of talk in a general way about the rule of the negro. When this campaign started I had not heard anything about the evils of negro rule. I took pains to ask about it from many sources—reliable it seemed to me. I learned that in some of the negro counties there were some negro magistrates—a very few county commissioners, & some school committeemen. In no case did I hear that they were disposed to abuse the privilege. They were reported not to be self-assertive & as a rule presided over courts in company with white men. They were disposed to be guided in their action by the advice of white men. They were reported to be quiet. The democratic press opened up on the negro question. Considering the violence of its attack it seems to me the negro has acted admirably. Villified, abused, denounced as the unclean thing he has kept his peace; he has been patient. He has borne what no other people in history have borne. He has done it largely because he is a coward in the presence of white men.

Since the election is over there is some reäction of opinion against the violence and passion of the past few days; but the great majority of people are in support of all that has been done. The democratic press approves of it openly so far as I can see—You must know that there is not a daily paper in the State that is not Democratic. I have tried down in my portion of the vineyard to cause men to think. I have spoken as clearly as a teacher ought to speak on a partisan question; but I have had but little effect. I am going on in my way. But there is not much hope that I shall be able to reform the State. What would you do to meet the disease if you were the physician? Tell it not in Gath—but do you know, the white man will continue to run over the negro until the negro learns how to defend himself. If about 25 white men were dead as the result of the Wilmington riot the whites would be a little more careful of how they go into a race riot there again. As long as the negro question is in politics so long will these things occur.

Now I have said my say. You may not have cared to hear it; but it occurred to me you won't have a chance to hear this side of this miserable affair from many North Carolinians. Good night. I will send you some printed matter soon.

Yours very sincerely—

J. S. Bassett

157 — From Berthold Fernow

Trenton, N. J., Nov. 21/98

My dear Mr. Adams,

I do not know yet, whether I shall be able to attend the meeting of the Am. Hist. Assn. at New Haven next month, but I want to go on record as in favor of adopting the Review as the organ of the Association.

In this connection let me tell you of a step I took some ten years ago. I had a plan to start such a review as a private undertaking and for that purpose had secured the promise of the leading historical writers of Europe, Central and South America to become contributors. Some of them are dead now, Ranke, Cesare Cantù and others, but there still are enough remaining, who could occasionally write an interesting article on American history from the outsider's standpoint.

But retournons à notre mouton, the Review. A good advertising agent should be able to secure for such a high class publication sufficient advertisements to pay for the printing of it. Another suggestion is, to make the whole Association provide the publication fund as follows: Raise the annual dues to $5.00, give $2.50 to the Review and keep the other 2½ for the Association.

I want your help in another direction. In my work here on the early Jersey records, I have come upon an Indian vocabulary, which my slight knowledge of Algonquin tells me is not pure Algonquin, but, as I suspect, intermixed with Finnish. To whom could I submit it for ascertaining what it is? The State Library here has no dictionary, which I could consult.

Very truly yours

Fernow

Prof. Herbert B. Adams

158 — From John S. Bassett

Trinity College
Durham, N. C.
Dec. 16, 1898

Dear Dr. Adams.

Your letter of today is not the first time that you have said something to me that has encouraged me. I am deeply gratified at your kind words. You have shown me my duty many times before this. I see it now more than ever. If I can set a limit to this wildfire of prejudice that is in the South I will do it. It is a difficult task, and a delicate one: the point is to come at the people—not through blows & kicks; but through kindness. Tell the Northern philanthropists that *the way to help the Negro in the South is to educate the white man.* I think it would have a most fortunate result if the Northern Presbyterians would give a certain amount of money to the Southern Presbyterian colleges. It might be for any purpose—perhaps for a loan fund would be best. $5000 a year for this purpose to a college like Davidson would be ample. It would give the North a *raison d'etre* for its Southern sympathy—which I think the South does not always appreciate:—Of course I refer to the masses in the South. Do you think this could be worked? You have so much & we so little. Of course this would apply also to other denominations. The way to appeal to the Southerner is through his religion. The way to work the reform is through the church, but it will take a broad churchman to do it. This is no time to lose one's head. I am pleased that my remarks met the approval of Dr. Gilman & of Dr. Steiner. They are both men qualified to know; Dr. Gilman by experience, & Dr. Steiner is, it seems to me, a man of great good sense. I don't think this trouble at Wilmington merely will set us back any more than the social & intellectual conditions behind it—which we have had all along. I cannot believe that any outside capital will ever develop the South: it must come from the Southern people themselves, if it comes at all.

I wish I could go to New Haven; but it is an impossibility. The program seems very good—perhaps better than usual. Sometime ago I had a circular in reference to the adoption of the Am. Hist. Review. I should vote for the proposed plan; but why not form a stock company, shares to be taken by members of the Association at $50.00 each and each holder of a share to get the review free? Would not company management be more efficient than Association management? I wish a man of my complexion were needed to do the office work of such a review & I could get the place.

The History of Slavery I think I can furnish sometime in the late winter or early spring. I am thinking of writing two or perhaps three lectures on the Negro—one on the Slave period—& one, or two, on the present & future. An historical approach to the subject is perhaps the best way into it.

By the way, I hope you found all your books & other office furniture O. K. on your return from your vacation. I enjoyed my summer greatly & drew much real good from it. With kindest regards to Drs. Steiner & Vincent & to yourself I am

Yours very sincerely

J. S. Bassett

159 — From James A. Woodburn

Indiana University,
Bloomington.
Dec. 26, 1898.

My dear Dr.

I have been waiting an opportunity all fall to write to you. I presume the American Historical Association is willing to increase its membership. I should be glad to nominate a number of worthy Indiana people,—Superintendents and Principals of High Schools who are especially interested in the study and the teaching of History. We have organized an historical section of our State Teachers' Association, and I feel sure a number of these teachers would be glad to join

the American Historical Association, if invited to do so. If
it is the desire and policy of the Association to enlarge its
membership among teachers of History in secondary schools,
I should be glad to send in a list of names during the next
year of persons who would accept membership. I think it
would not be at all difficult to enlarge our membership in this
way. I should be glad to see the Association adopt the American Historical Review and send it to the members at the
present fee, if it can be done; if not, then for a larger yearly
fee. I wish, also, that the Association would appoint a strong
committee to bring the proper influence upon Congress to
secure a regular, systematic, and well-edited publication of
historical documents. Such a set of government publications
as Richardson's " The Presidents Messages " might well have
been under the control of our Association. There is a great
opportunity for government work in historical publications,
and our Association ought to take the leadership and direction
of the work. I wish very much that I could be in New Haven
this week, but it seems impossible. We owe certain duties to
our State Association of Teachers, and I have not been at its
sessions for several years.

I have been wishing to seek your judgment and advice
upon a subject which has been of interest to me for some time.
That is, as to the advisability of an attempt, in which several
might co-operate, to publish a series of monographs on
American Political History,—such a series as Putnams'
Quootions-of-the-Day series. 1 can think of thirty good sub
jects for such a series; and 1 believe a number of small vol
umes on important subjects would prove to be very useful to
the student, the teacher, and the general reader. Is there
not a possibility of a useful work in this direction?

I asked the publishers to send a copy of my edition of
Lecky's " American Revolution " to you. I am using it with
one of my classes this year and it works splendidly. It is
in use also in the Chicago University. I wish I had as good
a study on " The Old Confederation and the Making of the
Constitution "—though it need not be so long. I shall look
with much interest for the report of the Association this

week. Can you not send me a New Haven daily for a couple
of days, or leave my name with the enclosed stamps with a
news agent at the hotel?

I wish you would propose for membership in the Association
at this time, Mr. Charles F. Patterson, Supt. of Schools, Edinburgh, Ind. and Mr. N. C. Heironimus, 207 National Road,.
Richmond, Ind.

With best wishes for the season, I am

> Very sincerely yours,
>
> James A. Woodburn

160 — From Samuel Macauley Jackson

> 692 West End Avenue
> New York City.
> February 13, 1899.

Prof. H. B. Adams, Ph. D. Ll. D.
Johns Hopkins University,
Baltimore, Md.

Dear Mr. Adams:

My paper on "Zwingli and the Baptist Party in Zurich"
is a chapter in my biography of Zwingli and there I hope it
will appear. I had not intended to submit it to Mr. Cyrus
Adler's censorship. Dr. Norcross's paper on "Erasmus" will
not be published by the Association, nor should it be as it
is not scholarly enough. Dr. Richard's paper on "The Beginnings of Protestant Worship" was so almost entirely limited to Luther that I told him to call it "Beginnings of
Lutheran Worship." I told him also to send it on and I hope
Mr Adler will kindly allow it to be printed. If he does not
then it will be incumbent upon me to announce to my clerical
friends whom I ask to write papers for the Association that
their papers will not be published because a Jew says they
must not be![1]

---

[1] The article by George Norcross on "Erasmus, the Prince of the
Humanists" was published in the Annual Report of the American

Allow me to call your attention to Annual Report of the
American Historical Association, 1896, Vol. I, p. 22, 1. 7.
" The programme committee . . . of which the secretary of
the [Church History] section shall be ex-officio a member,
and no such paper shall be published without his consent."
This clause has been entirely overlooked. I had no part in
the programme or publications of 1897 and 1898.

Very truly yours,

Samuel Macauley Jackson.

161 — From John S. Bassett

Durham, N. C.
Feb. 18, 1899.

My dear Dr. Adams,

I am glad to know that the Historical Association is to
issue the American Historical Review. I regret that I did
not go to New Haven; but expect to attend the next meeting,
at Boston. I have not received the Reports of the Association
since 1896. Can you tell me to whom I should write to investigate the matter? Ought the Jan., 1899, number of the
Review to be sent to me? I have not had it. What would be
a good subject for a paper to offer to the Association? And
would a suitable paper be taken by the committee on program?

The " white man's government " is in full blast in this
State. They are arranging a suffrage amendment which will
disfranchise the negro and not disfranchise the ignorant
whites. At best it is an enamelled lie. If it honestly provided for an intellectual standard for suffrage it would be a
good thing. It is one more step in the educating of our people
that it is right to lie, to steal, & to defy all honesty in order
to keep a certain party in power. They are introducing a
Jim-Crow-car law & it will likely be passed. They introduced
a Jim-Crow-bed law—i. e., a law to prevent white men and

Historical Association for 1898, after some editorial censorship. Dr.
Richard's paper was not published. See letter No. 166.

negro women occupying the same bed but that is hung up in committee. It will not pass, for fear it would overthrow the "white man's government." They are about to pass an election law which will throw the election machinery into the hands of one party & with the suffrage amendment it is probable that the "white man's party" will be in power for years. There is not a daily paper in the State that is opposing any of these laws as to principle. A dozen weeklies—Populists & Republicans—are raising the weakest kind of a protest. The Democrats of the legislature are entirely in the hands of populistic theorists. They are passing a law forbidding a trust to collect a debt in the State courts, & forbidding any college to acquire any stock in a trust. The latter is a blow at Trinity & Wake Forest & is inspired by Clark. They are passing a law to tax railroads from 2% to 3% on gross earnings and quoting Drs. Ely & H. C. Adams as authority. The citation to Ely seems to be legitimately made. I am not able to say about that to Adams. The people at Trinity are disappointed but not despairing. I shall continue to protest against this spirit. A few have heard me—a few will continue to hear. Do you know anybody who would present to the Trinity College Historical Society a picture of Lincoln? I should do it myself but it would have a bad effect. If I could get such a picture I should prepare an address on Lincoln and deliver it when the picture was presented. I think some good could be done in that way.

I am working away on the negro. I think you will have it by April, although I have had some interruptions. I am glad to have outlines of your lectures to teachers. We are doing something somewhat similar in connection with our Library. I shall send you some printed matter in connection therewith in a few days. I have decided to make some changes in my courses of instruction for next year which I can best explain by sending you the catalogue on which the printer is now at work. I have, among other things, offered a course preparatory to law. Before Xmas, I offer [a] course of lectures on basis of Holland's Jurisprudence & Markby's Elements of Law. It deals with the nature of law & with legal definitions.

After Xmas, I offer a course on the history of law, beginning
with Maine—going through Roman law—mediaeval law—
Canon law & giving some attention to the history of great
English lawyers. The following year and alternating with it
I shall offer Administrative development before Xmas, &
American Politics after Xmas. Another feature is narrative
history. France, Germany, England & the Nineteenth Century
will have one-half year each. These two lines of study are to
be open to Juniors & Seniors & are electives. The Freshman
& Sophomores will have completed Anct. & Med. History.

I return a clipping you sent me sometime ago. Thank you
for sending it. Thank you also for an account of the New
Haven meeting of the Hist. Association. Anything which will
serve to keep closer my connection with the world up there
will always be welcome to me; and more welcome still the
kindness which prompts you to send it.

Yours very sincerely,

John S. Bassett

162 — From Elroy M. Avery

Cleveland, March 6, 1899.

Professor Herbert B. Adams,

Dear Sir:

Your letter of February 22nd is at hand.[1] I am much
obliged to you for its suggestion but I am not willing quite
yet to let you go. I am wholly in sympathy with your idea
that I ought to lay more stress on the nineteenth century
than on the aborigines or on colonial America. It is largely
to this end that I want stakes stuck along the stream of
American history dividing it into twelve such parts that each
of the parts may be approximately equal in importance to
each of the other parts. I do not intend these stakes to

---

[1] On Feb. 18, Avery had written announcing his plan for a history
of the United States "from Pre-glacial Man to Dewey and Otis,"
in twelve volumes. He asked Adams to suggest the dates for each
volume so as to have a " well-balanced " history.

measure Procrustean limits for the several volumes but rather to blaze my way as I go. For instance, fifty years of American history covering the settlement of the slavery question is entitled to more space than the corresponding fifty years of the seventeenth century; therefore, the volume that covers the history of the seventeenth century ought to include more years than the later volume just mentioned. Now what I still want you to do is to help me stick these guiding stakes something as follows: The first volume to include the story of pre-historic America, the account of early geographic knowledge, Prince Henry of Portugal, Columbus, Vespucius, St. Dié, etc., to the end of the period of American discovery. The second volume to take in the period of exploration, Ponce, Balboa, Cortez, DeSoto, Coronado, etc., to the second stake which I want you to stick for me; and so on for the twelve volumes ending with the year 1900. These stakes having been stuck by you and some of them perhaps shifted a little by me will be of great assistance in the final revision of my manuscript. I think that you will see that the sticking of the stakes can be best done by one who knows nothing about my manuscript, because the *only* object sought is that the work when finished may be well balanced. You mention Winsor and Bancroft; I have in mind the sad fate of the Bryant's history that Sidney Howard Gay wrote, in which considerably more than three volumes are devoted to the story anterior to the adoption of the constitution and considerably less than one volume to the history of the United States proper. I do not expect anything more than suggestions from you that may be comparable to the rough free hand pencil sketch of the architect from which later are made plans drawn to scale. I know, of course, it would not be fair to hold you in any wise responsible for the distribution of my material and I agree that there shall never be any embarrassment coming to you on account of any suggestions that you may make to me in accordance with this request.

Now then, can't you help me?

Yours very truly,

Elroy M. Avery

163 — From James Bryce

House of Commons
Mar. 21/99

Dear Professor Adams

Thank you very much for your very interesting paper on Tocqueville & Jared Sparks.[1] Their letters are curious and instructive: and it was specially noteworthy to find that Tocqueville's view about the Tyranny of the Majority, which made such an impression in Europe upon J. S. Mill & others, & was a text for anti-democrats for many years, was criticized so acutely, and, on the whole, so justly, by Sparks on its first appearance in the world.

I was interested also in being reminded of our " Tocqueville night " at Johns Hopkins univ many years ago; and of the contributions to views of local Verhältnisse and Volksbewusstseinformen made by Albert Shaw & others.

I trust you are well & thriving.

Sincerely yours,

James Bryce

164 — From John S. Bassett

Durham, N. C.
April 3, 1899.

My Dear Dr. Adams,

I will accept the position of representative for the A. Hist. Assoc. in N. C. which you as Secretary recently offered me. I had already thought of some new members, thinking that with the new arrangement the Association would like more members. I had spoken to two gentlemen both of whom are willing to join. One is Hon. H. G. Conor, of Wilson, N. C. He is an ex-judge recently speaker of the House of Reps in N. C. & in every respect would be worth having. Another is Mr. W. K. Boyd of Durham, N. C. He is a very promising man. His paper on Holden is the best study on Reconstruction

---

[1] *Jared Sparks and Alexis De Tocqueville* published in the sixteenth volume of the *Studies*.

in N. C. that I have seen. He teaches history in the Trinity
Park High School; but I hope to get him to go to J. H. U.
next year. He is in many ways a better man than Weaver
and he is of the new way of thinking in the South. When
Sikes heard him read a portion of the Holden paper he (Sks)
remarked that you would be pleased with the paper at the
Hopkins seminary. I have some others in mind but will write
them first.

I have for some time wanted to see the real students of
history in N. C. united into an organization: yet I do not
believe in sectional organizations. Do you think the national
organization would consider a plan by which the members
in North Carolina might organize themselves into a N. C.
chapter or section. Such articles as would be prepared by the
N. C. section for publication to be submitted for acceptance
to the national officers? This State has had so little real historical interest in it that it cannot support an historical
society outright. I think it would be possible under the suggested plan to get something less than 20 members who would
be really interested in the matter and who would form the
nucleus of a movement which would eventually build up considerable interest in history. If you think anything could be
made of this I will confer with some of the N. C. men &
present a definite memorial to the national association.

I have read " Red Rock." It is, so far as I can form an
estimate of the times, an exaggeration, at some points a
caricature. Page has not an historical mind. His studies in
the Old South are absolutely inaccurate. His negro char-
acters are idealized, and his Southern gentlemen ditto. Yet
his negro stories—as Meh Lady—are the best he has written.
He has one good story of the whites—" Run to Seed "—a
short story in the volume with Elskit, I think. In fact I have
seldom seen a Virginian who could see slavery & the South
generally in a clear historical light. As for N. C. it rallied
against the populistic legislation and defeated much of it in
the Senate committees. The next issue is the suffrage amendment. It will pass, because it will be voted on under the new

elections law which is the worst since the days of reconstruction.

I hope to send you the slavery ms. by April 15. Can you give me the address of Prof. Emmott?

Kindly remember me to Drs. Vincent, Steiner & Ballagh.

Yours very sincerely,

J. S. Bassett

165 — From George W. Knight

Ohio State University
Columbus

April 18, 1899

My dear Professor Adams:—

I am looking for a man to fill a newly created assistantship in American History, for next year, and doubtless you have among your men one or two whom you may recommend—if available.

I should like to run upon a man who has done a good bit of specializing in American history, who is fairly up in American bibliography, who can take in hand much of the special topic and special report work of our younger undergraduates in American history courses, and who can handle students in our initial course (sophomores, mainly) in American history, along the lines of Hart's "Formation" and Wilson's "Division and Reunion" with supplemental lectures and special reports by students. Actual class-room work eight to ten hours per week (two sections) but with examination papers, etc. in higher courses to care for. Finally, I should prefer a man who has a little experience in teaching either in secondary or higher work.

We can give him the first year $700, but with gradual increases thereafter (if retained or reappointed) and an ultimate assistant-professorship. Nothing guaranteed beyond the first year, however.

If men are as plentiful as in other years the place ought to afford a fair opening for some bright fellow, tho' the salary be low.

Can you suggest some one, and tell me something in detail about him?

I have a man or two already named to me but the field is entirely open as yet. I shall hope to have made a selection in time so that the formal appointment can be made when the governing Board next meets—about the middle of May.

Yours truly

Geo. W. Knight

Professor Herbert B. Adams
Johns Hopkins Univ.
Baltimore, Md.

166 — From A. Howard Clark

Washington, D. C., Apl 22 1899.

Dear Doctor Adams

The Report has gone to the Public Printer and I do hope the work may go on promptly to completion.—The Secretary [1] decided to leave out Professor Richards paper as there was doubt about the advisability of printing it—It is interesting but would perhaps provoke some opposition. In the paper on Erasmus some rather too strong paragraphs were omitted.[2]

Very truly yrs

A Howard Clark

---

[1] The Secretary of the Smithsonian Institution, the governmental agency through which the reports of the American Historical Association have been published.

[2] See letter No. 160.

167 — From Reuben G. Thwaites

The State Historical Society of Wisconsin
Madison

April 28, 1899.

Dr. H. B. Adams,
Johns Hopkins University,
Baltimore, Maryland.

My dear Dr. Adams:—

Yours of the 25th at hand. When the list of members is included, 3 or 4 copies of the pamphlet would probably suffice for me.

My suggestion for the Bibliographical Committee is this: I would like to have done for the various publications of the Historical Societies— national, State, and local,—together with historical serials not emanating from such societies, what is done for general periodical literature by Poole's Index. A great deal of interesting and often quite important matter gets into these historical publications which is as good as lost except to the members of the several societies, or to those others who are in the habit of consulting them. As it is now, any man engaged in historical research, has to look over, at great waste of time and patience, great heaps of Transactions and journals which *may* have something he wants. I myself have wasted days at this sort of thing, and of course as a librarian see many others engaged in the same manner. It might be supposed that these scattered publications cover certain well-defined fields, and only an investigator in those fields would think of examining them. But as a matter of fact, they often go far afield. One often comes across in them, stray information of which he wishes he knew, when engaged in some previous work.

I have talked this project over with Professor Turner, who agrees with me fully, and thinks it ought to be pushed as a boon to students of American history.

The field is, I think, an important one, and deserves consideration by our Committee. If you think so, I wish you would synopsize the above, and send it out to the other mem-

18

bers. If adopted, we should probably have to ask the Association to give us a small appropriation for cataloguing and publication of an annual Bibliography. But these are details which may be arranged after conference. I am going to the national library meeting at Atlanta, a week hence, and then spend the rest of May in the East, inspecting library appliances. After June I shall be at home for the rest of the summer.

1. The following is a partial list of current historical serials, which are worth indexing regularly: American Catholic Historical Researches. (q.) Phila.; Annals of Iowa. (q.) Des Moines; Dedham Historical Register, (q.) Dedham, Mass.; Essex Antiquarian. (m.) Salem, Mass. Essex Institute Historical Collections. -(q.) Salem, Mass. Iowa Historical Record. (q.) Iowa City; Kansas University Quarterly. Lawrence; Maine Bugle. (q.) Rockland, Me.; Maine Hist. and Gen. Recorder. (q.) Portland; Maine Historical Society, Collections. (q.) New York Genealogical and Biographical Record. (q.) New York; Old Northwest Gen. Quart. Columbus; Putnam's Monthly Hist. Magazine. Salem, Mass.; Revue Canadienne. (m.) Montreal; Rhode Island Historical Society Publications. (q.) Providence; Southern History Association, Pubs. (q.) Washington, D. C.; Virginia Magazine of History and Biography. (q.) Richmond; William and Mary College Quarterly Historical Magazine. Williamsburg, Va.

2. Then, there are numerous old files, which need indexing—some of them of great value. The following are merely samples—all of them containing excellent historical material, and not covered in Poole: Olden Time; Magazine of New England History; Salem Press Hist. & Gen. Register; Massachusetts Magazine; Pennsylvania Magazine; Columbian Magazine; American Magazine; Canadian Antiquary; Canadian Magazine; British American Magazine; Revue de Montreal; Quebec Literary and Historical Society Pubs.; Genius of the West; Chicago Magazine; Western Magazine; Western Messenger, and Western American Review.

Yours very sincerely,

R. G. Thwaites
Secy. & Supt.

168 — From James Schouler

Intervale, N. H., June 15/ 99.

My dear Adams:

Yours of 13th has reached me here. You are indeed my true & faithful friend; and if I may at any time do you a service in return I shall not fail you. But you have somewhat misconceived the tenor of our conversation, last winter, as I recall it. I knew that the Johns Hopkins conferred no honorary degrees and I had not the slightest idea of having an exception asked in my favor. What I desired was, that Prest Gilman & you would present my name at some other institution, such as Harvard recognizes in her Quinquennial Catalogue, so that I might find a place there in its coming issue. Not only Yale, Columbia, Princeton or the like would serve, but Amherst, Brown, Univ of Virginia & various others of less endowment, occupied with undergraduate work. Why I mentioned President Gilman was, because of a circumstance which I thought he had remembered, but presume now that he has forgotten. About five years ago, & with this same object in view of not having my doctorate ignored in the Harvard catalogue, I addressed President Gilman with reference to an " LL D " at Yale. He was pleased in his reply to say that I ought to have the degree; but he added that he could not then apply, for the reason that he had just done so on behalf of another person, whose name he mentioned, & who, I think, was one of your Hopkins faculty. The impression I received was, that Presidents of various institutions influence mutually the conferring of honorary degrees, & that Hopkins, though giving no such honors, looked after her friends upon other opportunities elsewhere.

Let it all pass, now. I shall never appear again as an *applicant* for earthly honors as long as I live. Very likely, after my final volume of history is issued, next October, I shall take up a post-graduate study at Harvard, with the view of *earning* a " Ph. D." in course there. In that way I may get into the green pastures.

I wish very much you could bring up your valise & make me a few days' visit some time during your coming vacation. Do think of this, my friend. My wife & I will be here & hereabouts, quite constantly, this summer, & delighted to have you for a guest.

Yours very truly,

James Schouler.

P. S. Was it not four lectures on " Founders of the Republic," you expected from me next year? (Franklin—Washington—Hamilton & Jefferson.) If so, I think I can prepare them—not, however, to be delivered until next March.

169 — From Albert Bushnell Hart

15 Appian Way, Cambridge.
January 2, 1900.

My dear Professor Adams:

At the recent meeting of the American Historical Association the Council appointed as a committee to consider a monographic history of the United States the following persons:—

Charles Francis Adams, Boston
Herbert B. Adams, Baltimore
William A. Dunning, New York.
John Bach McMaster, Philadelphia.
Frederick J. Turner, Madison, Wis.
Moses Coit Tyler, Ithaca, N. Y.
Albert Bushnell Hart, Cambridge,—Chairman.

The mandate of the Committee is expressed in the following votes of the Council:

(a) " Voted, That a Committee be appointed for one year to consider the expediency of a history of the United States, including the colonial period, to be prepared on the cooperative method.

(b) " Voted, That the said Committee investigate the desirability of such a history; the problem of general editorship; and the prospects for publication on such a commercial basis that the authors may have a reasonable payment for their work.

(c) "Voted, That this Committee be instructed to report at the Detroit meeting of the Association.

This inquiry arises out of the suggestion that perhaps the time has come for the preparation of what may possibly become a standard history of the United States. Should such a work be possible and desirable, the Association would be the natural centre from which it might spring. The difficulties and defects of the cooperative method are obvious, and no one stands committed to the proposition that it must be a function of the Association to take any responsibility for the proposed publication. The work of the Committee is, therefore, simply one of inquiry with no prejudgment of the question.

It is not expected that the committee will take much of the time of the members. Perhaps it may be found convenient to hold a conference on the subject on the day of the Council meeting in New York next November. Before very long, however, I will send out to the members of the Committee some inquiries with a view to arriving at a method of investigating the question. You will notice that all the members of the Committee are men who have had some experience in writing on American history.

Very truly yours,

Albert Bushnell Hart

Professor H. B. Adams.

You were very much missed at the meeting as the official action of the Association will show.

170 — From A. Howard Clark

American Historical Association
Office of the Assistant Secretary.

Smithsonian Institution, Washington, D. C., —May 17, 1900.

My dear Adams —

The Association has grown so that the expense of printing extra copies of the Report will be a continued heavy drain on the Treasury unless we can get the law changed and I have, I hope, without any fuss or correspondence made the way clear for such change. The chairman of the House Committee on Printing is a personal friend of mine and I showed him the need of more copies of the Reports to supply the demands on Senators and Members as well as for the Association. I drew the accompanying Resolution and Mr. Heatwole put it through the Committee himself and yesterday got it passed by the House without objection.[1] I have asked Senator Hoar to say a word about it to Senator Platt, chairman of the Senate Printing Committee, and am confident it will pass the Senate without objection or attracting attention. You notice that the measure appears to be something Congress wants for itself and the Association as benefitting incidentally. This is a very much better way, I think, than to have the Association appealing to Congress. You remember how easily we got the law fixed in 1894 by a simple letter from you to Senator Gorman asking him to amend the Printing Act so as to include the Hist. Reports.

Very truly yours

A Howard Clark

---

[1] House Joint Resolution 255, 56th Congress 1st session, provided that "there be printed of the annual reports of the American Historical Association, beginning with the report of the year eighteen hundred and ninety-nine, two thousand five hundred copies in addition to those provided for under existing law, of which five hundred copies shall be for the use of the Senate, one thousand copies for the use of the House of Representatives, and one thousand copies for the use of the American Historical Association."

171 — *From A. Howard Clark*

American Historical Association
Office of the Assistant Secretary.

Smithsonian Institution, Washington, D. C., May 22, 1900.

My dear Adams—

I do not think the Association needs more members unless it be historians or those positively interested in it, and who will consider membership an honor and be an honor to the Association. To appeal to the public to " join " for what they may get in the shape of publications is the lowest of motives. Last winter Doctor Bowen sent me draft of a circular that Macmillan proposed to issue and as it was a clear mercenary, publishers circular, telling what could be gained by subscribing for the Review and the Reports, and how much pleasure and profit would be derived by mingling with eminent men in meetings of the Association, I opposed the plan strongly. Doctor Bowen replied to my criticisms that he and Hart would no doubt be able to modify the circular to meet my views and have the Association issue it—but it was not done just as I expected. A circular was printed and a copy was sent to me, which I enclose, bearing my name " for the Council." I immediately wrote to Bowen objecting to the issuance of the circular but he replied that my objection came late as some were already distributed. I presume many have been distributed since, for replies come occasionally as you know.

Now the Council had no meeting to discuss this circular and although the form was doubtless shown to several of them it was not an order of the Council or for the Council as I am made to say in print. This entire plan of getting more and more members seems to me to aim at getting more money for the Review, as Professor Hart practically admits. I told Doctor Bowen a year ago that the Association is now on a splendid national foundation, and while we want to help the Review in every proper way, we must not subordinate the

Association to a publishing concern. I said that the Review appeared to me to be of more expense to the Association than needful for the reason that the Board of Editors consume the allowance. This hint brought the statement from Professor Hart " that of the $2400 received from the publishers for editorial expenses about $1200 go for the managing editors meagre salary and about $800 for articles, leaving about $400 for the railroad fares of the editors in attending the quarterly editors' meetings."

I enclose clipping from the Washington Post of recent date, I think last Monday, that may be of interest. I do not know what Committee or Association sent Prof. Hart to the President—it is rather a bold stroke for any Association.[1]

Very truly yours

A Howard Clark

Dr. Herbert B. Adams.
Baltimore.

172 — From Frederic Bancroft

Paris, July 26, 1900
Aux Soins de Monsieur Beydon
54 rue Caumartin.

My dear Adams:

I meant [to] send you a few lines and my hearty thanks, shortly after receiving your friendly note.

The weather and the Exposition (here as at Chicago in 1893) confirm the axiom that like causes produce like results, and that historical meetings and congresses should be held far from the ordinary crowd.—Hearing Brunetière filled me with reproaches for not having gone to Baltimore to follow his course there a few years ago. There have been some pleasant features to the Congress, but the weather is so hot that it destroys nearly all curiosity and all sociability. Official

---

[1] The clipping states that Professor Hart called upon President McKinley and presented the plans of a " committee which has been organized to obtain and publish the facts relative to the Philippine problem."

France knows how to be gracious and entertaining, but not much appreciation is shown by the delegates. Heat, no doubt.

Otherwise I have been having what I needed—an entire change and an easily-going life among old French friends from whom I could learn much without an effort, go bicycling and sightseeing without having any plans of my own, and an opportunity to read much French literature in very pleasant surroundings.

Latterly, I have been working with some system, reading the historians and critics and comparing them with those (or the lack of them) in some other countries or generations.

Has it every occurred to you that none of our schools of history has ever produced a historian of special merit as both scholar and writer?—Do you remember our conversation years ago about the superiority of the French to the Germans as historical writers etc.? I am following some thoughts and investigations growing out of our common opinion. I am also thinking of the best method, style etc. to present the " History of the Confederacy." In a few days I settle in the country with my French friends. In October I shall meet the literary and historical world here. I may return to Washington in Nov. or Dec. I hope you are entirely well and happy again.

Cordially yours,

F. B.

173 - From Albert Bushnell Hart

15 Appian Way,
October 25, 1900.

My dear Adams:

Now I do mean to talk business. You are one of the committee appointed by the Association to consider the question of a general monographic history under the auspices of the American Historical Association. I mean to hold a meeting of that committee on Friday afternoon, November 30, in New York; but meanwhile will you write me your views on the general subject? I enclose another copy of the outline suggestions to refresh your memory: it is possible that I did not send you one in the spring, knowing that you were out of the country.

There is no doubt that several large publishers would be very willing to take the financial responsibility for such a work.

Sincerely yours,

Albert Bushnell Hart

Professor H. B. Adams.

QUERIES AS TO A COOPERATIVE HISTORY OF THE UNITED STATES UNDER THE AUSPICES OF THE AMERICAN HISTORICAL ASSOCIATION.

At the meeting of the American Historical Association, December 29, 1899, the following persons were appointed a committee to consider the question of a cooperative history of the United States, and to report thereon to the Association at the meeting in December, 1900.

Albert Bushnell Hart, Cambridge, Chairman.

Charles Francis Adams, Boston.	John Bach McMaster, Philadelphia.
Herbert B. Adams, Baltimore.	Frederick J. Turner, Madison, Wis.
Wm. A. Dunning, New York.	Moses Coit Tyler, Ithaca, N. Y.

This appointment arose out of a suggestion which was placed on the docket of the Council meeting of November, 1898, and was taken up again in 1899, that perhaps a new activity of the Association might be the undertaking of a general history of the United States on a large scale, to extend from the discovery of America to the present time.

The first task of the Committee is plainly to find out its own mind upon the questions involved in this proposition, questions which may be stated as follows:

1. Is there need of a comprehensive general history of our country, embodying the results of the latest scholarship?

2. Is a competent individual likely to attempt this task?

3. Can the work be accomplished on a cooperative plan?

4. Is such a plan commercially practicable?

5. Can the American Historical Association take the responsibility for organizing such a work?

I. QUESTION OF THE NECESSITY OF A GENERAL WORK.

The argument in favor of a broad and thorough going history of the United States is that there is no such work at present. There is hardly a single one volume outline of merit except the school histories: there is as yet no two volume or larger accurate work which covers the whole field; and no work of historical value on a large scale has ever been completed; Winsor's *Narrative and Critical History* practically stops at about the War of 1812, and the projected complete histories of Bancroft and Hildreth fall short; while the principal recent historians have chosen limited areas. The argument against such a general history is the very considerable labor of preparing it, and the fact that this history of the country is now accumulating so fast that any comprehensive work after a few years begins to pass out of currency.

II. QUESTION OF A GENERAL HISTORY BY AN INDIVIDUAL.

An ideal general history would of course be written by one man, who should avail himself of the great monographic literature of the last twenty-five years. Perhaps some member of the Committee is acquainted with the right man for this task. No person of the requisite learning, judgment, youth, good health and presumptive long life is known to the chairman. Mr. John Fiske is the only man whose writings include considerable parts of the whole area, and he is of course not available for a more detailed account of the same field.

III. QUESTION OF A COOPERATIVE HISTORY.

If no individual comes forward, can the work be done by a combination of individuals? The advantages of a division of labor and of specialization are apparent; the disadvantages of the cooperative system are well illustrated by Winsor's unrivalled work, in which there is a lack of coordination between the various parts, and there are also many great gaps. One of the serious questions for the Committee to consider is, whether it is possible so to subdivide the great field into periods and movements that have a unity of their own as reasonably to cover the ground. It will be noted that the critical apparatus in the Winsor work is not a necessary part of a cooperative history.

IV. COMMERCIAL QUESTION.

Any such work must involve a heavy initial expense: the authors ought to be paid in proportion to such work elsewhere, and the books ought to be handsomely manufactured. If, as has been suggested, there be twenty or twenty-five small volumes, instead of gathering the history into a smaller number of great volumes, the expense of publication is proportionately increased. It is of course impossible for the Association to take any financial responsibility; if the work is done at all, a publisher must be found who has faith enough in the scheme to risk his money in it. The success of Winsor's work, and the republication of the Lord Acton series in this country seem to show that there is a market here for historical works on a large scale.

V. PARTICIPATION OF THE AMERICAN HISTORICAL ASSOCIATION.

This is the most serious point of all. Participation is not necessary in order to secure the work, for if the plan is in itself practicable, doubtless some publisher would be ready to take it up as a private venture; the *imprimatur* of the Association would undoubtedly be a very great commercial advantage, and would make more easy a proper return to the authors. On the other hand, the Association has something to gain from making clear to the world its ability to take the direction of a great historical work; responsibility will give it a raison d'etre. The question for us to consider is how far, through a committee appointed for that purpose or otherwise, the Association can exercise real control over such a scheme, so as to give a guaranty of scholarship and soundness to a work for which the Association took responsibility; and also how far the Association would stimulate a knowledge of our own history and aid historical science by undertaking the work.

VI. SUMMARY.

The five questions stated above come down to three:

1. Is a general history of the United States on a large scale by the cooperative method worth while?

2. Is such a work commercially so promising that a good publisher would take it up?

3. Ought the American Historical Association to take any part in such a work?

Upon all the points here suggested, and upon other considerations which may present themselves to the minds of other members of the Committee, the Chairman requests you to express an opinion. If it is the decided judgment of the Committee that the thing is not worth while, will not pay, or is not a function of the Association, our labors will be speedily ended. If, however, the Committee think the scheme worth a deeper investigation, the Chairman will collate the replies, and will raise questions of detail as to organization, subdivision of the field, selection of writers, and so on, as a centre for further discussion; it will then be time to consider whether the scheme, though perhaps in itself desirable, can be worked out on a practicable basis.

VII. CONSULTATION WITH PUBLISHERS.

Upon several of the questions here proposed the opinion of publishers is desirable, and I therefore suggest that before replying to this circular, each member of the Committee consult some large publisher, not only on the commercial question, but also on the questions of the desirability of the work, the method and the participation of the Association. Publishers will also have some ideas as to the most efficient way of organizing such a scheme, as to illustrations, as to the amount and kind of apparatus, as to the most available form of volume, etc, all of which will be helpful to the Committee.

ALBERT BUSHNELL HART.

Cambridge, Mass., January 17, 1900.

174 — From Albert Bushnell Hart

Cambridge, Mass., November 10, 1900.

My dear Sir:

Of the problems which the committee on a monographic history of the United States has to solve one is conclusively settled, namely, the commercial question. Two publishers in Boston and four in New York have been asked to give an opinion upon the general scheme of a monographic history to be issued in small separate volumes under the auspices of the American Historical Association, but entirely at the financial risk of the publishers. Five of the six publishers would be glad to take such a series; and three of them, Appleton, Harper, and Macmillan, are extremely anxious to secure such a work. In our further deliberations, therefore, we may assume that such a history would find a publisher and market, and consequently a sale.

This leaves for us to consider before making our report in December the two main questions of expediency; first, whether a cooperative work of the kind suggested can be carried out so as to be a real contribution to historical literature.

It seems to be the opinion of publishers that such a piece of work can be made to hang together sufficiently to form a reasonably well ordered whole, but we shall have to approach the question from the point of view of historical writers, who see the difficulties of the subject and the differences of method.

If we come to the conclusion that such a series is worth while, the other great question for us to decide is whether the American Historical Association ought to take any action in the premise. The farthest responsibility proposed is that the Association should appoint at its next meeting a committee on monographic history, and authorize such committee to select a general editor and arrange with a publisher; thenceforward, the committee to act as advisor; any expenses incident to the work of the committee to be met by the publisher; on the other hand, the title page to bear the statement that it was published under the supervision and auspices of the American Historical Association. The only further detail would be the question whether members of the Association should have any special opportunity to buy the book.

In order to have a face to face discussion of these questions, I hereby call a meeting of the committee to be held at the Metropolitan Club, New York, at three-thirty P. M., on Friday afternoon, November 30, just preceding the meeting of the Council of the Association. Should we come to any result it can then be communicated to the Council for its information and any such action as it may see fit to take. Should you be unable to be present may I ask you to send me your views on the pending questions in writing. Since Professor Turner is out of the country I have asked Professor A. C. MacLaughlin to sit as his alternative.

Very truly yours,

Albert Bushnell Hart

Chairman

Prof. H. B. Adams

175 — From Clarence W. Bowen

New York, Nov. 24, 1900.

My dear Adams:—

I have your letter about resigning and I sincerely hope
that you will not insist upon it. If you resign I feel like
resigning myself for I can work so much better with you
than with anyone that I have ever been associated with. The
work is greater for both of us now than it was years ago.
You have written that you cannot come to the meeting of the
Council next week but I have assumed that you would be at
the meeting in Detroit. If you go to the meeting in Detroit
that will relieve me from the necessity of going there. I will
do everything in my power to attend to the work necessary to
be done at the Council meeting next week. You and I agree
on all points connected with the policy of the Association to
such an extent that I am anxious to have the same relationship continue awhile longer. I personally want to do as you
would like to have done but aside from our personal relations
you know that I have at heart the best interests of the Association. Mr. Lea's name has been suggested as the 2nd Vice-
President. There are three other names that I thought we
should add to the list of 2nd Vice-Presidents: Daniel C. Gilman, John Fiske and John Hay. Mr. Gilman was the first
one who ever suggested the idea of forming an association.
I heard this from the lips of Moses Coit Tyler a year ago.
This was a year before the Association was formed in Saratoga. You know what John Fiske has done and he certainly
deserves the honor, and John Hay might come along after
him. I have looked over the list of members and these three
men seem to me the most eminent. Now after this list has
been disposed of we could take the younger men who would
come along whom you know intimately and some of whose
names were suggested awhile ago by Mr. Hart. After the
three names first spoken of have been made 2nd Vice-President during the next two or three years I thought if you
insisted upon your resignation to elect you 2nd Vice-Presi-

dent. I wish now to state, however, that if you insist upon
your resignation as Secretary I shall suggest to the Council
and to others that we select you as our 2nd Vice-President.

I have written the above to you as I have thought it out
for that is the way I have always done. The point that has
been criticised of what we have done during the past year has
been the work done by Macmillan in getting names for the
Association in order to increase the circulation of the magazine. Hart has been in favor of this but I have not been particularly in favor of it but have yielded to the influence of
others; now the Council will decide definitely what must be
done on this point. I think the only way to do is to have men
nominated regularly after their permission has been obtained
before election. This is the way we have always done in the
past and it has worked all right. Hart has made many suggestions to me and I have acted on some of them early in the
year without consulting you simply for the reason that your
health was so poor that I did not wish to bother you in any
way and that has been his desire as well. We have wanted
to relieve you of as much work as possible.

* * * *

I am, as always,

Your sincere friend,

Clarence W. Bowen

176 - *From James Schouler*

(Confidential) 60 Congress St., Boston, Mass.,
Dec. 1st., 1900.

Prof. Herbert B. Adams,
Johns Hopkins University, Baltimore, Md.

My Dear Friend Adams:—

At our Council meeting, yesterday, I brought up the
matter of soliciting subscriptions for the Review by soliciting memberships, and I think I put the matter in such a

19

way that there was a disposition to check such business. I proposed that our subsidy should be for the next year a gross sum, so as to ignore an increased or diminished membership; but Dr. Bowen seemed otherwise disposed, and so I deferred to his intimate knowledge of our financial interests. I even went so far as to express my dislike of book reviews, etc., such as institute comparisons or make invidious remarks as between members of the Association; referring in this connection to a rule of our Massachusetts Historical Society which forbids all such comments, reflections or criticisms, concerning members still living; but this, of course I intended merely for general effect and not for specific action. In the whole matter I have carefully avoided committing you or referring in any way to your possible views on the subject.

As you know, I have from the outset disliked this alliance between our Association and the Historical Review under existing conditions. I have been cognizant of several instances where the opinions printed by the editors (usually, however, expressed by some outside writer who has sent in his contribution) are such as to produce rankling and ill feeling among our leading members, while on the other hand others have the good fortune to be praised and courted. It is one thing to have an organ, for some purposes of our own, and quite another to make ourselves responsible for a pet magazine with ambitious purposes apart. I fear that if such conditions continue our Association will be ruled in aims and membership by the editors and publishers of such a magazine; that they will control the membership, guide the counsels, and choose the officers who are nominally to appoint them; besides using the money of our treasury to support contributors of their own selection. Already a job seems to loom up in the horizon for a grand cooperative history of the United States, under the auspices of our Association, as you will see by the prepared brief which I enclose to you.

Dr. Bowen gave us a fine dinner, last evening, and I only wish you could have been there yourself. Besides many members of the Council there were several professors—Jameson,

Stephens, MacDonald, Judson, etc. Senator Hoar was present, also Charles Francis Adams, Rhodes, and the two assistant secretaries.

Yours very truly,

James Schouler

177 — From John S. Bassett

Trinity College
Durham, N. C.

December 7, 1900.

Dear Dr. Adams—

Your letter should have been answered some days ago, but just at the time I received it the Gottis—Kilgo trial came on and I lost a week out of my work waiting around a court house to be called on the witness stand; and all my work has got so much behind that I am only now beginning to catch up somewhat.

The dates for the lectures I leave entirely to you. I had expected to make one on the Negro in Africa—one on the Negro in American Slavery, and one on the Negro in American Freedom. I propose to make the treatment historical rather than sociological, although it will not be possible to avoid a mention of problems of today. If you desire to make the number only two I can arrange to cut my treatment down to that number. The compensation you mention is satisfactory. There was no agreement about this when we first corresponded on the subject.

I have been much surprised to hear of Dr. Gilman's determination to resign. He has been a great force in American education. His service in planning the Hopkins on the lines of research & German method can never be forgotten by American educators. I never realized this so fully as during the past summer when I was on my visit to Cambridge. There will, of course, be much said about Dr. Gilman's successor. I stand for you for the place, and if there is anything I can do to secure your election I shall gladly do it. If I only knew to whom I might write as the representative of your interest in the matter I should write at once.

Our college goes on well. We have just selected the design of a pretty gray brick library building which will cost $40,000 and hold 100,000 vols. The N. C. Literary and Historical Society has just been launched with good prospects. One of its sections is a Committee on Libraries. I hope it will be able to do some really good work in establishing village libraries.

The Gottis case went against us. He swore that he had been damaged by the publication of Dr. Kilgo's speech in the Clark—Kilgo matter and the jury gave him $20,000 damages. The suit was against Dr. Kilgo, B. N. Duke, & W. R. Odell— the latter being trustees & rich men. The jury were prejudiced against Duke on account of the tobacco trust. Everybody concedes that it was a political verdict. It does not affect Kilgo's standing at all. The Conference of the Church has just given him a unanimous endorsement. We hope to get the decision in the Supreme Court to which we have appealed.

Yours very truly—

J. S. Bassett

178 — From John S. Bassett

Durham, N. C.
18 December, 1900.

Dear Dr. Adams,

Prof. F. W. Moore, of Vanderbilt, is making efforts to get the 1902 meeting of the American Historical Association in Nashville, Tenn. I hope it will be possible to secure the adoption of his project. There is an appreciable revival of interest in the teaching of history in the South. It is probable that this meeting would do much to intensify such a revival. Nashville is no more inaccessible to the men of the North-west, and to the men of the middle west, than New York.

The only men inconvenienced would be the men from states
north of the Potomac & east of the mountains, and these, I
think, would not mind some inconvenience if they do us some
real good. I hope you can see your way to giving your influence to get the Association to make this missionary journey
into the South.

I received this morning the program of the Ann Arbor
meeting. It is a very attractive one. I greatly regret that I
cannot attend. I never before felt so much of a desire to
attend a meeting. I hope it will be possible for me to attend
all the meetings after this.

With the program is an announcement of a history of the
United States on the Coöperative plan. It seems to me a
good thing. Under that plan it will be possible, I hope, to
write the history of N. C. without catering to popular prejudices in Mecklenburg matters etc.

Yours very sincerely,

J. S. Bassett

179 — From John H. Finley

Princeton, N. J.
January 2, 1901.

Dear Dr. Adams:

As I come to my desk this morning to begin the work of
a new year and a new century, I make it my first duty and
pleasure to write to you, for it is to you that I owe first of all
many of the opportunities that came to me in the old century,
and to your advice that I am indebted for guidance when I
was in doubt as to the road I should take. Looking back over
these few years, since I left the University, from this ground
of vantage I feel that the issue has commended the several
decisions which have led to it. The way has been circuitous
but I doubt if I could have found a better one, for every
prospect which it has presented has seemed more promising
than that immediately preceding.—But I must not be talking
in this fashion about myself. My only excuse for saying so

much is that you have a right to a good share of the credit, if indeed there is enough credit to give anyone satisfaction in the claim to the greater part of it.

I have not known what to say in answer to your letter about the Shaw lectures. I am working out a course on the " Expansion of Europe" which will involve a discussion of the phenomena of the spilling over of Europe into the other continents, the processes under which the expatriates have conquered and occupied new lands and erected new States and the relations of the new to one another and to the old. I shall come by this way to our own expansion problems. Whether I shall in the working out of this course uncover any pay ore in diplomacy I cannot now predict with any certainty. I can only say now that to go back to Johns Hopkins under such auspices and in such service, would be most gratifying to me, if only I could do something worth while.

I have been hoping to get down to Baltimore before this, but as I still keep my New York connections I have to go that way nearly every week. Can't you come up and spend a few days with us? I have only a hut of a house here and it is full with my little family and guests, but the Inn is just around the corner and we can temporarily annex it. Vincent or Willoughby told me that you were not so well again. An outing here in this peaceful town might be a restorative. At any rate I should be delighted to have you come up and I am sure Woodrow Wilson would as strongly urge your coming.

With the heartiest and best of all good wishes for the new days and with grateful remembrance of the old days

Sincerely yours

John H. Finley [1]

---

[1] John H. Finley was a graduate student under Adams during the years 1887-1889.

180 — From James Schouler

Boston, Jan. 6, 1901.

My dear friend Adams:

That was a good long letter for you to write, considering that you were in quarantine. I was glad indeed to get it, but you must take good care of yourself and get thoroughly restored before you use the pen much. Your paper arrived before the letter, & hence I sent you a copy of that *New York Herald* article, not supposing it had met your eye. Strange is it, however, that a friend's vision will peer into the immense recesses of a Sunday casual paper & discover what one would think was buried from sight. I wrote my " Century " essay upon request, was well paid for it, & furthermore read it in somewhat modified shape, last December, before the girls at Radcliffe College & the sedate men, fellowmembers, of the Massachusetts Historical Society. It may now be passed out of sight with all the vast literature of a kindred nature drawn forth by the departure of old 1900.

Your article in the *Baltimore News* I read with great interest. I felt the same fascination about your good city with its hospitable people & Monument Square, in those happier years when the Johns Hopkins University seemed rich & prosperous & I felt myself an integral part of its instruction corps. Perhaps some day again, if you are there still, I shall make Baltimore my spring headquarters; but just now Washington pulls more strongly & my wife prefers it.

I had not felt quite assured of what transpired at Detroit, though Mr. A. Howard Clark made me a call here, early last week, and stated that the slate, as made up when he left for this State, Saturday morning, proposed our desired list of new officers. I hear since to the same effect from your Professor Vincent, though particulars are not stated. This, of course, means that you are put into the progression groove as Vice-President, & for this I am heartily glad. Yes, we will close up a little before next year's gathering at Washington. Clark's promotion to Secretary in your place was the right

thing. They tell me that the Detroit meeting was very successful & full of enthusiasm. Yet, what a strange meeting in
some respects! You, our "original Secretary," absent &
tendering your resignation; Clark, the acting Secretary &
assistant, called away by telegram to attend his mother's
funeral; Eggleston, the President, sick & unable to appear;
Moses Coit Tyler, the designated President of the new year,
dying at his home within twenty-four hours of the moment
when his election would have been carried. Not the least of
the pleasures & responsibilities that now await you, will be
the "November recess" meeting of the Council in New York
City,—especially if some one gives the body as handsome a
dinner as did our Treasurer the last time.

I have, of course, read with great concern & regret of President Gilman's intended resignation at the Hopkins. The
"obituaries" are quite seasonable, &, as you say, he must
have enjoyed reading them. I rather thought, from something he said to me, last spring, following his only partial
success with your close-fisted legislature of Maryland, that his
intended European excursion was preliminary to taking such
a step. Certainly, so far as educational work goes & lifting
the standard of our University before the country, Dr. Gilman
is good for ten years more, & it is doubtful whether any successor will improve upon him. But perhaps he does wisely,
both for himself & the rest of you, in retiring just at the
present time. It affords a good opportunity for a dramatic
presentation of the needs of the Hopkins, & for rallying
friends & contributions; & I hope Dr. G. will still keep in
Baltimore (or perhaps New York City?) & give things his
counsel & countenance. But for a successor just now—& in
fact it seems the requirement of all such high officials—the
man wanted should be one who can rake in the money, &
furnish the much-needed financial endowments. Either a
President who can supply the funds from his own coffers or
those of near relatives & family—as some have done—or else
one who can smite the rocks—(Rockafellers?)—and make
them gush out. President Gilman has well given public

notice & made general appeal; indeed, during all these years he has done much more; but we are getting now to where College Presidents must individualize in their appeals, buttonhole the rich; or, as I have heard said of one highly successful educator in this respect, get an aged rich man to write his will in favor of the institution, & then lock up the instrument in the college safe. How do the candidates you mention promise in such functions? Maryland ought to be liberal with such a University, as Virginia has been with the University which Jefferson founded. A Virginian in this city, a friend of mine, says that the Old Dominion, in all her poverty, has appropriated $50,000 a year regularly for the University of Virginia, thus giving the educational staff a sure & comfortable support. As you are an expert in University details, you will know whether or not that statement is correct.

I have written Professor Vincent, in response to his inquiries, & he has arranged suitable days for my four lectures in March—the first of them set for my next birth-day anniversary (March 20th). I presume Donovan Hall, at the 4 P.M. or 5 P.M. hour, is intended; if so, all right. To-morrow I mean to send you the long-delayed presentation copy of my volume 6—I had hoped to give it to you personally last summer at my mountain home. " Civil War " is to be bought separately, specially bound & lettered with that title; if preferred to the title of " Vol. 6." There has been little advertising, nor have reviewers, with a few exceptions, helped this final volume much; and yet it has sold out three editions already & circulates handsomely, bringing up the whole set well besides.

Yours very truly,

James Schouler

P. S. Mrs. Schouler joins me in sending a " happy new year," & thanking you for your good wishes.

181 — From David Kinley

Berlin, Germany,
Feb. 16, 1901.

Prof. H. B. Adams, Ph. D., Balto.

Dear Dr. Adams :—

The enclosed list came to hand this morning and I have corrected it as well as I can from memory. Doubtless you can easily verify the additions I have made. The article on Trusts and ,that on the Census are important items in my list and should not be omitted.

I am glad to get this word from you,—it shows me that you are well enough to be at work again. I am very glad to know it, and hope you may keep well.

You will be surprised to find that I am over here. You will remember that I was offered the position now held by Prof. Falkner. Had I found an opportunity to lecture with you I would have taken a position in Washington. But my College Faculty kindly sent me an urgent request to remain, colleagues on the other College Faculties in the University also urged me to stay, and various members of the Board of Trustees kindly did the same. I asked no promises for the future, but felt assured that any reasonable requests of mine would, under such circumstances, be granted. So the Trustees gave me a year off on half salary, and have asked the legislature for an appropriation of $15,000 a year for the development of the political sciences. There are at present six of us at work in these lines and the above amount, if obtained, will enable us to do great things in our section.

I have been in Germany (Eisenach, Göttingen and Berlin) since Nov. 1. Of course I am not attending lectures, although I " visit " the various lecture rooms and am " looking over " some of the educational institutions. I shall visit Halle, Leipzig, Vienna, Munich, Frankfurt A. M. Köln, Paris, & various British Universities, besides taking a flying trip of two weeks to Constantinople.

I think far less of Germans, German education and German educational institutions than I did six months ago! I cannot help feeling that they (especially the *Prussians*) are a narrow people, outwardly polite, but at heart somewhat coarse. I wonder why American students come here to study in any lines except such as Germanic philology, Roman jurisprudence, German history, art, and other subjects in which the material can be found only here. It seems to me that in all technical education, and in university subjects like Economics, chemistry, all history *except* German, mathematics, Literature, &c &c., Germany has nothing to offer that our students cannot get better in our own country. I visited the famous Charlottenburg Hochschule in company with one of our profs. of Chemistry, spending the better part of three days in the process. We went directly to the head men and they kindly took us about, showing us the inside of things. We agreed, after our visit, that with the single exception of the *artistic* side of Architecture, the institution can hardly be put in the same class with the Mass. Inst. of Tech., Troy Polytech. Inst., the Sheff. Sci. Sch. &c &c, or with our own work in Illinois. I have visited the seminaries of Lewis & Cohn and have seen something of the work here in Economics. But it is in no way superior to our own and, I think, is much *below* our *best*.

The temper of the people at present is not pleasant! They are breathing hatred towards England, and—with not much less intensity—towards the U. S. The real reason, veil it as they may, is that England, and, in less measure, the U. S., stands in the way of their colonial and commercial ambition. That is the answer I have gotten—when I pressed my questions -from Thüringen to Berlin! A recent magazine article puts it in a nutshell, thus: "Wir brauchen Neuland für unsere Bauern, da steht uns aber in Südafrika und sonst der Brite im Wege. . . . Raum für alle hat die Erde—das ist die Weisheit einer friedlichen Märchenzeit,"—and so Germany would have England vacate and the U. S. stay, at home!!! But enough of this!

I had an hour's chat with Wagner the other day,—mainly

political. He is still a believer in the Bismarckian policy!
He declares that the higher tariff on wheat *must* pass, that
Germany must protect her agriculture so as to raise farmers,
since they make the best soldiers; and also that retaliation on
the U. S.—for our high tariff is justifiable!

Frankfurt opens a school of polit. science next October;
Köln, a Handelshochschule in April; Aachen's Handelshoch-
schule is flourishing, as is also that at Leipzig. Mannheim,
Hannover and Berlin " project " similar institutions!

I wish I could be in the country in time to visit the J.H.U.
while in session, but it is hardly possible.

I hadn't been very well last winter & spring (grip) but am
getting into pretty good shape. I am pegging away on a
work on the theory of Money and Credit. It is mostly written,
but I don't know when it will be ready.

I hope all goes well with you. Ambassador White told me
of Pres't. Gilman's resignation, but he knows nothing further.
I shall watch with great interest what the issue shall be.
Good luck now and always to the J.H.U.!!

Please excuse this " scribble " and remember me to Drs.
Sherwood and Vincent and my other friends.

With best wishes and sincere regards I am

Very truly yours

David Kinley [1]

---

[1] David Kinley had been a graduate student during the years 1890-
1892.

INDEX

Acton, Lord, 284.
Adams, Brooks: letter from, 173; paper on suffrage, 173.
Adams, Charles Francis, Jr., 43, 276, 282, 291.
Adams, Charles Kendall: letters from, 78, 147; address by, 127; at Association meeting, 72; consulted about a historical journal, 49; extension lectures, 211; on history at Michigan, 79-80; on teaching of history, 8; praise of Adams, 147-148; work at Michigan, 86.
Adams, George B.: letter from, 244; extension lectures, 211; on relations of Association and Review, 244-245.
Adams, Henry: letters from, 33, 201; Adams asked to review history of, 153; apology for absence when vice-president of Association, 201; offered position on Hopkins faculty, 13-14; on Washington's diary, 33; reviewed von Holst, 38; work praised, 237.
Adams, Henry Carter, 127 n. 2, 186, 266.
Adams, Herbert Baxter: letters from, 27 (2), 31, 35, 40, 54, 69, 71, 72, 82, 99 (2), 126, 131, 145, 148, 150, 152, 155, 177, 209, 216, 221, 225, 229; career at Hopkins, 7, 8, 12-15, 16, 17, 39, 82-87, 145-146, 151, 152, 156, 221; Chautauqua lectures, 17, 211-212, 246; consulted on a historical review, 47-50, 52; contract for biography of Sparks, 81 n. 1; cooperation with historical societies, 54-55; correspondence of, 7, 9 n. 5, 11; death of, 8, 9; description of Curry, 42-43; German studies of, 11, 27, 28-31; influence on historical profession, 9, 10, 16-18; interest in students, 10, 18, 73-74, 94, 100, 178, 242, 293; invitations to lecture, 136-137, 138, 140, 211; on a

national university, 101, 103; on appointments to fellowships, 54-55; on Anglo-American cooperation, 55-56; on French scholarship, 99; on Germanic origins, 113-114; on Gross, 69-70; on Jefferson MSS, 132; on Virginia politics, 41-42; on Wilson, 91 n. 1; plans of study, 17-18, 28, 32, 99; positions offered, 14, 16, 67 n. 1, 85-86, 96, 138, 145, 150, 152, 220-230; proposed cooperative history, 276, 282; proposed series on American government, 209-211, 215, 216-217; rejection of Chicago offer, 147, 150, 155-158, 164; rejection of presidency of Ohio State, 221-230; secretary of Association, 12, 16, 71-72, 126, 296; sketch of by Vincent, 12 n. 11; suggestions of study to Turner, 169; teacher at Smith, 13, 39, 40; title of professorship, 146; trustee of Amherst, 221, 238, 254, 255-256; use of Washington's resources, 32, 131, 148, 157; visit to Virginia, 40; Wilson's opinion of, 90 n. 1; work praised, 18, 32, 33, 34, 46, 57, 63, 64, 70, 108, 111, 131, 147-148, 151, 152 n. 1; writings of, 7, 17, 31, 32, 33, 34, 35, 45, 57, 60, 63, 69 n. 1, 80-82, 103, 106, 108, 115, 119, 164 n. 1, 173, 177, 181, 199, 205-206, 210-211, 215, 269.
Adams, Samuel, 109.
Adolbert College, 234, 249.
Adler, Cyrus, 264.
Allen, William F.: letter from, 87; bibliography by, 60; on history at Wisconsin, 87-88; Turner hope to succeed, 123; work on Rome, 120.
American Historical Association: absence of Henry Adams, 201; censorship of publications, 264-265, 272; connection with Review, 111, 121, 127, 244-245,

301

260, 262, 263, 265, 279-280, 289, 290; creation of Adams, 12, 16, 108; Lodge's resignation, 207; membership drive, 262, 269-270, 289, 290; meeting in South asked, 292-293; officers discussed, 288-289; organization meeting, 71-72; plan for bibliographical work, 273-274; policy of no endorsements, 177; proposed cooperative history, 276-277, 281-286, 287-288, 290; publications of, 126-127, 163, 166, 172, 212, 263. 264, 278; relations with local societies, 126, 128; reports published by government, 278; Rhodes urged as president, 237-238; Schouler on annual programs, 247-248, 290; suggested by Gilman, 288.

American Nation Series: authors professional historians, 9; relation with Association, 276-277, 281-286, 286-287, 290, 293.

Amherst College: Adams a student, 28, 30, 32; Adams a trustee, 221, 238, 254, 255; honorary degree sought, 275; Jameson on, 134; need for lay president, 254, 256; publications by, 84; Wilson proposed as president, 254, 256.

Andrews, Charles M., 56 n. 1, 160.

Angell, James B.: letter from, 98; Adams offered professorship by, 85, 98; suggested as reviewer, 170; World's Fair program, 199.

Ashley, William J.: letter from, 112; on conditions at Oxford, 112; course by, 240.

Atchison Champion, 150 n. 1.

Atkinson, William P., 63.

Atlantic Monthly, 129.

Attainder, in revolutionary Virginia, 124-125.

Avery, Elroy M.: letter from, 267; plan of history by, 267-268.

Baker, Newton D.: letter from, 201; courses at Hopkins, 202; plan for research, 202-203.

Baltimore News, 295.

Bancroft, Frederic: letters from, 73, 76, 237, 280; letters to, 9 n. 5, 72, 99, 131, 148, 177; consulted by Adams, 177; on German professors, 11 n. 9, 76-77, 281; on Grow, 238; position recommended to, 100; plan for history of Confederacy, 281; praise of Rhodes, 237; progress on life of Seward, 238; studies in Germany, 73-74, 76-78; studies of Negro, 73; superiority of French historians, 281; visit to France, 280-281; work praised by Adams, 177.

Bancroft, George: letter from, 32; history by, 135, 268, 283; on Gadsden, 218; referred to, 13, 48, 135.

Ballagh, James C., 239, 246, 271.

Barker, Wharton, 67 n. 1.

Bassett, John S.: letters from, 238, 242, 245, 256, 261, 265, 269, 291, 292; advice on Weaver, 245-246; attitude toward teaching, 242, 246, 259; on a cooperative history, 293; on conditions at Trinity College, 11, 239, 243, 246, 256-257, 292; on Gilman's resignation, 291; on race riots, 257-259, 261; on Review, 262; request for Association meeting in South, 292-293; research on negro and slavery, 238-239, 246, 262, 266, 291; seminary of Southern history, 204; start of publications at Trinity, 242-243.

Bemis, Edward W., 217.

Benjamin, Judah P., 45.

Bigelow, John, 111.

Birney, William, collection of materials on slavery, 162.

Black, James William: letters from, 194, 213; on extension, 195; on Oberlin finances, 195, 213-214; plans of, 214, 215; work at Oberlin, 194-195.

Blackmar, Frank W.: letters from, 149, 248; book by, 131; cooperation suggested by Turner, 160; isolated in Kansas, 248; work in University of Kansas, 149-150, 249.

Bluntschli, Johann K.: letters

from, 29, 33; Adams a student of, 27, 29-30, 31; on American edition of book, 34; on English policy about Turkey, 34.
Boggs, William E., 141.
Bolles, Albert S.: letters from, 67; on availability of Scott, 67-68; on McMaster, 68; resignation of, 107.
Books mentioned: Adams, Henry, 153, 237; Adams, Herbert see Adams, Herbert, writings; Bancroft, History of the Formation of the Constitution, 135; Bryce, American Commonwealth, 188, 203, 209, 210, 236; Bryce, Holy Roman Empire, 46, 95, 104; Centz, Republic of Republics, 45; Colin, Introduction to Study of the Constitution, 203; Curtis, History of the Constitution of the United States, 135; Curtis, Life of Webster, 118; Diesterweg, Methods of Teaching History, 60, 71, 88; Doyle, English in America, 61; Duruy, History of France, 167; Epochs of American History, 119, 120, 165, 194, 271; Federalist, 203; Gardiner, History of England, 167; Gibbon, Decline and Fall, 107; Gneist, Constitutional History, 203; Green, History of English People, 45; von Holst, Constitutional History of the United States, 36, 38; Hosmer, Samuel Adams, 109; Hosmer, Sir Henry Vane, 109-110; Johnson, Normans in Europe, 95; Johnston, United .States Constitution, 167, 170; Lecky, England in the Eighteenth Century, 95, 263; Lodge, Short History of the English Colonies, 45; Lodge, Modern History, 95; McMaster, History of People of United States, 61; Mommsen, History of Rome, 167; Morse, Jefferson, 61; Nitobe, Intercourse between the United States and Japan, 104; Oman, History of Greece, 167; Pertz, Aus Stein's Leben, 77; Poore, Charters and Constitutions, 203; Rhodes,

History of United States, 237; Ritchie, Darwinism in Politics, 189; Ritchie, Principles of State Interference, 189; Seeley, Stein, 104; Staples, Rhode Island in Continental Congress, 59; Stubbs, Constitutional History of England, 113-114, 203; Stubbs, Select Charters, 88, 160; Taswell-Langmead, English Constitutional History, 165, 203; Taylor, Constitutional History, 203; Thwaites, The Colonies, 165; Wilson, Congressional Government, 92 n. 1, 254; Wilson, Division and Reunion, 120, 271; Winsor, Columbus, 176; Winsor, Narrative and Critical History, 9, 175-176, 205, 268, 283, 284; Wright, American Constitutions, 203.
Borgeaud, Charles, 181.
Boutmy, Emile, 99, 130.
Bowen, Clarence W.: letters from, 121, 206, 288; discussion of officers of Association, 288; on Adams's Sparks, 206-207; on Lodge's resignation, 207; on relation of Association to Review, 121, 245, 279-280, 289, 290.
Boyd, William K., 269.
Boyesen, I. K., 191.
Brackett, Jeffrey R., 151.
Bright, John, 110.
Britannica, encyclopaedia, 167.
Brown University: history in, 127-128; honorary degree sought, 275.
Bryant, William C., 268.
Bryce, James: letters from, 51, 53, 70, 186 (2), 187, 269; aid to American scholars, 109, 136, 186-187, 188; American Commonwealth, 188, 203, 209, 210, 236; contributor to Studies, 209, 269; Holy Roman Empire, 46, 95, 104; interest in William and Mary, 186; lectures at Hopkins, 46, 51-52, 90; on a historical review, 53, 55, 57; on American universities, 71; on Freeman's death, 186, 187, 188; on de Tocqueville, 70, 269; subjects sug-

gested by, 187; Wilson on, 90
n. 1; wish for Hopkins Studies,
187.
Bryn Mawr College: advantages
of, 100; Wilson on faculty, 86,
100.
Burgess, John W., 72, 96.
Butler, Benjamin F., bad influence of, 62.

Caldwell, Howard W., 65, 66 n. 1.
California, University of: history in, 95; position in, 75.
Callahan, James M., 234-235.
Cambridge Thursday Evening
Club, 205-206.
Cantù, Cesare, 260.
Centz, P. C., 45.
Chamberlain, W. I.: letters from,
220, 222, 228; letters to, 221,
225, 229; offer of presidency
of Ohio State to Adams, 220-
223, 228-229.
Chamberlin, Thomas C.: on extension teaching, 144-145, 159;
plans for publication, 169;
president of Wisconsin, 123,
161.
Channing, Edward: letter from,
50; at historical meeting, 71;
courses by, 51, 240; on Harvard faculty, 83.
Charleston, S. C., libraries in,
204.
Chautauqua, 17, 211-212, 246.
Cheyney, E. P.: letter from, 208;
plan for publishing texts, 208.
Chicago, University of: Adams
offered position at, 16, 138,
147, 150, 155-158; extension
activities, 163, 169; von Holst's
seminar, 191; Jameson's inaugural lecture, 9 n. 4; progress of, 191, 192; use of
Lecky, 263.
Chicago World's Fair: architecture, 192; history papers at,
193, 198-199; protest against
loan of Declaration of Independence to, 196-197, 198.
Clark, A. Howard: letters from,
196, 272, 278, 279; association
publications censored, 272; on
government publication of
Association reports, 278; on
moving the Declaration of In-

dependence, 196-197; on officers of Association, 295, 296;
on relations of Association and
Review, 279-280.
Colorado, University of, Adams
offered presidency, 138.
Columbia University: history in,
8 n. 2, 84, 107; honorary degree
of, 275; to start publication
of studies, 78; Trent on faculty,
124 n. 1.
Convention, Federal of 1787, opposition to a national university, 103.
Cooley, T. M.: offer of position
at Hopkins, 13, 86; resignation
from Michigan, 98; reviewer
of von Holst, 38.
Coppinger, William, 170.
Cornell College, Iowa, 215.
Cornell University: comparison
with Ohio State, 220, 223, 233;
desire for Adams, 147; Gross
recommended to, 70; history
in, 66, 84; Wilson lectures at,
89.
Cromwell, Oliver, 100.
Curry, J. L. M., 42-43.
Curtis, George T., 118, 135.
Curtius, Ernst, 28.
Cyclopaedias: biographical, 163;
Britannica, 167.

Dartmouth College, 255.
Darwinism, 7, 189.
Davidson College, 261.
Declaration of Independence:
Baker's study of, 202, 203;
protest against moving, 196-
197.
Dewey, Davis R., 75, 86.
Diesterweg, F. A. W., Wegweiser
zur Bildung für Deutsche
Lehrer, 60, 88.
Diman, J. L.: influence of, 59;
offered position at Hopkins,
13, 39.
Doyle, John A.: English in
America, 61; wanted for Re-
view, 111.
Duchesne, Abbé L. M. O., 185.
Duke, B. N., 292.
Duke University, see Trinity Col-
lege.
Dunning, William A., 189, 276,
282.

Dwight, Timothy, 75.

École Libre, 99.
École Pratique des Hautes Études, 185.
Education, Bureau of, Adams's connection with, 17, 106, 115, 157, 164, 210-211.
Eggleston, Edward: letter from, 10 n. 6, 253; lecture at Hopkins, 253; on American opinion, 253; president of Association, 296; study of history for its own sake, 253.
Eliot, Charles W., criticised in Kansas, 150 n. 1.
Ely, Richard T., 70, 85, 86, 87, 130, 164, 185, 266.
Emerton, Ephraim, 71, 83, 123.
Emmott, G. H.: introductions by, 236; on Hopkins faculty, 187 n. 1; notes on lectures of, 165; visit to Bryce, 187, 188.
English Historical Review, 85.
Erasmus, paper on censored, 264, 272.
Erdmannsdörffer, B., 63.
Erickson, Lief, 119.
Extension, see University.

Fairlie, John A.: letter from, 239; education of, 239-241.
Federalists, lectures on, 135.
Ferguson, George D.: letter from, 133; on methods of teaching history, 133.
Fernow, Berthold: letter from, 260; connection of Association with Review, 260; on Indian language, 260; wish for a review, 111, 260.
Finley, John H.: letter from, 293; lectures on expansion of Europe, 294; relations with Adams, 293.
Fiske, John, 237, 283, 288.
Foster, William E.: letters from, 44, 58, 61, 63; on differences between North and South, 45; on history of Providence, R. I., 58-59; on Mc Master's history, 61; on Morse's Jefferson, 61; political views of, 61-62.
Ford, Paul L., 121.
Ford, Worthington C., 177.
Fortnightly Review, 53.

Forum, 153, 254.
France: attitude of Germans toward, 77, 105; College de, 178; scholarly contacts with, 85, 92, 99, 130, 133, 178-180, 183-184, 185, 280-281.
Franklin, Benjamin, 276.
Fredericq, Paul: article by, 133, 185; on work at Hopkins, 85.
Freeman, Edward A.: attack on, 187; biography of, 188; Bryce on, 53-54, 186, 187; contact with Hopkins Studies, 55, 85, 209; death of, 186; lectures at Hopkins, 47; mention of, 112; praise of Adams, 57, 108; visit by Vincent, 181.
Friedenwald, Herbert: letter from, 197; request for aid in finding data, 197-198.

Gadsden, Christopher, rôle in American revolution, 218-219.
Gardiner, Samuel Rawson, 109, 186.
Gates, Merrill E., 220, 222.
Gay, Sidney Howard, 268.
Georgia, University of: extension activities, 170; local opinion on history taught, 167-168, 170; position in history at, 141, 143; work in history at, 166-167.
Germany: historical journals, 35, 36, 48, 85; inferiority of scholarship in, 11, 76-77, 281, 298-299; scholarly contacts with, 11, 17, 27-31, 33-34, 35-37, 63, 71, 73-74, 76-78, 79, 85, 92, 99, 104-106, 108, 110, 130, 180, 298-300; spirit of, 77, 105, 299.
Gibbon, Edward, 107.
Gide, Charles, 130.
Gilman, Daniel Coit: letters from, 39, 46, 57, 69, 72, 130, 152 n. 1, 227; letters to, 27, 30, 31, 40, 54, 71, 90 n. 1, 99, 145, 150, 152, 181; book by, 57; inducements offered to Adams by, 67 n. 1, 152 n. 1; interest in report on race riot, 257 n. 1, 261; offer to Wilson, 90 n. 1; on appointments to Hopkins faculty, 13, 39, 70,

130-131; on cooperation with Bryce, 57; on discussion of current problems, 227; on salaries, 152 n. 1; resignation from Hopkins, 291, 296-297, 300; suggestion of Association, 288; visit to French scholars, 130.

Gilmore, James R., 163.

Gluck, James F., 80.

Gneist, Rudolf, 73, 76, 203.

Goldman, Eric F., 67 n. 1.

Goodell, Abner C., 176.

Gorman, Arthur P., 278.

Göttingen, University of, 116, 117.

Gould, E. R. L.: article by, 53; fellow, 54-55; in series on government, 217; introductions by, 183.

Great Britain: British Museum, 109, 180, 188; German attitude toward, 299; official publications not given, 187-188; opinion on American Revolution, 251; scholarly contacts with, 11, 53, 55, 69, 85, 95, 109-110, 112, 113-114, 133, 180, 181, 186, 187, 188, 209, 235-236, 251, 252, 269, 298; visiting scholars from, 11, 46-47, 51-52, 70-71, 252.

Green, John R., 45, 52.

Grimm, Hermann, 28.

Gross, Charles: Adams on, 69-70; consulted, 196; course by, 240.

Grow, Galusha A., 238.

Guild Merchant, 69.

Guizot, Francois: translator of Sparks's Washington, 82; book used in courses, 87, 107.

Hadley, A. T., 83.

Hall, G. Stanley: letter from, 60; editor of Methods of Teaching History, 60, 71, 88.

Hamilton, Alexander, 62, 276.

Hancock, John, 197.

Harper, publishers, 286.

Harper, William R.: letters from, 138, 211; letter to, 155; extension activities, 163, 211-212; offer of position to Adams, 138, 150, 152, 155-158.

Harris, T. L., 236-237.

Hart, Albert Bushnell: letters from, 276, 281, 286; asked to protest moving of Declaration of Independence, 196; at Harvard, 83; courses by, 240; Epochs of American History, 119, 120, 165, 194, 271; in proposed series on government, 217; plans for cooperative history, 276-277, 281-286, 286-287; relations of Association and Review, 279-280, 289; suggestions for officers, 288.

Harter, Michael D., letter from, 181.

Harvard University: age of graduates, 205; efforts to attract students, 175; graduate work in, 40, 66, 151, 240-242; history in, 51, 71, 83, 240; honorary degree, 275; Jameson on atmosphere, 135; president of criticised, 150; Ticknor at, 117-118; to publish monographs, 84.

Haskins, Charles Homer: letters from, 161, 162; comparison of Hopkins and Wisconsin students, 161-162; on dissertation, 162; on history at Wisconsin, 162-163; prospects at Wisconsin, 161; recommended by Turner, 123; request for information about cyclopaedias, 163; student at Hopkins, 156 n. 1; study of Pennsylvania education, 163; suggested as reviewer, 170; work at Wisconsin praised, 151.

Hay, John, 288.

Heath, D. C.: letters from, 254, 255; qualifications of Amherst president, 255; wish for Wilson as Amherst president, 254, 256.

Hegel, G. W. F., 113.

Heidelberg University: Adams at, 27, 28, 29, 30, 31, 33-34, 100; lack of contact with, 63; moral conditions at, 100.

Henry, Patrick, 124-125, 193, 218.

Hildreth, Richard, 283.

Hirsch, E. G., 191.

Historians: French, 281; German, 76-77, 281; positions for,

8, 16, 75, 98, 103, 141, 161;
professional, 7, 12, 16, 83-84,
128, 149, 164; Roosevelt on,
122; salaries, 14, 68, 85, 93
n. 1, 98, 99, 100, 138, 142, 149,
152, 154, 157, 167, 183, 195,
213, 239, 243, 248, 271; teaching loads, 12-13, 65, 87, 100,
149, 154, 163, 165, 167, 171,
182, 271.
Historische Zeitschrift, 35, 36, 85.
History: Anglo-American, 55,
113-114, 251-252; courses in,
12-13, 51, 73-74, 76-77, 83, 87,
95, 107, 123, 131, 135, 163, 165,
182, 194, 195, 202, 266-267;
local societies for, 54-55, 57,
127, 128, 138-141, 269-270;
materials for, 44, 57, 109, 162,
167, 200, 204, 208; methods
of teaching, 12, 14-15, 60, 66,
71, 79, 83-84, 88, 106, 133, 136,
163, 165, 167, 185, 194, 208;
of Revolution written by north-
erners, 218; plans for a cooperative, 276-277, 281-286,
286-287, 290, 293; scholarly
journal for proposed, 47-50, 52,
53, 111, 127, 260; scientific,
7, 17, 47, 63, 64, 69, 133, 156,
167; subjects studied, 12-13,
14-15, 17, 27, 28, 30, 31, 33,
42, 44, 51, 52, 70, 73, 75, 77-
78, 79, 87, 107, 124, 135, 146,
151, 154, 158, 161, 163, 165,
167, 176, 187, 191, 193, 200,
202, 236, 239, 240, 266-267;
university neglect of, 8, 65, 82-
83, 87.
Hoar, George F.: letter from,
101; aid in securing appropriation, 278; at council dinner, 291; on a national university, 101.
Hodder, Frank H., 97.
von Holst, Hermann Eduard:
letters from, 34, 37; addresses
of, 191, 192, 211; career of,
36, 37, 38; Chicago seminar
of, 191; history by, 36, 38;
interest in the Hopkins, 191;
lack of American materials,
35; offered position at Hopkins, 13, 39; reviews of his
history, 38; visited by Ban-

croft, 73-74, 77-78; wanted for
Review, 111; Wilson to review,
97.
Hopkins, Stephen, 58, 59.
Hosmer, James K.: letter from,
108; on Vane, 109-110; praise
of Adams, 108.
Howard, George E., letter from,
64.
Hoyt, John W., 101 n. 1.
Hughson, Shirley: letter from,
204; research on negro history,
204.
Hull, Charles H., 79.
Hull, William I., 164 n. 1.

Indiana University, 193.
Ingle, Edward, 54-55, 63.
Iowa, University of, presidency
offered to Adams, 85, 96.
Iyenaga, Toyokichi, 129.

Jackson, Andrew, 62.
Jackson, Samuel Macauley: letter from, 264; on censorship
of Association publications,
264-265.
*Jahresberichte der Geschichts-
wissenschaft*, 184.
James, E. J., 86, 155, 158.
James, James A.: letter from,
151; on faculty of Cornell College, 215; on history at Wisconsin, 151; praised by Turner,
169, 175, 212.
Jameson, John Franklin: letters
from, 127, 134; appointment
urged, 87; article by, 53; assistant to Gilman, 57; at Council dinner, 290; book by, 141;
cooperation suggested by Turner, 100; historical work at
Brown, 128; inaugural address
at Chicago, 9 n. 4; lectures
at Hopkins, 134-135, 162; member of Hopkins faculty, 127 n.
2, 130; on Amherst affairs,
134; on Harvard atmosphere,
135; on influence of professional historians, 9 n. 4; on
number of history professors,
8 n. 3; opinion of local historical societies, 127-128; report of Adams's plans, 17-18;
to criticise Haskins disserta-

tion, 162, 163; unable to write volume on government, 216; work in New York, 55.

Japanese students: examination of, 129; preference for Germany, 104-106.

Jefferson, Thomas: connection with attainder case, 124; economic views studied, 191; founder of university, 297; lecture on, 276; manuscripts, 131-132; Morse's life of, 61; removal of William and Mary, 102; spirit of, 62; Ticknor and plans for university, 115-118.

Johns Hopkins University: Adams at, 7, 8, 12-15, 16, 17, 39, 82-87, 145-146, 151, 152, 156, 221; Adams's opinion of, 155-158; alumni feeling, 143, 151, 293; Baker's courses in, 202; Curry interested in, 43; discussion of current problems in, 227; fellowships in, 12, 27, 30, 54, 82; financial condition of, 97, 152 n. 1, 295, 296-297; history in 11, 12-15, 82-87, 90 n. 1, 156, 179, 182-183, 202; influence of, 64-65, 108, 111, 151, 156, 167, 184, 252; library, 44, 162, 187, 188; policy on honorary degrees, 275; project for a Hopkins American history, 123; proximity to Washington, 32, 131, 148; publication by, 14, 49, 55-56, 63; reputation in France, 184; resignation of Gilman, 291, 296-297; southern history the opportunity of, 162; students compared with those of Wisconsin, 161-162; Turner to send students, 175; unlike Ohio State, 220; visits by English scholars, 46-47, 51-52, 70-71, 252.

Johns Hopkins University Studies in Historical and Political Science: anticipated, 49, 52; Bryce's wish for set, 187; in demand, 72, 184, 187, 209; influence of, 14, 65, 78, 84, 108, 111, 133, 156; introduced by Freeman, 55, 209; not sent to

Germany, 63; plans for, 14, 56, 100; publication in, 12, 158, 160, 168, 173-174, 175, 181, 192, 209, 217, 236; reputation in France, 184; started, 14.

Johnston, Alexander, 61, 167-168, 170.

Judson, Harry P., 163, 291.

Kansas, University of: handicaps of faculty, 248-249; position in, 149.

Kasson, John A., 148.

Kilgo, John C., 291-292.

King, John A., 207.

Kinley, David: letter from, 298; hostile German public opinion, 299; inferiority of German universities, 11 n. 9, 298-300.

Kirchwey, George W., letter from, 111.

Kirk, John Foster, 107.

Knies, K., 30.

Knight, George W.: letters from, 146, 154, 271; history of Ohio State, 226; on education in Ohio, 146-147; position in history vacant, 154-155, 271-272.

Lafayette, General M., 118.

Lake Forest College, 193.

Lea, Henry C., 288.

Lecky, W. E. H., 95, 263.

Leete, Governor William, 165.

Levermore, Charles H.: letters from, 10 n. 7, 74, 94; at University of California, 86, 94-95; interest in Latin-American history, 75.

Liberia, history of, 168.

Library, resources, 32, 67, 86, 100, 109, 125, 131, 136-137, 139-140, 143, 149, 151, 162, 165, 167, 168, 178, 180, 185, 187, 188, 192, 204, 208.

Lincoln, Abraham: anticipated by Vane, 110; on state sovereignty, 45; picture of wanted in South, 11, 266.

Lodge, Henry Cabot, 207.

London School of Economics, 252.

Longmans Green & Co., 120.

Low, Seth, 216.

Lynch law, study urged by Bryce, 187.

Macdonald, J. Ramsay, 252.
McKinley, President William B., 280.
McLaughlin, Andrew C., 170, 289.
McMaster, John Bach: at Pennsylvania, 14, 85; consulted, 196; on committee for cooperative history, 276, 282; opinion on history by, 61; qualities of, 68.
Macmillan & Co.: letters to, 209, 216; interest in cooperative history, 286; plan for series on government, 209-211; work for increased membership in Association, 289.
McPherson, John H. T.: letters from, 166, 170; attacked by southern paper, 167-168, 170; in University of Georgia, 166-167; journals to review work by, 170; on extension activities, 171.
Macvane, Silas M., 240.
Madison, James, 118.
Magazine of American History, 53 n. 1, 63 n. 1.
Mahan, Alfred T., 245.
Mahon, Lord, 207.
Mahone, William, in Virginia politics, 41-42.
Maine, Sir Henry, 69, 85.
Marburg, Theodore: letter from, 188; on English conservatives, 189-190; studies at Oxford, 189-190.
Marshall, John, 125.
Maryland Historical Society, 32 n. 1, 57.
Massachusetts Historical Society, 207, 290, 295.
Massachusetts Institute of Technology: Dewey on faculty, 86; historical laboratory of, 63.
Mather, Cotton, 166, 172.
Matthews, Brander, 8 n. 2.
Meekins, Lynn R., letter from, 200.
Merriam, Lucius S., 214.
Miami University, 146.
Michigan, University of: graduate work in, 66; history in, 8, 13, 79-80, 107; offers to Adams, 85, 98; prospects of, 223, 233; to publish monographs, 84.

Mill, John Stuart, 269.
Miller, T. Ewing, 232-233.
Mommsen, Theodore, 108.
Monod, Gabriel, 85, 183, 185.
Monticello: Jefferson at, 117, 118; visited by Adams, 40.
Monumenta Germaniae Historica, 31, 133.
Moore, Benjamin P., 81 n. 1.
Moore, F. W., 292.
Moore, John Bassett, 177.
Morley, John, 53, 236.
Morrill Act, 141.
Morse, John T., 61.
Moses, Bernard, 95.
Motley, John L., 218, 237.
Murray, Nicholas, in charge of Hopkins publications, 163, 168, 175, 185.

Nation: article in, 110; on a biographical cyclopaedia, 163; quoted, 35; review by Adams in, 45; reviews in, 38, 61, 176, 199; wish for a historical review, 127.
Nebraska, University of: history in, 65; presidency offered to Adams, 85.
Newberry Library, 192.
New England Historical and Genealogical Register, 57 n. 1.
New York Herald, 295.
Nitobe, Inazo [Ota]: letter from, 104; monograph by, 104; on German universities and life, 104-106.
North American Review, 38, 189.
North Carolina, race riots in, 257-259, 261.

Oberlin College: finances of, 195, 213-214; history in, 194-195, 214.
Odell, W. R., 292.
Ohio State University: dismissal of W. Q. Scott, 230-234; enrollment and faculty, 220, 222; finances of, 146-147, 220, 222, 223-224, 233; history position in, 154-155; political and religious influences on, 220, 231-234; powers and tenure of president, 224-225, 226, 228-229, 230-234; presidency offered to Adams, 16, 220-230.

Ohio University, 146.
Ota, *see* Nitobe.
Otis, James, 218.
Otto, Emil, letter from, 29.
Oxford: on Freeman's successor, 186; tutorial system criticised, 112; work in by Marburg, 189-190; Woodburn to study at, 235.

Page, Thomas Nelson, works criticised, 270.
Page, Walter Hines: letter from, 153; on book reviews, 153-154.
Parkman, Francis: on Puritan characteristics, 172; work praised, 237.
Paton, J. B., letter from, 251.
Peabody Education Fund, 42, 43.
Peabody Library, 55.
Pennsylvania, University of: Adams offered position in, 67, 85; consideration of McMaster, 67-68; history in, 84, 106-107.
Periodicals, historical, listed, 274.
Perrin, John W.: letter from, 191; on seminar of von Holst, 191; on University of Chicago, 191-192.
Phillips, Josiah, attainted in Virginia, 124-125.
Pickering, Lizzie Sparks, 81 n. 1.
Pinkertons, study suggested by Bryce, 187.
Plymouth, local trade of colony, 58.
Political Science: at Hopkins, 14-15, 82-87, 99, 202, 252; at other universities, 78, 83, 84, 107, 189-190, 214, 240-241, 298; scholarly journal proposed, 47, 49; series on American government planned, 209-210, 215, 216-217; studied by Adams, 27, 28, 29, 30, 31, 34; subjects studied, 92, 99, 112, 209-210; Wilson's lectures on, 87, 89, 93, 99, 241.
Political Science Quarterly, 84.
Poole, W. F., 122.
Poole's Index, 273.
Princeton University: history in, 84; honorary degree sought, 275; Wilson at, 90 n. 1, 254.
Providence, R. I., interesting history of, 58-59.

Providence Journal, 176.
Publishing: Association, 263, 264-265, 272; at universities, 14, 84, 169, 242; by local historical societies, 54, 55, 127-128, 139; cooperative history, 277, 282, 284, 286, 286-288; Harper, 286; Henry Holt, 74; Houghton Mifflin, 72, 109; Macmillan, 209-211, 215, 216-217, 286, 289; monographs in history, 84; papers of statesmen, 131; Putnam, 219; scholarly journal, 47, 49, 50, 52, 53; source materials, 208.
Puritans, characteristics of, 172.
Putnam, publishers, 219.

Quellenstudien, 31.

Radcliffe College, 295.
Randolph, Edmund, 125.
Ranke, Leopold von, 260.
Rathbone, William, 70.
Renick, E. I., on Gadsden, 218-219.
Review, judicial, 124-125.
Review, The American Historical: anticipated, 47-50, 52, 53, 111, 260; connection with the Association, 121, 127, 244-245, 260, 262, 263, 265, 279-280, 289, 290.
Revue des Deux Mondes, 85.
Revue Historique, 85, 183, 184.
Rhode Island: history of, 58-59; politics in, 61-62.
Rhode Island Historical Society, 128.
Rhodes, James Ford: at Council dinner, 291; praised by Bancroft, 237-238.
Richardson, D. N., letter from, 96.
Ritchie, D. G., lectures of, 189.
Rockefeller, John D.: founder of University of Chicago, 211; on salaries, 152; supporter of universities, 296.
Rome, visit by Adams, 28.
Ross, Edward A., 156 n. 1, 193.
Roosevelt, Theodore: letter from, 122; on Association members, 122; paper by, 122.
Round, J. H., 187.
Rutgers University, 68.

Salaries, 13, 14, 68, 85-86, 93, 96, 98, 99, 100, 138, 142, 149, 150, 152, 154, 157, 167, 195, 212, 213, 223, 239, 243, 248, 271.
Sale, Lee, 54.
Sanford, Albert H., 164, 169, 174.
Scaife, Walter B., 131.
Scharf, John T., collection of historical materials, 162.
Schouler, James: letters from, 247, 275, 289, 295; article on nineteenth century, 295; connection of Association and Review, 289-290; finances of universities, 296-297; lectures at Hopkins, 247, 248 n. 1, 276, 295, 297; on needs of Hopkins, 296; presidential address of, 247; proposed book on state government, 216, 217; sale of history by, 297; views on Association programs, 247-248, 290, 296; wish for honorary degree, 275.
Schurz, Carl, 74.
Scott, Austin: on Hopkins faculty, 13; paper by, 72; recommended by Adams, 67; situation of, 68.
Scott, Walter Quincy, on his dismissal as president of Ohio State, 230, 234.
Scott, W. H.: letters from, 223, 224; on Ohio State, 223-225; relations with trustees, 222, 223, 224-225, 231.
Seelye, Julius H.: letter from, 30; recommendation of Adams, 30; reference for Adams, 27, 28, 32; resignation from Amherst, 134.
Seligman, E. R. A., 217.
Seminar: Adams in German, 11, 31; Adams placed in charge, 14; first in United States, 79; von Holst's at Chicago, 191; Monod's, 185; papers before Hopkins, 69, 70, 179, 218, 270; physical arrangements of, 69 n. 1, 166-167, 185; praise of by Bryce, 71, 269; Turner's modelled on Hopkins, 151.
Semple, James, 102.
Sewanee, see South, University of the.
Seward, William H., 238.

Shaw, Albert: article by, 53; lectures, 294; on local history, 269; proposed book on government, 216, 217.
Sherwood, Sidney, 161, 164.
Short, John T.: letters from, 47, 48, 52; death of, 232; proposal of scholarly journal, 47-48.
Simms, W. G., 143.
Small, Albion W.: recommended to Chicago, 158; student at Hopkins, 156 n. 1.
Smith College, Adams on faculty of, 39, 40, 85, 100.
Smith, Goldwin, 245.
Smithsonian Institution, connection with Association, 126-127, 264-265, 272.
Sorbonne, 178, 185.
South, The: conditions in, 41-44, 250, 257-259, 261, 265-266; education in, 11, 101, 141-143, 166-168, 171, 239, 243, 249-250, 256-259, 261, 266, 291-292; history of, 135; Hopkins opportunity, 162; local government in, 45, 257-259, 265; public opinion and history, 167-168, 170, 246, 266, 270, 292-293.
South, University of the: conditions at, 142-143, 249-250; Trent on faculty, 124.
Spanish-American War, lack of interest in, 10.
Sparks, Jared: Adams's life of, 17; Bowen on Adams's biography, 206-207; contract for biography, 81 n. 1; contrast with de Tocqueville, 269; editorial work of, 132, 177, 207; materials for biography, 80-82, 205; Winsor on Adams's biography, 205-206.
Sparks, William E.: letter from, 80; materials for biography, 80-82.
Sprague, William, in Rhode Island politics, 62.
Springfield Republican, 62.
de Staël, Mme., 116.
Stanford, Leland, 152 n. 1, 193.
Staples, Carlton A., 59.
State Department: archives of, 148; custodianship of Declara-

tion of Independence, 196-197, 198.

Steiner, Bernard C.: letter from, 164; courses by, 241; interest in race riot, 261; on teaching at Williams, 164-165; remembered, 271; writings of, 165-166.

Stephens, Alexander, 168.

Stillé, Charles I.: letter from, 106; on history in the University of Pennsylvania, 106-107.

Stovall, Pleasant A., 170.

Stubbs, Bishop William: books by, 88, 113-114, 160, 203; interest in Adams's work, 69.

Suffrage: Brooks Adams on, 173; Bryce lecture on, 51; in North Carolina, 270; paper by Adams, on, 31.

Sumner, William G., 75, 83.

Switzerland, scholarly contacts with, 179, 181.

Taine, Hippolyte A., 184.

Taylor, Hannis: letter from, 113; on Teutonic origins of constitution, 113-115.

Thompson, R. E., 67 n. 1.

Thwaites, Reuben Gold: letters from, 138, 167, 273; Adams invited to lecture by, 136, 138-141; author in Epoch Series, 119, 194; list of historical periodicals, 274; on work of Wisconsin Historical Society, 138-141; plan for bibliographical work, 273-274; trip abroad, 159, 164.

Ticknor, Anna E.: letter from, 115; on George Ticknor, Jefferson and education, 115-118.

de Tocqueville, A., Bryce on, 70, 269.

Tolman, William H., 149.

Toner, Joseph M., 177.

Toronto, University of, 112.

Torrey, H. W., 71, 83.

von Treitschke, Heinrich: Adams a student of, 27; course by, 74; lectures incomprehensible, 76.

Trent, William P.: letters from, 124, 141, 249; on education in the South, 11, 141-143, 249-250; researches of, 124-125.

Trevelyan, Sir George Otto, 122.

Trinity College, N. C.: finances of, 239, 256-257, 266, 292; library of, 292; study of history in, 11, 242-243, 246, 266, 267.

Turner, Frederick Jackson: letters from, 119, 123, 136, 144, 158, 159, 168, 173, 174, 212; asked to write for cyclopaedia, 163; attendance at Association meeting, 164; bibliographical plans approved by, 273; courses taught, 123, 151, 163, 174; definition of history, 160; examination for degree, 123; invitation to write on northwest, 169; on committee for cooperative history, 276, 282, 287; on Epochs of American History, 119; on extension work in Wisconsin, 136, 137, 144-145, 159, 169, 174, 175; on historical activities in Wisconsin, 136-137; on prospects at Wisconsin, 123; on publishing dissertation, 158-159, 168, 173-174, 175; opinion of own dissertation, 173-174; opinion of Sherwood, 161; paper on significance of frontier, 212; praise of James, 169, 175, 212; proposal of a collection of texts, 160; recommendation of Olson on Norse, 119-120; seminar modelled on Hopkins, 151; student at Hopkins, 156 n. 1; subjects studied in his seminar, 169; to send students to Hopkins, 175; use of Wisconsin Historical Society, 139; work at Wisconsin described, 151.

Tyler, John, 102.

Tyler, Lyon G.: letter from, 101; on education in Virginia, 101-102.

Tyler, Moses Coit: at first Association meeting, 72; death of, 296; on committee for cooperative history, 276, 282; recommendation of Hull, 79; said Gilman suggested the Association, 288.

Tyler, W. S., reference for Adams, 27, 28, 32.

University Extension, 17, 119,
  136-137, 159, 163, 169, 171, 174,
  175, 195, 202, 211-212, 236.
University, National, views on,
  101-103.

Vanderbilt University, 292.
Vane, Sir Henry, sketch of, 109-
  110.
Vespucius, A., Winsor on forg-
  eries, 199.
Vincent, John Martin: letters
  from, 178, 182, 184; Association affairs, 295; book on historical research, 179, 182;
  courses by, 179, 182; custo-
  dian of library, 162, 182, 185;
  on Hopkins faculty, 87, 130,
  182-183, 184, 262, 271, 294,
  297; plans for career, 179-180,
  183; sketch of Adams by, 12
  n. 11; student at Hopkins,
  156 n. 1; study in Paris, 178-
  180, 183-184, 185; Swiss
  studies, 179, 181 n. 1.
Virginia: attainder case in, 124-
  125; education in, 101-103, 115-
  118; generous to the University, 297; politics in, 41-42;
  views on the Revolution, 193.
Virginia, University of: aided
  by state, 297; honorary degree
  of, 275; position at, 143; relations with William and Mary,
  102; Ticknor and Jefferson on,
  115-118; visit by Adams, 40-
  41.

Wake Forest College, 243, 266.
Walker, Francis A., 129.
Ward, A. W., 53.
Washington, resources in, 32,
  131, 148, 151, 157.
Washington, George: editions of
  writings, 177; lecture on, 276;
  plan for a national university,
  101 n. 1, 102-103.
Washington University, 108.
Weaver, Charles C., 245-246, 270.
Webb, Sidney: letter from, 252;
  visit to Hopkins, 252; Wood-
  burn anxious to meet, 236.
Weeden, W. B., 129.
Wendell, Barrett: letter from,
  171; on Puritan character-
  istics, 171-172.

West, The: Adams's opinion of,
  155-158; education in, 66, 75,
  80, 85-86, 95, 96, 98, 108, 136-
  137, 139-141, 144, 149, 151,
  161, 163, 169, 174-175, 191,
  194-195, 213-214, 220-234, 248-
  249; intellectual relations with
  East, 137, 150, 169.
Wharton, Francis, 178.
Wharton School, history in, 106-
  107.
Wheeler, A. M., 176.
White, Andrew D.: letters to,
  9 n. 5, 69, 126; address at first
  Association meeting, 71-72; at
  Michigan, 8, 79, 86; news of
  Gilman's resignation, 300; on
  lack of history professors, 8.
White, Horace, 38.
Wilhelm, Lewis W., 54-55.
William and Mary College: his-
  tory of, 101-103; interest of
  Bryce in, 186 (2).
Williams College, history in, 164-
  165.
Williston Seminary, Adams a
  teacher in, 28, 30.
Willoughby, Westal W., 156 n.
  1, 217, 294.
Willoughby, William F.: letter
  from, 218; on Renick's account
  of Gadsden, 218-219; to write
  in series on government, 217.
Wilmington, N. C., race riot at,
  10 n. 6, 257-259, 261.
Wilson, Woodrow: letters from,
  88, 91, 93, 97, 103, 120, 129,
  215; academic position of, 86,
  100; Adams's opinion of, 90
  n. 1; Angell interested in, 98;
  anxious to see Adams, 294;
  as a historian, 120; Congressional Government, 92 n. 1,
  254; considered for history of
  North Carolina, 72; cooperation suggested by Turner, 160;
  departure from New England
  regretted, 128; Division and
  Reunion, 119, 120, 271; law
  partner, 219; lectures at Cornell, 89; lectures at Hopkins,
  87, 89, 93, 97, 99, 120, 241;
  offered Adams position at Hopkins, 90 n. 1; on a national
  university, 103; on Iyenaga's
  examination, 129; opinion of

Adams, 90 n. 1; plans for study in Europe, 89, 91-93; praised by Boutmy, 130; proposed as president of Amherst, 254, 256; recommended by Turner, 123; to review von Holst, 97, 103; unable to write book in series, 215-216 (2).

Wilson, W. L., 187.

Winkelmann, Eduard A.: letter from, 30; on work at Hopkins, 85; recommendation of Adams, 30.

Winsor, Justin: letters from, 175, 198, 205; at first Association meeting, 71; books on explorations, 199; comments on Adams's Sparks, 205-206; Narrative and Critical History, 9, 175-176, 205, 268, 283, 284; on historians at World's Fair, 198-199; on Puritans, 172; on reviews of his Columbus, 176; protest against loan of Declaration of Independence, 196, 198; to help on review, 111.

Winston, Ambrose P., 175.

Winthrop, John, 166.

Winthrop, Robert C., 207.

Wisconsin Historical Society: activities of, 138-141; relations with University, 136-137, 140, 151.

Wisconsin, University of: extension teaching, 136-137, 144-145, 159, 163, 169; history in, 87-88, 151, 161, 162-163, 169, 212; like Ohio State, 220, 223; publication plans, 169; relations with historical society, 136-137, 140, 151; students compared with those at Hopkins, 161-162; work in Norse, 119.

Witchcraft, paper on, 75.

Woodburn, James A.: letters from, 192, 234, 262; consulted by Haskins, 161; editor of Lecky, 263; on Association activities, 262-263; on reviews of his book, 192-193; plans for publishing, 263; plans for study in England, 235-236; praise of paper by Harris, 236-237; student at Hopkins, 156 n. 1; subjects suggested by, 193; suggested as reviewer, 170.

Wyoming, University of, presidency offered to Adams, 138.

Yager, Arthur, 54.

Yale University: contest over presidency, 75; history in, 83-84; honorary degree sought, 275; represented at first Association meeting, 71-72.

Zwingli, paper on, 264.